Off the Mic

Off the Mic

The World's Best
Stand-Up Comedians Get
Serious About Comedy

By Deborah Frances-White and Marsha Shandur

Bloomsbury Methuen Drama
An imprint of Bloomsbury Publishing Plc

B L O O M S B U R Y
LONDON • NEW DELHI • NEW YORK • SYDNEY

Bloomsbury Methuen Drama

An imprint of Bloomsbury Publishing Plc

Imprint previously known as Methuen Drama

50 Bedford Square	1385 Broadway
London	New York
WC1B 3DP	NY 10018
UK	USA

www.bloomsbury.com

BLOOMSBURY, METHUEN DRAMA and the Diana logo are trademarks of Bloomsbury Publishing Plc

First published 2015

British Library Cataloguing-in-Publication Data
A catalogue record for this book is available from the British Library.

ISBN: PB: 978-1-4725-2638-0
ePDF: 978-1-4725-2212-2
epub: 978-1-4725-2719-6

Library of Congress Cataloging-in-Publication Data
Frances-White, Deborah, interviewer.
Off the mic : the world's best stand-up comedians get serious about comedy / by Deborah Frances-White, Marsha Shandur.
pages cm.– (Performance books)
ISBN 978-1-4725-2638-0 (paperback)
1. Stand-up comedy. 2. Comedians–Interviews. I. Shandur, Marsha, interviewer.
II. Title.
PN1969.C65F73 2015
792.7'6028092–dc23
2015000834

Typeset by Fakenham Prepress Solutions, Fakenham, Norfolk NR21 8NN
Printed and bound in India

To Robin Williams and Joan Rivers – two comic giants who died while we were writing this.

To my long-lost, newly found family who gave me the inspiration for my BBC Radio 4 comedy show which I recorded while we were writing this. And my friend Phill, who helped me get there.

– Deborah Frances-White

To Lenny Love, who brought me into the world of interviewing stand-up comedians, and Scott Shaw, who taught me how to navigate it.

– Marsha Shandur

Contents

Introduction

This book was suggested after *The Improv Handbook*, which I wrote with Tom Salinsky, was pleasantly received by the international improvisation community. I was asked to write a similar book about stand-up comedy but the obvious obstacle was that, while improv has shared principles that can be debated, stand-up is a game for loners. Everyone does it their own way. I was sure there'd be trends in finding inspiration, craft and performance styles, but the only way to identify patterns or outliers would be to interview a lot of comedians. When Marsha Shandur interviewed me for her XFM radio podcast *Marsha Meets…*, she really did a number on me. I told her stuff I didn't even know I knew. She's such a skilful interviewer, I discovered I had a whole new Edinburgh show in me during our discussion. It was clear I wasn't going to be able to do this book without her, and I knew I wouldn't have to try when her eyes lit up at the suggestion of a book that meant she'd have to spend her time in bars psychoanalysing comedians.

We are pullulating with gratitude for all the comics who gave their closely guarded time, deep thoughts and funnies. Without you this would be a series of empty pages devoid of the insight and self-deprecating wit you have brought us.

My essays throughout are not about how they do it, but about how you might. That is because if you're reading this book, then you're interested in what stand-ups think about when they lie in bed till lunchtime and what they talk about at roadside services after midnight and that probably means you're a little bit tempted to try it. Yes, you are. Even if you only do one open mic gig, far, far, far from your house, you'll have done it and that's more than nearly everyone else can ever tell anyone else about, ever. If the idea of stand-up brings you out in some kind of undiagnosable rash, it may be the essays are useful for any place you have to make something up or tell more than one person a story.

The wonderful thing about stand-up comedy is that it is a job you have to play at. In Western society we have an idea that work is the only way to create worthwhile results. The truth is that work and play are both processes that can be responsible for wonderful things. They're both good tools; it just depends what you want to make. If you're digging a hole, I'd say work will get you where you need to be faster than play. Play might keep morale up if you have a team of people digging many holes over a long period of time, but the holes won't be any better or deeper and they'll probably take longer to dig.

If you want come up with good ideas for screenplays, then play is definitely your go-to guy. Sitting with a great friend, playing spit-balling games and joking around will up the quality of your first movie ideas, massively. It will almost certainly yield better results than making yourself stare at your laptop for five hours in a library. A Protestant work ethic is usually no friend to inspiration. Having said that, do you know anyone who doesn't have an unfinished screenplay? I don't. The only people I know who don't have unfinished screenplays are people who have *finished* ones. They're in a tiny minority because that's where the work comes in. Coming up with ideas is a playful pursuit. First drafts can be wonderful fun. Third drafts require graft and craft.

The thing I noticed most keenly from reading our collated interviews – what made the page and some of the brilliant stuff that sadly had to be stashed in drafts – is that working, living, breathing, comedy-loving stand-ups are all playful hard workers to an individual. When you're starting out, you're in the flirtation period. First, second, third dates with comedy are not serious. The stakes will never be lower, so play at it. Have you ever had sex with someone who was working at it? Ghastly? Don't make your honeymoon earnest.

Once you've been in the relationship for a year or two and comedy wants to move in with you and get serious, you'll have some decisions to make. Some of them will be sacrifice-based. Many potentially brilliant comedians have bailed at that point, for good reason. I mean, if there's anything else you can consider doing for a living, you should definitely do that. If there isn't, keep playing at it. If you enjoy it, work at it. If the work feels too hard, try playing at it again. If you're still going in five years, Marsha and I will come and interview you for the second edition.

Deborah Frances-White

Figure 1 Deborah Frances-White © Isabelle Adam

PART ONE

Preparation

Chapter 1
Inspiration

Where do ideas come from? Making a living out of thin air.

DEBORAH FRANCES-WHITE: If you are considering doing stand-up comedy but don't know where to begin, it may be because you feel you lack ideas. Now, if you are just dying to rant about the little or large things in life and you feel you have to do comedy, you probably already have 'a voice' and just need to know how to use it – but you may feel the comedians you admire are more talented than you because they seem to overflow with inspiration. 'Where do you get your ideas?' is asked of comedians as often as 'How do you deal with hecklers?'

The secret is, people we consider to be 'talented' listen to the thoughts that occur to them in the privacy of their heads and allow them out into the world. They don't censor their personal sparks of originality and kill them before they're born. All children have innovative ideas – in that adorable 'kids say the darnedest things' kind of way. Eddie Izzard's conceit that his cat is drilling behind the sofa seems brilliant. You no doubt said things like that when you were a child and somebody replied, 'Don't be silly, darling, it's purring', so you stopped saying whatever occurred to you out loud. You grew up, which meant that fewer and fewer behaviours, emotions and verbal games were available to you. The truth is – most comedians never allowed the growing-up process to rid them of playful and childish connections, observations and juxtapositions. (If you envy this, you can comfort yourself that a lot of natural born comedians aren't very mature in other ways either. Many comics live with their mums, eat too many sweets and can't use a washing machine. Their delightful refusal to let the adult world drown out their whimsy is part of a wider problem.)

Most people simply allow their interior censor to be louder than their inventor. You may think you never have original misunderstandings or quirky observations as a grown-up and can't even remember a time when you did. If this is the case, then you have just trained your brain to censor them out, really quickly. Luckily, the brain is very plastic and you can retrain it to come up with ideas for stand-up comedy in about a month.

When people say they can't think of anything, they really mean they can't think of anything good or worthwhile. The first thing you have to do to overcome this feeling is change your metric for success. You are no longer seeking quality ideas. You are seeking quantity. There is a reason the editor does not follow the director around on a film set whispering into his or her ear: 'I wouldn't bother shooting that… We won't use that… There's no point improvising… That's an unusable angle.' Most directors shoot for months to get a ninety-minute film you can watch in a cinema. What they are shooting is choice; lots and lots of footage to choose from. The lower budget your film, the less choice you can afford to shoot. In terms of stand-up comedy – the lower budget your imagination, the fewer ideas you will allow yourself to come up with, in case some of them are unoriginal or 'bad'.

If your mind is completely blank, are you are sitting in an empty, silent room? I am willing to bet you are not. Look around the space you are in now. What can you see? Is there a wobbly table? A bowl of aging fruit? A birthday card? An iPhone charger? These are all ideas. Write one of them down. The first one is the best.

Wobbly table.

Good. You have your first idea.

Now write things you observe about the wobbly table. I'm improvising as I go here, so I have no idea if I'll come up with anything usable. I'll just begin a list…

- One leg shorter than the others.
- Propped up with a magazine.

- Things can slide off it.
- The cat nearly falls when it jumps on it.

Now write about your relationship to the wobbly table. Here's mine...

- Should have bought a new one ages ago.
- Wish I could fix it. My dad could fix it. Why can't I fix things?
- Could leave it outside my flat to get rid of it.
- Think I actually got it off the street when I was a student.

Now write a few sentences about *one* of those ideas. Let it flow like a stream of consciousness. Again, I'm improvising as I write, so there's no quality control here. I promise not to rewrite this. This is just process.

My dad could fix that table. He could fix anything. Except computers. How come I can fix his computer but I have to get him to fix my table? A table is a much simpler piece of technology than a computer. A table is one of the earliest technologies. I mean it might have even come before the wheel. Cave people probably put their cave food on a table-rock. Surely my generation should be expert table and computer fixers. But we're not. We skipped tables and went right to laptops. Do you think our kids will be able to fix hover-boards and mind chips but will have to get their dads to turn their phones on and off?

Now, pick another idea and run with that...

I'm going to leave my old table on the street. The thing is I actually got it off the street, so it's like I'm returning it back into the wild. The thing is I'll probably leave it on the street in the morning, go to work, come home, see it and think, 'Ooh – I need a table. I'll have that.'

Now think of what a wobbly table might be like.

- The coalition government – the Lib Dems are the short leg.
- Your family at Christmas – alcohol is the thing you prop the table up with.
- A pigeon with one leg you saw in the park.

Write a few sentences expanding on one of those, and so on.

Maybe your ideas are more surreal. You think there's a little family of pixies living under one leg and that's what makes it wobble. Maybe the pixie family are dysfunctional alcoholics and that's why the table keeps falling over. Maybe the table thinks *you're* the wobbly one and talks back to you. Maybe it's you that's come home smashed, and the table tells you its legs are fine and it's your perception that's at fault. Are you being bullied by your furniture? Does your bed then accuse you of being lazy?

Maybe you want to write comedy songs. So what rhymes with wobbly table? Who might own a wobbly table? Is the wobbly table the last straw for a hapless character? A ride at a funfair for a mouse? I'm not suggesting for one minute these ideas are good. We're just playing here. It doesn't take long to come up with ten, twenty or fifty ideas. And you only need one you really like. Unlike footage on a film set, the ideas you throw away cost nothing.

When you've exhausted wobbly table, disused fireplace and old dog-basket, go into another room – or more radically, leave the house.

Get on public transport. A trip on the tube or bus is a goldmine of ideas if you're looking at posters and litter, observing haircuts and tattoos, reading over other people's shoulders and seeing their reactions, watching people's pets, listening to conversations – noting everything down – then hitting a coffee shop and expanding on those ideas.

If the process seems intimidating, this is a good place to start.

Just set aside one hour a week to get ideas down in a notebook. Window-shop in your own house, go for a walk taking an unusual route, get on a bus, go to a park, museum or restaurant. Note down everything you can. A word. A phrase. The shape of a cloud. Try sketching an image or recording a noise. Mix up your process. This is just footage. Later you want choice. Right now, you're just stimulating your brain.

Then each day, choose one idea from your scrapbook to write about – for just one minute. Write as fast as you can. Don't take your hands off the keyboard or pen off the page. Write gibberish if necessary. Be curious as to what comes out. This is not your censor's time to speak. Your only metric for success is quantity. Try a word that inspires you one day and an image that doesn't the next. Compare those two processes. Was the 'difficult' one actually easier because you thought you'd have nothing to say and surprised yourself? Or did it make you freeze up? Part of the discovery is establishing your most creative process.

Write for a minute a day for six days. On day seven, go over the one-minute ramblings and see if there's anything you find funny or interesting. Something that makes you laugh out loud is especially good. You only need one thing from your six minutes of speed writing.

Spend five minutes writing as fast as you can, expanding on that idea. If you get blocked writing prose, put the idea in the middle of the page and draw lines away from it with different associations in every direction.[1] Anything will do. No one is going to see this. You are looking for lots of stuff, *not* lots of good stuff.

After a week or two of doing this, your brain will start to take over for you. You will get on a bus and your mind will automatically see material rather than a dull commute. You will find yourself reaching for your notebook or texting yourself ideas, turns of phrase and little images. You will find that the ideas start to come to you in Stage Two: 'table as early technology', rather than Stage One: 'table – oh god – what's funny about a table?' Inspiration will come to you unbidden, especially when you are relaxed – as you are falling asleep, in the shower or riding a bike.

Stand-up comedians are like magpies looking for shiny things. They see them because they have trained themselves to see them. Sometimes when two comedians are joking around, an idea will spring up between them in the conversation which will make them laugh. You see the look in their eyes: 'Who owns this?' One of them will politely cough and enquire: 'Do you want that?' They see treasure in the recycling. In other words, they never walk past an old table in the street and dismiss it as junk.

Stand-up, unlike improvised or sketch comedy, is not a collaborative art form so every comic will have a different way of finding their voice. Note your processes, because they will be personal. If you hear of an interesting way of creating inspiration for yourself, then try it. Be curious

---

[1] I learnt this technique at Nat Luurtsema's Sketch Writing Workshop and have found it very useful.

as to whether it works for you. If it doesn't, it's not a good procedure for you. Find ways of exciting your brain and making it rain ideas. Your imagination is like a magical creature in a cave. You can tempt it out to play because that's what it wants to do, but you can scare it away with judgement, pretty easily.

We interviewed comedians about where they find inspiration and this is what they said.

ADAM BLOOM

Adam Bloom is a British comedian with a fast-paced, almost hyperactive style of delivery. He has played the Edinburgh Festival for many years, once winning a Punters Award. He appeared at the Melbourne Comedy Festival in 1999 and 2000, winning a Stella Artois award for the former appearance. He has also appeared on *Mock the Week* and *Russell Howard's Good News* and starred in the BBC Radio 4 show *The Problem With Adam Bloom*.

My fifth gig ever, I did a joke – I had a goatee beard and I said to them, 'There's a lot in my beard. I actually grew it to cover up a tattoo that I regret having. It's a bit of a Catch-22 though because the tattoo says "wanker".' I just came out with it off the top of my head, when someone commented on my beard offstage. Then I took it on stage and it worked. It stood out head and shoulders above the rest of my set. I realized, OK, when I do something that has got that little self-contained, clever little flip, the idea – you got a beard. You shave it off. It says wanker. It's a cerebral way of saying 'I'm like a wanker with a beard', isn't it?

This little story illustrates the gap between a funny idea, a bit of banter between two friends offstage, and a piece of well-crafted comedy material. But a lot of those onstage jokes begin life in ordinary events offstage.

RICHARD HERRING

Richard Herring began his comedy as part of the Lee and Herring double-act with Stewart Lee. They produced two television series in the 1990s, *Fist of Fun* and *This Morning with Richard Not Judy*. Since then, Herring has returned to solo stand-up comedy, taking a new show to the Edinburgh Fringe every year since 2004, as well as podcasting, writing and failing to win televised quiz shows.

I had a fight on tour with someone in Liverpool. It had nothing to do with the show and it was a sort of pathetic fight. So when I did the first preview, two days later, I decided to talk about this fight because it was in my mind. Maybe I could use it but I wasn't really trying to put it in the show.

I told the story once, came off stage and thought, 'If I get four more jokes in there and just tighten it up a bit, that's a really good routine'. Now it's a major routine of that show. It's easy when it's a story that has a beginning, middle and end. You get to tell it and if it's true, that makes it easier. A lot of my stuff is a flow of an argument and it's a logical argument and it may go crazy, but you've got to make sure the logic of the argument gets in the right place.

Some comedians (although not many) even get visited by sudden inspiration while they sleep.

SARA PASCOE

Sara Pascoe writes, acts and improvises in addition to her stand-up comedy. She has been seen on many TV panel shows and appeared on *Live at the Apollo* in 2012. In 2014 her solo show *Sara Pascoe vs History* was nominated for an Edinburgh Comedy Award.

I have almost entire routines – this is very rare, about 10 per cent – where I have a dream and I dream the material or it's just before I fall asleep or it's just as I'm waking up, something happens in my brain, and it's a scenario and it's almost ready-made and I know it's good. And then all I have to do is try and say it as much as possible on stage. And then eventually it clicks in.

Then there's other times where I have an idea of something and it takes a hundred attempts at trying to write it on stage. I can see it's interesting. I know that people are interested in the idea but I don't know how to make it a routine yet. And other times, something feels very exact. In my last show I wanted to talk about burqas, and that's not something I ever felt comfortable about riffing on stage about, because I had to be so careful in the words that I chose. I had to write it down and look at it from every moral angle, and look at it from an audience's perspective before I ever said it in front of anyone. So there are times when it's actually lots of typing and looking at exact phrases before putting it on stage at all.

Some comedians become associated with comedy only on certain topics, not necessarily by choice. Lewis Black is largely known today for his political material, but this was not always the case.

Figure 2 Sara Pascoe © Idil Sukan/Draw

LEWIS BLACK

> Lewis Black never meant to be a comedian, doing a degree in playwriting and writing and producing hundreds of one-act plays in the 1980s; however, his literate, impassioned and apoplectic performance style has ensured that he is in high demand on the US stage.

I didn't actively choose to talk about politics. When I broke in as a comic really young, I talked about my sex life because it was funny and then I moved on to other things. I had always talked about politics. It's always been of interest to me, but it was maybe 20 per cent of my act. It's consumed more and more of my act – but it's not so much politics that interests me as much as how it affects people.

Comedy has the power to allow people to stand back from the situations and the reality we find ourselves in. So it allows them at least the moment to take a breath and look at it again, as opposed to being all wrapped up in it and losing their minds. So in that sense, maybe it gives them the energy to deal with what's happening a little more.

But if you're not telling funny stories, but instead dealing with serious issues of the day or tackling weighty themes like politics, should you really be on stage in a comedy club, where the person after you is just going to be doing jokes for twenty minutes?

TODD GLASS

Having been a successful professional comedian for over two decades, Glass came out as gay on Marc Maron's podcast in 2012 and has talked about both the relief he has felt ever since and the warm reaction of the American comedy community.

I always want to be funnier than I am preachy. That's my rule: have I been preachier than funny? You get the right audience that happens to agree with you and you get a round of applause. But that's not what I want. Jimmy Dore says most people pick their religion because of the parents. Why are you Jewish? That's what my parents decided. You take their beliefs. Jimmy goes, 'You wouldn't let your parents buy you jeans or music'. That's not just being silly. If your parents go, 'We're going to go to the mall. We will pick you up jeans', you would be like, 'No fucking way! You're not buying me jeans!'

Oh, what about the religion? Oh, you probably got that right. We will go that way with your religion. Jeans, you don't know how to buy. Music, no way, but religion, yeah. I think that could make a younger person go, oh my god – you know.

Margaret Cho also rejects the role of preacher.

MARGARET CHO

Margaret Cho began doing stand-up comedy in a club adjacent to her parents' bookstore. From there she went on to open for Jerry Seinfeld. In 2000, she released her first live DVD *I'm The One That I Want* to great acclaim.

You're not preaching, you're *celebrating*. Celebrating what you feel, and what you think, and what *they* think. I think that's the nature of comedy; we laugh because we agree and that is wonderful. I think when you just say, 'Okay, this is who I am, this is what I'm doing, this is what my journey is', that's really exciting. You let go of pretence and of trying to act cool and you're admitting to everything – and I'm guilty of *everything*.[2]

One way of developing material is to work under more than one heading. Some comedians set themselves topics to write on.

NATHAN CATON

Since winning the Chortle Student Comedian of the Year in 2005, Nathan Caton has become a popular headliner on the UK circuit and has written and performed one series of his Radio 4 show *Can't Tell Nathan Caton Nothing*.

[2]Taken from *Satiristas: Comedians, Contrarians, Raconteurs & Vulgarians* by Paul Provenza, published by It Books May 2010 and used with permission. Anyone reading this book should go and buy that book immediately.

Mostly what happens is I'll be reading a paper or something or I'll be brainstorming and then something will come up in my head. Then I'll write down the topic that I want to talk about. Actually, I've got two notebooks now. One is a topical notebook and one is storytelling and family stuff. I'll sit down for I don't know how long that is. But I must do it in the daylight between 11 and 4 because that's when I have the most quiet time to myself. And I just write jokes about that certain topic that I'm writing about.

Then what I might do, if it's a short joke, I'll check on Twitter or Facebook. I'll see what kind of reaction it gets. If it gets a good reaction, then I might try it on my brother as well. Some jokes, he will get. Some jokes, he'll be like, 'What are we talking about? Are we talking about something?' He's kind of young and in tune for everything that's going on. So I'll try it on him. If he laughs then I think, 'Okay, it's worked on Facebook. He's laughed. It's ready for a comedy club.'

Other comedians begin by talking about subjects which are outside of themselves and then discover a more personal voice as they get older – they morph from joke-smiths to personal storytellers. For some, telling personal stories is the most important thing a comedian can do. Stephen K Amos only came out as gay after five years as a comedian.

STEPHEN K AMOS

Already a successful circuit comedian, Stephen K Amos really made a splash with his 2006 Edinburgh Fringe show *All of Me*, wherein he announced that he was gay. A well-respected compere and headliner, he got his own BBC TV show in 2010.

I spent quite a lot of years kind of just being funny and not really getting anything out of it, apart from just being funny and not letting anything of myself be seen. When I first started, I didn't think for one minute an audience would be remotely interested in what I had to say personally about my own life. But then I thought, actually, we've all got a story to tell.

Every single one of us on this planet has a story to tell. We often have the same kinds of stories – particularly growing up in England, South London. A lot of people grew up in England and South London. So a lot of experiences are generally the same.

However, on that same journey, I take a left route as opposed to taking a right path and obstacles happen and how you overcome those is quite an interesting story. But it is also very, very personal. For years, I didn't think I was ready to do it. I never thought when I started I would ever, ever talk about myself or my family or my personal views. With a job like this, you're your own self-censor – in the live arena anyway, there is nobody else telling you what to do. I think when you're ready for yourself, it's up to you to speak your truth because you could be, without trying to sound too grand, helping other people.

Comedy is certainly a powerful force, and has been since the earliest days of humour.

ROBIN WILLIAMS

A true comedy superstar, Robin Williams shot to fame in the TV series *Mork and Mindy*, which found a marvellous way of harnessing his quick-fire improvisation skills. He later earned an Academy Award nomination for his sensitive performance in the movie *Dead Poets Society* and won in 1997 for his role in *Good Will Hunting*.

You know, if you go back in history to the fool ... The fool's purpose was to point out to the king himself all the king's foibles and weaknesses, and as best he could, make the king go 'Ha ha' about them. His job was to remind the king, 'You are not a god'.

True story: In Germany, I was on this very dry German talk show with a woman hosting it and at one point she said, 'Vy do you zink zere's not so much comedy in Germany? Ve have some, but not a lot.' And I said, 'Did you ever think it's because you tried to kill all the funny people?'[3]

Some comedians who are known for political material, or whimsy, also tell personal stories about themselves from time to time, but drawing on your own experiences doesn't have to mean confessional storytelling. A lot of new comedians begin by asking themselves 'what subjects can I talk about which other comics aren't?' Judah Friedlander found a rich vein of ideas in a childhood obsession.

JUDAH FRIEDLANDER

The self-styled 'world champion', Friedlander's ironic bombast and laid-back approach led to him starring memorably in all seven seasons of *30 Rock* as the mother-obsessed comedy writer Frank Rossitano and headlining comedy shows all over the world.

I always did sports as a kid. I was always athletic and loved the *Guinness Book of World Records*. When I was eight, I tried to break the pogo stick record. I did it for an hour straight without missing. For an eight-year-old, an hour is like forty days or something. I could have kept going – I wasn't tired or anything, I was just bored. I think the record was twelve hours. I thought, 'Forget this. I've got other things I can go do.'

But I was obsessed with that. So I started writing jokes about ridiculous world records I've broken. I also always did a lot of art as a kid and I've been making my own hats for about twenty years. Then I decided to incorporate that into my act.

---

[3] Taken from *Satiristas*, op. cit.

Some comedians have drawn from different wellsprings of inspiration as their careers developed. Marcus Brigstocke is very much associated with political comedy, but his shows have spanned an enormous range of topics and approaches.

MARCUS BRIGSTOCKE

Few things are more illustrative than the title of Marcus Brigstocke's only DVD to date: *Planet Corduroy*. Brigstocke's educated and vituperative style has led to him being a Radio 4 regular and his love of snowboarding has led to multiple broken limbs.

I was politically engaged, then the build-up to the Iraq war happened and then for the first time in my life I had some very strong feelings politically of 'this is not right'. And so I started talking about that on stage. And I'd say that was when I found my voice. I then imposed a rule that had come about organically, and the rule was: never talk about anything you don't care about.

Now what's happened is the thing I cared about last happened to be silliness. So the 'care-about' before was theology, politics, the economy. But the last show I did was silly, and fart stories, and dancing – that's what I care about at the moment. It's not 'telling you my story', but being silly. I see the joy in that. My kids at that time were seven and ten, and I was surrounded by silliness.

For me, ideas for shows are parasitic really. They're like a thing that pops into my system, and the persistent ones cannot be ignored. And they grow out into a show eventually. The next show, the parasite that won't go away at the moment, is getting an audience to do the Chancellor's budget. The vague plan is I'll have cardboard cut-outs of what we spend the money on, and I will get the audience to decide: here's what we raise in tax at the moment, do we pay this much or more? Who's willing to pay a bit more? Who thinks we should raise less? Then we'll come up with a figure and decide what we spend it on. And get them to devise the budget.

I want the core idea to be boring, in order that when the thing comes along, the laugh is a good 'un, it's really unexpected, like, 'Holy shit – what happened there? How did we start laughing about that?' It gives me enormous pleasure. And it's not just, 'Ah, this makes me look clever', it's that these are the things that interest me, so the challenge then is there must be a way to put this in a pretty enough bow that people say, 'Ah! How delightful!'

Stand-up comedians working in Britain today do so in the shadow of the early 1980s 'alternative' comedy movement, which swept away what were suddenly seen as old-fashioned and reactionary comedy performers. While it was a useful label at the time, it scarcely seems to apply now, certainly not as a useful description of the kind of places people look for inspiration.

ROBIN INCE

Robin Ince is an English stand-up comedian known for his passionate interest in science and for his willingness to try different show formats and approaches. He started his career on *The 11 O'Clock Show* as a writer and impressionist and to this day regularly impersonates his idol Carl Sagan and co-host Brian Cox on their long-running Radio 4 series *The Infinite Monkey Cage.*

I mean now, stand-up is so broad. And even though some people still call the area that we're in 'alternative', that is of course preposterous because in the 'alternative' is Micky Flanagan and Michael McIntyre and you can't call it 'alternative' if you're doing twenty-two nights of 12,000 people per night.

I mean, when I was first getting into alternative comedy, Channel 4 was an alternative channel. It was a dark and mysterious channel with these gritty and unpleasant dramas and strange programmes of naked people – 'Ooh they're suddenly throwing on porn again' – Derek Jarman films, and all of these kinds of things, and Alan Bleasdale's *GBH*. And there was an alternative sensibility of the comedian as outsider.

Music, it's quite acceptable that it has many different genres. You can love music, and by that you might mean that what you love is free jazz, or that you love 1960s Motown and Atlantic, or you love punk or whatever it might be. Stand-up is the same thing. There are lots of different genres of stand-up, but the lines aren't that specific.

One problem faced by a lot of comedians is that some topics are seen as too hot to handle. But there is a pigeonhole for the 'controversial comic' as well as for the 'political comic'. Jim Jefferies is often described in the press as controversial. In 2005, he faced criticism from right-wing political advocacy group Christian Voice which attempted to have his show banned on the basis that his routine was both 'sick and repellent'. He rejects the 'controversial comedian' label.

JIM JEFFERIES

Jim Jefferies is an Australian comedian known for his confrontational style. He tours internationally, making regular appearances at comedy festivals all over the world, and often features on British TV panel shows including *Never Mind the Buzzcocks* and *Have I Got News For You*. His show *Legit* began airing on FX in 2013.

No, I don't think I'm the most controversial comic at all. It's just what I think is funny. Every comic is doing the comedy that they enjoy watching themselves. But there are a lot of clean guys who think 'I'll make a lot more money if I'm clean'. I've had cleaner comics tell me, 'I wish I could say the things you say, but you know, I've got this audience that are…'

But I liked listening to dirty comedy when I was a teenager. I feel like comedy should be depressing. They're the things you're meant to laugh at. You're not meant to laugh at the joyous moments in life. There's nothing funny about them. For me personally, comedy's a form of cheering yourself up. So if you can laugh at something that's really sad, then it makes it a little less sad, you know?

When it comes to material which is in questionable taste, or which might shock or repel an audience, most comedians will tell you that they have a personal line which they prefer not to cross. But most will also tell you that articulating exactly where that line is can be very, very difficult.

MARK WATSON

Mark Watson was born in Bristol to Welsh parents, and initially performed with a strong Welsh accent. He won the Edinburgh Panel Prize in 2006 and has regularly presented format-stretching shows, including marathon performances lasting 24 hours or longer. He has presented several radio series for the BBC including *Mark Watson Makes the World Substantially Better*.

I don't think there are rules. I'm sure people could find examples of jokes I've made which could be viewed as offensive and I certainly don't think that there's an objective standard of offensiveness. For example, I'm not remotely offended by any foul language really at all, unless it's racially offensive.

But the C word, the F word – I'm not offended by those and I don't emotionally understand people who are because I just can't connect with the idea that a word can be that offensive. But other people are massively offended. So that one example shows that you literally can't prove it.

So I don't think there are rules, really, and I do think that there's plenty of opportunity for comedy to be really mean. It's not like I've never laughed at a joke that I thought was really wrong. But if there is a rule, I think you should avoid targeting groups like disabled people that really are defenceless. Because it doesn't quite seem right that a rich, able-bodied person could be making gags about the disabled.

A joke about being disabled that's fun for disabled people, fine. A joke that encourages 90 per cent of people to laugh, but not the 10 per cent of people who have got an illness, maybe not fine. But as I say, you can't really be scientific about it. I just think you could try not to really hurt people.

Comics rightly say, 'Look I'm not going to go through my life worrying, because everything offends somebody'. But the answer to that is, yes, but you're not an idiot. You know when you're risking offence with an edgy joke or when you're just being a bully. It's to do with avoiding bullying and the mentality of bullying. I was going to say I don't think that any of these comedians are bullies, but they underestimate how many people take every word they say more seriously than they might expect.

For Richard Herring, it's not so much about subject matter, but the reason that the comedian has for making this joke at this time.

RICHARD HERRING

I think you can cover any subject – and I do cover all of the subjects; I do jokes that are about paedophilia, that you could say were about rape, and are about race and are about sexuality and sex. So you're doing jokes about the subjects but it's the way you do them. You've got to go to bed at night thinking, 'Have I done the right thing? Are people laughing for the right reasons?'

> There are things that I don't like other comedians doing. I don't like most rape jokes. I don't like sexism and this ironic sexism that's pervasive in a lot of comedy. I don't like people doing jokes, thoughtless jokes about disabilities which just use the buzzwords as the punchline.

Richard Herring is broadly of the opinion that comedians can make any joke they like, but they have to be willing to stand by the joke. Marcus Brigstocke agrees that it's the target of the joke, not the subject matter that makes all the difference.

MARCUS BRIGSTOCKE

Some comedians, I think, are just psychopaths. When people talk about 'meta-bigotry', they can sometimes be acting out the psychopath's role of disassociating themselves from the consequences of their actions. It can be about the normalization of concepts like rape. It's 'No, this isn't so horrific'. Don't get me wrong, I did a really long, really in-depth bit about rape. But I would argue in the strongest possible terms that it served precisely the opposite function.

My neighbour was a UKIP-y type person. Well, a racist. And we were talking about immigration where we were both exaggerating the way that we are. So I was saying, 'We should throw open the gates and not only let, but encourage them to come over, and I think we should put them into the building directly opposite'. And he was doing 'Yes, ha ha, yes we could do that. Until one of them rapes your wife.' And then the whole routine that followed from that was me going, 'So one of them rapes my wife?' The whole routine was about immigrants coming here only to rape my wife.

It was the only thing I ever checked with her. Because it went as far as, 'I wonder if there are men in the Sudan right now, who have lost their children, and their houses, and they've seen their friends and family machete-d to death, and they're saying, "All this is well and good, but what I really wish, what I really wish is that I was fucking Mrs Brigstocke without her permission. If only I could find some way to get to Britain to do that." And maybe, as conscientious liberals, we should take my wife to Gatwick, we could arrange it with customs, and then people could fly here, rape her, and fly back again without even coming in the country. Or perhaps we go on tour!' So it was all about the horror of being casual about rape.

Another common point of view is that everything can be funny, but the jokes have to be worth it.

TODD GLASS

Every fucking thing can be funny. Some people hear what I say and they go, 'Oh, Todd wouldn't like that comedian'. They're wrong. But it just doesn't get a blanket acceptance. Your rape joke might just suck.

I know there might be someone reading, going, 'Can there be a good rape joke?' It's very hard to explain. It's usually not about describing the act of rape as being funny. No. Of course there's nothing funny about that. But I do know a comedian has a joke where he makes fun of people that legitimize date rape. Brilliant! That's a rape joke and it's a good rape joke. But put it to some test. Don't just think you're being edgy – it could just be a shitty joke. Because comedy is an extremely powerful tool. It really is.

The other thing that I really despise is this: if somebody is sexist or homophobic, and then they have a homophobic joke in their act, believe it or not, that doesn't really get me fired up. But when somebody says, 'Oh, that's just a joke for my act. I don't feel that way.' Well, why don't you fucking write a joke about the way you feel? I can't help but guess the answer. 'Oh, because that's hard.' The stereotypical jokes have already been written. They're easy. But a joke about the way you feel? You have to put some work into that. So that would be my other piece of advice: understand what a powerful tool comedy is. I don't mean you should have to be social. Some people don't want to deal with that.

Jim Jefferies has a slightly different way of looking at the more eye-catching parts of his act.

JIM JEFFERIES

Only the stories are true. The rest of it… of course I don't think that.
Or they're things that I believe in for five to ten minutes when I'm in an
argument with a girlfriend or argument with a friend. You know, when
I'm angry. They're not things I believe twenty-four hours a day. They're
moments of insanity that I repeat every night on stage.

Of course, it's impossible to know in advance that nothing you say will
offend anybody, but Richard Herring doesn't think that lets him and
other comedians off the hook.

RICHARD HERRING

Every joke is going to offend someone, it really is. I think you've just got
to think what point am I making and is it worth the fallout? Sometimes
you do go too far. And I think if you do go too far, you apologize.
　　Certainly, anything in my stand-up, I've thought very hard about why
I'm doing it and what point it's making, what results I'm trying to get. I
think the thing with disability jokes is – the mongs and stuff that was
coming up a couple of years ago – don't just use those disability words
as punchlines in themselves. We've all done those kind of jokes and
your joke is being maybe ironic about it. But you need to ask whether
you would do the same joke without the racial or disability effect in the
middle.

For other comedians, their admiration of the joke may override
concerns about the tastefulness of the subject matter. Jim Jefferies is
well known for making jokes about a lot of 'hot button' topics, but he
maintains that nothing is truly off limits.

JIM JEFFERIES

No subject is out of bounds. Not if you do it funny. I believe that most racist jokes are out of bounds just because most of them aren't funny. If you can find a real funny one, everyone will laugh at it. I don't have any problem getting into stereotypes because they're there for a reason. Everyone knows them because they're stereotypes. Not as long as it's funny.

The edgier the subject, the harder it is to make it funny. It's very easy to make light subjects funny and pull funny faces. That's how you entertain babies, shaking car keys and rolling your eyes. To make a dangerous subject funny is more difficult and that's why people think these jokes are off limits, because so few comics do them very well. But any subject can be done as long as it's done brilliantly.

I don't censor myself on stage though. The only time I edit myself is if I think the audience won't laugh. Sometimes there might be a joke in my head that I think is really funny, but I don't think enough people will find it funny for me to say it. I'm not going to stick by my guns to the extent that I'm not going to entertain the crowd. My main job is to entertain the actual crowd.

Richard Herring is prepared to describe some of his personal boundaries.

RICHARD HERRING

There are obviously some things I wouldn't do – I wouldn't want to do a joke that punched down. I think punching down for no reason and mocking the weak above the strong is a weird thing to do. Doing a joke that will perpetuate a racial or sexist stereotype, to me, is a weird thing to do.

So I'm all for freedom of speech. People should be allowed to try things. It was interesting with the Frankie Boyle case about racism, because he is certainly not a racist comedian. He uses racist language, as many comedians do, to highlight a racist character. So you've got to be allowed to do whatever you want. I think you've just got to make your own decision yourself about it and whenever I get criticized about things I've said I will always think about it.

Whereas Jim Jefferies doesn't see himself as a controversial comic, Andy Kindler is struck by the need for some comedians to court controversy deliberately.

ANDY KINDLER

Andy Kindler is an American voice artist and actor who featured regularly on the TV show *Everybody Loves Raymond*, who also now appears on Marc Maron's show *Maron*. In his stand-up comedy, he regularly criticizes other comedians for being too predictable.

It's a weird situation. It depends on what you mean by controversial comedy. Adam Carolla says that women are less funny than men. That's not controversial comedy. That's a misinformed man acting out, isn't it? If what you're trying to do is provoke people just for the sake of provoking people, I don't think that's necessarily funny.

I notice people are always trying to protect when someone says something – like when Tracy Morgan had that outburst where he said if he found out if his son was gay, he would stab him or something. Then people were defending him. Bill Maher is famous for that. He will defend Rush Limbaugh. Why is he defending Rush Limbaugh? Because he says terrible things about people.

Everybody mixes up the concept between free speech and paid speech because you can say anything you want. But if I was running a network, I would not allow *The Nazi Hour* to go on. I would not approve a show called *Cooking With Skinheads*. You have to be able to have some kind of your own morality. So, just like it's free speech for you to say something that's horrible, it's also free speech for me to go, 'I don't like what you said'.

So it's kind of hilarious that comedians who are all, 'let me say what I want', but then as soon as you object, like, 'Oh, you can't do that'. As though the freedom should go one way.

With some comedians, their approach changes over the years. The need to do more 'groundbreaking' material (i.e. likely to offend) sometimes lessens with age.

MARC MARON

Marc Maron is a politically inclined American comedian, who also hosts the *WTF with Marc Maron* podcast and acts occasionally, notably in episodes of Louis CK's FX show *Louie*. In 2013 IFC began airing *Maron*, a sitcom he created in which he plays a fictionalized version of himself. He has published two books: *Jerusalem Syndrome*, a book version of his first stand-up show, and *Attempting Normal*, a memoir.

You've got to present yourself as yourself and whatever form of yourself lives on stage. But you can get away with just telling jokes for a long time.

I've had a lot of fights with a lot of women over things I said on stage. I don't know that I do it the right way or that I would recommend it because when you're honest, I think a lot of times, it's hard to differentiate between getting a laugh because people are shocked or uncomfortable or getting a laugh because you've written something good or your joke is good. It's hard to tell. It really doesn't matter, but the honesty at different points of my life had a different tone. I was very angry and bitter for a lot of years and that didn't really work.

I got my ass handed to me by a woman. You can't really assume that people will identify with bitterness. There's a difference between anger and bitterness. If you're righteously angry, you're pointing your satire at something. People can see the validity of that, but I think that bitterness in and of itself is just cynicism a lot of times. It's just some sort of amplified self-pity and I think people don't go to comedy clubs necessarily to hear a guy angrily complaining about this or that.

Even the great angry comics are limited in their success with audiences a lot of times. I don't see much of it around any more. I mean, there has only been a couple that both sacrificed getting over on an audience for their own point of view. That's still a rare comic who will continually risk bombing to service their voice. It's not marketable. So it's not popular. So there are never that many of them.

I was never ever everyone's cup of tea really. But after a while, I realized, it doesn't matter why people laugh at me. If they laugh at me because they identify with me or if they laugh at me because I'm crazy or just ridiculous. It doesn't really matter and it's a different quality of laugh but it's still getting laughs. So I think that the humility of that realization was some sort of turning point but then there was also the fact that I used to think I was angry about things, that I think I was just angry.

Once I addressed some of the real causes of my disposition, a lot of that is based on fear and so you're moving through the fear. You get to a different place. So I'm not as angry as how I used to be.

You don't have to be making racist jokes or tackling subjects like rape to run the risk of offending people. If you tell personal stories, you may offend the other people in your stories.

NATHAN CATON

My brother is fine with me talking about him on stage. I think everyone else is. I think the only person who might have a bit of a problem is my grandma, my very old-school, traditional grandma. She has never been to any of my shows because I know she'll probably kill me if she came and she saw that I was doing jokes about her. But I did some jokes about her on *Mock The Week* and she saw that. And I was doing jokes about how she's quite backward when it comes to interracial relationships and stuff. Again, it was nothing malicious. Just jokes, just having a laugh.

And then I went to her house a few days afterwards – the first time I've been to her house since doing *Mock The Week*. I walked in the door and I said, 'Hey, grandma. How are you doing?' She just looked at me and said, 'Because of you, everybody thinks I'm a racist'. And she walked away. I said, 'Grandma, it's just a joke. It's just a joke. Don't take it personally.' Yeah, she won't come to any of my shows. Every time I'm doing a gig where I'm on TV, she's like, 'You're going there to joke about me'.

Not everything a comedian says on stage about themselves or the other people in their life is 100 per cent true. Comedians walk a fine line between confession, exaggeration and invention, and while many cheerfully admit to making up a lot of what are presented as true stories, on stage they are careful to give the impression of fidelity.

JO CAULFIELD

An Edinburgh Fringe regular since 2001, Jo Caulfield has written for Joan Rivers, Graham Norton and Alistair McGowan and in her own sets is well loved for her informal, caustic delivery that belies her canny joke-writing abilities.

I think it's a trust issue. My audience, they pretty much know a lot of what I'm saying is exaggerated and not true but they know that when I talk about my husband that I've been with for a long time, they know that's true. If they then found out, 'oh she split up with him five years ago, no she's seeing some 25-year-old now', that audience will then go, 'I'm never seeing her again', because I would've lied to them.

But more than that, what I think about stand-up is that it is you. It's you at your funniest because you're not there to bore them. I feel like it's disrespectful to an audience to go, 'yeah but I'm just doing that to make you people make a noise'. Some people who are doing one-liners and nothing makes sense and it doesn't matter because the audience aren't believing it, but if you're selling your real personality and then you've lied to them in that kind of way, I do feel they have a right to be annoyed and it's upsetting.

I know they want me to be in control and they want me to be not affected by things that might affect them. You know, I'm there to go, 'oh, fuck that. If they say that to you well I just say this.' They don't want me to be too needy and vulnerable. I can tell a funny story where I am the butt of the joke and I have been an idiot and I do that. But it's not Jo going, 'oh, I'm really weak and I need some help'. I'm going, 'I'm a fucking idiot but I got over it because I had three glasses of red wine'.

It's also the person that I would probably much rather be all the time. She seems so much fun and she's much more 'fuck-you'.

When your life takes an unexpected turn, it can provide fantastic fodder for a storyteller comedian. Sarah Millican famously started by telling audiences about her divorce, and you can't move on the circuit for thirty-something new dads telling stories about their babies. But sometimes, an unexpected development in your personal life – even a very positive one – can screw up your emerging stage persona completely.

NAT LUURTSEMA

Nat Luurtsema is a British stand-up comedian, one-third of the sketch outfit Jigsaw along with Dan Antopolski and Tom Craine. After several successful Edinburgh Fringes, the trio recorded a version for Radio 4. As well as stand-up and sketch, Luurtsema also wrote and acted in the award-winning short film *Island Queen* and is now working on her first feature.

When I fell in love my stand-up just died in the water. I had no idea what to write about because I was really happy. That's when I got the Russell Kane tour. Which was very bad timing. Quite a lot of dates in front of the biggest audiences I'd been in front of and I had no new material and for me it's all about new material. I'm not really into a honed twenty, I've always got something new on the go and that's what keeps me interested.

Anyway, I was having to flog stuff that was dead things in my mouth. I didn't know the person who'd written these, I didn't understand them. I was gigging about being on dates and being alone and it made no sense to me. It's not healthy but I think I'm at my best as a stand-up when I'm isolated. Then the audience are sometimes my first, certainly my strongest, human interaction all day. That really makes you need the laughs. But I know how unsustainable that is, it's just how it was when I started, I was at such a low ebb and the evening's gig would be everything to me.

It is strange, though, to write material when you're in one mindset, it works so you hang onto it, but six months later you feel like a different person. I am a bit emotionally turbulent, to be fair; maybe other people have more consistent personalities.

Storyteller comedians are essentially assembling a cast of characters from the people in their life, exaggerating some of their characteristics to make them more vivid, just as they do with themselves to create an onstage persona. Then the stories need to be honed and refined, to move them from rambling dinner-table monologue to sharp onstage comedy material. This is not a trivial skill by any means.

GREG DAVIES

Six-foot-seven Davies rose to prominence as part of anarchic sketch group We Are Klang. His first solo stand-up show *Firing Cheeseballs at a Dog* was nominated for an Edinburgh Comedy Award in 2010. He is also a popular TV actor, appearing in *The Inbetweeners* and *Cuckoo*, and has written and starred in two series (and two Christmas Specials) of his own show on Channel 4, *Man Down*.

There is an art to what you include and what you don't include. I know that me accidentally farting on a Spanish man's hand is funny. And I always knew it was going to be a big enough punchline. It is just funny.

That story in its entirety is, 'I was at a Catholic religious festival. I had eaten a lot of meat and cheese. I farted on a Spanish man's hand and he went, "Hey!".' If you were telling your mum, that's the story she would get. It's mildly amusing in that state. But if you start layering up the jeopardy, if you make it very clear that this is a very formal and religious ceremony, if you describe the atmosphere as being a terrible atmosphere for someone to fart on a man's hand – if you build that up enough, then incrementally that punchline becomes funnier.

So it's about feeding them stuff. It's about layering up the jeopardy, which is very similar to writing a sitcom. If you start layering up this place, the audience will automatically start thinking, 'Well, I'm getting a flavour for what's going on here, and I know there are lots of different things that can happen that would be really inappropriate to happen here'. Then you just hope that the thing you give them is not entirely predictable and as funny as they want it to be. It's a weird thing; the audience are always on the side of the storyteller. They're thinking, 'Oh god. I hope this happens, but I'm not sure what exactly the awful thing that is going to happen is.'

The temptation, of course, is to try and improve on reality too much, or even to invent your own stories, and plenty of comedians' flights-of-fancy are pure invention. But there's a quality to true stories which make them especially valuable. However, just as not all plausible stories told by comedians are actually true, so too are not all true stories also believable.

TOM WRIGGLESWORTH

Tom Wrigglesworth is an English stand-up comedian, born and raised in Sheffield. In 2009 he was nominated for the main Edinburgh Comedy Award at the Edinburgh Festival. His storytelling style is regularly featured on BBC radio shows including *The Unbelievable Truth*, *It's Not What You Know* and *It's Your Round*.

Sometimes, I've tried to make up stories based on what happened and the truth is much better than anything I could make up. Sometimes, stuff's happened that's absolutely 100 per cent totally true, but when I tell it on stage, no one believes it and it just sounds like a rubbish version of something I might make up.

Remember I was on that Virgin train and I got arrested? The ticket inspector had made an old woman pay loads of money for a ticket, so I had a whip-round on this train. The first and second carriages, I did quite well. Third carriage, I got really complacent and I bombed. I actually tried to address this carriage full of people for a charitable cause and tanked … as a human. They were looking away, you know? And I got heckled. This was 11 a.m. I got heckled by a drunk black dwarf. Now, you say that to an audience and they don't believe you. They think that you're just being really inappropriate, but that's what happened. I had to take him out of the story.

My relationship with the stories is that I don't really edit along the lines of what's actually true and what's not. It's what is believable in the context of the story. It has to have integrity, but it can be absolute fiction. Some things that I say happened to me didn't; they happened to a friend. Or it was a totally different situation I've moulded and melted together, but it's a version of the truth.

I have arguments with my wife about whether I should lie on stage as much as I do or don't. My ending argument to all our discussions and rows we have about it is always, look, if you've paid to see me and I'm holding a microphone and I'm in a spotlight, I think that gives me a license not to tell the truth. I don't need to reveal that some of this is nonsense. Surely that situation explains that it's not *This is Your Life*.

My wife does object to being in the act sometimes. In this one story, I paint her out to be a politician-bashing drunk, who has a go at a current cabinet member – which is a true story. That was an almost unbelievable situation that I've managed to tame into being a truthful, jokey story. I've painted her with such broad brushstrokes that she's not really bothered. If I really go into detail, she gets a bit uppity then.

Chapter 2
Material

How does an idea become a joke? Making nothing into something.

DEBORAH FRANCES-WHITE: If you've generated a body of ideas to choose from using techniques from the inspiration chapter (or you had plenty of your own anyway), you've now got to go about killing your babies. I once heard that Paul McCartney's advice to young songwriters was, 'Don't write the tune down – if you can remember it the next day, it's good'. There's something to be said for that. How many of your ideas can you recall? What sticks with you? What have you thought about since? What are you really wanting to say? Is there anything you feel you need to get off your chest?

Sometimes I see Facebook arguments about artists being paid properly for their work. The way I see it is, I expect to be paid for craft, but art is anything I just can't help but put out into the world. In other words, if you want me to write jokes for your script, don't tell me it's good exposure or experience, I'll want to know what the fee is – but when I was finding my biological family (as an adoptee) I really needed to get on stage and talk about it. I had a slot at the London Storytelling Festival to do a show from my back catalogue. I phoned the comedian Sarah Bennetto, who was the Artistic Director of the festival, and said, 'I'm living a story, I have to talk about it', and she was excited to help me change the programme. I figure if the art is any good, it'll probably monetize itself at some point to some extent. But if it doesn't make much, it still serves a purpose. I get to express it. And an audience gets to hear it and identify with it.

So if some ideas are bugging you more than others, they're the ones you want to develop. Let them get under your skin. Generate lots of ideas around them. When you've got lots of choices on the table – it's time to edit. Get rid of anything you feel is derivative, a little dishonest, straining for effect or just doesn't really interest you – and see what's left.

After the film director has finished the shoot, they've got to work with a good editor to get rid of stuff and put what's left together in a usable sequence. This is your cutting room. Cut everything you can. It's a separate but valuable process to the quantity-driven game of generating ideas. If your end product is no good, it's probably because you didn't say 'yes' enough at the beginning or 'no' enough at the end.

Once you've cut most of what you've got, you will be able to see the few ideas that seem really fresh, original and 'you'. Then you need to craft them. I often work with a young comedian called Sadia Azmat, who talks a lot about being a young British Muslim Asian who wears a headscarf. I have very little insight into what it's like to be her, but I work with her on creating routines and punchlines. I go through her latest five minutes of material asking, 'Where exactly are the audience meant to laugh? There are a lot of funny ideas and concepts here but you need to be explicit about what you expect from an audience.' We work together on mining the best idea in the concept into the funniest turn of phrase, the most surprising example or the twist on what the audience were expecting.

Sadia works in a call centre and deals with a fair amount of casual racism from her callers. Customers often comment: 'You have an Indian name? I hope you're not _in_ India!' Sadia's joke was that she can't really respond as she'd like to because the incoming calls are recorded, but the outgoing calls are not recorded. We spent ages brainstorming funny things you could call up and say to a rude customer when you were off the clock. Sadia's first draft was woolly and we knew we could make it punchier. The more specific you are, the more laughs you're likely to get. When we hit upon Sadia phoning the caller and pretending to be an Indian, with a strong accent, from a call centre in Mumbai telling them they'd won a prize for being 'Mofo of the Month', it made us laugh a lot. The way Sadia pronounced 'Mofo' like a cheerful Indian call centre employee was the funniest thing we came up with.

This aspect of feeling like an outsider as a British-born woman from an Asian family was something Sadia felt strongly about sharing. It was her voice, her experience and her need to speak. We abandoned other, weaker examples of this type of encounter as less dynamic or relatable. When we'd hit on the one that seemed the strongest, we brainstormed twenty or thirty different punchlines until we had the one that made us laugh the most. I always encourage her to share her most personal stories because they're always more powerful and seem much funnier than her generic observations.

When I'm writing my own material, I often shape on stage. If I listen to early recordings of shows I've done, I'm always surprised how messy the set-ups are and how underdone the punchlines seem in the first few previews. The audience can make you reach for something funnier every time you perform a routine. There's nothing like that grasp to greatness in the moment. I remember being in the middle of a story, the first time I'd performed it, and realizing I'd worked out all the beats but had no punchline. I had nothing at all but I knew my best strategy was to relax into it and act as if I did have one – and because of that my brain gave me a great one that I've kept in ever since. I probably could have worked all day and got something half as funny. When you're starting out, record yourself every time you're on stage and listen back to where the laughs dried up so you know what needs work. It's also a great way to remember ad-libs you can use again that might otherwise be lost in the post-show adrenaline and beer-fest. My husband texts me ad-libs I make during my show, if he thinks I should add them to the routine, which is about as romantic as it gets for a comedian.

GARY DELANEY

A true master of the craft of joke construction, Gary Delaney is a regular on *Mock the Week* and has been able to tour on the back of his success on that show. He is the only person to ever have two jokes appear on Dave's Top Ten Jokes of the Fringe list.

I'm certainly not as disciplined as I should be. I'm much more disciplined when I'm writing for other people than for myself. If I had the discipline to go and write four days a week for myself nine to five, I would have much more material than I do. I tend to motivate myself by either a panic that I've got Edinburgh coming or that thing where there are a lot of new material nights now. There's quite a few of us who do those and you tend to be doing them with your mates and you put your name down a few weeks in advance. So often the biggest benefit of that is the social pressure that you've committed to it and the fact that people know you're going to be doing it. If you just cancel it, people know that you've probably just been lazy.

The business of writing is something which every comedian does differently. Some really do treat it like a business, so much so that they even have to go to an office.

NEAL BRENNAN

Neal Brennan followed his elder brother Kevin into stand-up comedy and has since eclipsed his success, writing for Jenny McCarthy, *Keenan & Kel* and Dave Chappelle's TV show as well as performing his own stand-up and hosting *The Champs*, a podcast with Moshe Kasher.

I'm a member of a thing in LA called The Writer's Junction, which is basically like a shared office space. It's 180 bucks a month. I go every day. I sit down. I read and I know that I'm there to incubate. I read the newspaper. I read Twitter. I read *The New Yorker*. I read fiction, non-fiction, whatever. I have a Kindle and read on there. I'm just putting myself in a position to think and shit. I'm sure a lot of comics do that thing where if you think of something, it will keep coming back. It will metastasize on its own.

Douglas Adams famously said: 'Writing is easy, just stare at a blank piece of paper until your forehead bleeds.' Andrew Maxwell describes the process similarly.

ANDREW MAXWELL

Irishman Andrew Maxwell began performing comedy in 1992 in Dublin. He was a regular warm-up comedian at television recordings in London throughout the 1990s and is now a regular on the comedy and festival circuit as well as a familiar face on panel shows. He hosts his own weekly late-night comedy gig *Fullmooners* in London and during the Edinburgh Fringe and he founded the Altitude Festival with Marcus Brigstocke.

It used to be just a sheet of A4 and a pen late at night. Sometimes marijuana-induced, sometimes not. Me downtime late at night when I'll be thinking about stuff. I'll always be writing something down.

Now, the notes are in my iPhone. I don't know I've written these things, and later I'm like, *what the fuck?* The latest was 'gays, you can have all your freedoms but we want the word "gay" back. We haven't had a decent word for picnic for years. We want the word "gay" back and now that you're getting married you won't need it so much.'

Over the space of the year I try to build up a joke and I don't plan it, but a joke will probably come on each big news hoo-ha and come together. They're merely ingredients. As I come closer and closer to time, it falls into place. It's just on a piece of A4. I write it out.

Even though a lot of successful comedians have a strong work ethic, this discipline doesn't always involve chaining yourself to a desk to write.

ORNY ADAMS

> Orny Adams rose to prominence as the parallel protagonist in the 2002 documentary *Comedian* about Jerry Seinfeld's return to the stand-up stage, and has since released two TV specials and been cast as Coach Finstock in *Teen Wolf* spin-off series.

My process is you never force anything. I write when I want to write. So if right now all of a sudden something came to me, I would get up and leave this interview. Because it's that important to me. I could come back and do this.

So I've got all my crazy pieces of paper with handwritten notes and then I type it out word for word. For example, there's this new bit I'm doing on expressions of time. It's about a three-minute bit right now and you chisel it down to about a minute and a half or whatever it is.

Some people get up, it's a routine, and they write from 6.00 am to whatever. I get up and I write when it's there. But sometimes you have to be in a weird mind-frame to make these connections, to pull this from this from this and see it. And sometimes it can be years. I have jokes that I was doing for years and I didn't understand why I was doing them. And then all of a sudden I go, 'Oh that's what it was. That's why I was doing that joke.'

Orny Adams is unusual in writing down every word he plans to say on stage, but he isn't entirely unique. Another writer-comedian is Jenny Eclair.

JENNY ECLAIR

Malaysian-born Jenny Eclair was the first-ever female winner of the Perrier Award in 1995 and her brand of confrontational, edgy humour has sustained her as a firm favourite on TV, radio and the comedy stages of Britain ever since.

I'm a writer. I sit down in my study. I have it all set up. I have a proper Mac – I can't write on a laptop. I do use notebooks. In the old days it was all longhand. I've still got the red and blacks in a lock-up. They're waist-high now.

It's the word with me. I love writing. Writing is incredibly important. I don't feel good if I haven't written in a day. I've started the fourth novel, but I've got the cast talking at me, I don't know what they're doing yet. That's upsetting. That's genuinely really keeping me awake at night, because I want them to settle and show me what they are going to do.

I've written three novels and every time I sit down to start one, I never know how it's going to work, how it's going to happen. Three times it's happened. I don't know whether it's going to happen a fourth time. It's like knowing you've made a dish and going back into the kitchen and sort of saying I can do that again but absolutely having no idea how you do it.

Other stand-ups who also write scripts or books as well find that the process is very different. A book must be written – there's no choice but to keep pounding away at the keys until you produce a readable manuscript – but a comedian does not necessarily need a script to memorize. And so, the same person may adopt very different processes for different kinds of writing.

MARK WATSON

With the other writing that I do, like books, I do have a discipline for writing. But for stand-up, I've never really been able to write by sitting down and trying to think of funny stuff. So I basically just wander around, collecting ideas by living my life. For a long time I did literally have notebooks that I would write stuff down in and I've still got some of those old ones, often with just baffling stuff. It will just be a word like 'duck' or 'plaster' and I will never know now what that funny thought was going to be, unfortunately.

These days, I note stuff straight into my phone, which means I am often rude, because at lunch someone will be saying something which I think is a really stupid thing to say. I'm definitely going to mention that on stage and I've got no option but to save myself a text within to remind myself. I frequently look like I'm texting someone when actually it's worse than that. I'm making notes about the people I'm with.

Mark Watson and Jenny Eclair are just two comedians who write a lot of material other than their own stand-up. As well as novels, they may also be writing screenplays, poetry, magazine articles and much else besides. And different forms of writing create different pressures.

NAT LUURTSEMA

Stand-up is so hard for me to write. Bizarrely, I can sit and write a film in no time. It takes me no time to write scripts and screenplays and things. TV's harder because I like an ending. That's why I like films. I like an ending. Bashed out my book in four months – 70,000 words in four months and every day was a joy. I let myself do two edits of each chapter and that was it, no more, because I didn't want to fiddle the life out of it. But stand-up, I write it in the back of the club before I go on. That's the only time I'll write it.

I feel like such a half-arsed dickhead. But stand-up to me only makes sense in a stand-up club. If seems facile when you're writing it in a cafe.

There's no beautiful language or anything but you can't take beautiful language up on stage like that. Writing ad-libs for people on panel shows taught me a lot. You have to write that really cleverly. You can't write something too smart or too intricate or too complex. It has to be like it just came to their mind.

I come up with a lot of my best jokes in front of the audience. I only learnt that because I used to write and write and write before I went on stage. That was fine and I felt sorted and I was really successful with that approach because it was okay for me to be quite stilted because I was brand new and I looked young and scared and the audience were rooting for me. Wherever I went in the country people were always kind. They were like 'she's clearly brand new but I like her jokes. You can smell the work on them. We like this.' Then you reach a certain point where you look comfortable and confident on stage and you have to bring something different because you can't have your overwritten jokes any more.

Writing for different mediums also means writing in different formations. The days of comedians like Bob Hope engaging small armies of gag-writers are largely over, but situation comedies, especially in America, tend to be a team effort.

HANNIBAL BURESS

Chicago-born Hannibal Buress has featured on a variety of TV shows, from *The Late Show with David Letterman* in America to *8 Out of 10 Cats* in the UK. He also wrote for *Saturday Night Live* and *30 Rock* and he currently hosts a weekly stand-up comedy show on Sunday evenings in Brooklyn.

With sitcom, it's more collaborative. On *30 Rock*, we would sit in a room together to kind of bounce ideas off each other. But for my stand-up, it's just really trying stuff in front of the audience and then seeing how it feels and add them based on that.

I've been thinking about trying to get one other person just to kind of help me write or just somebody that comes to all my shows and remembers the tags on the different stuff that I said and then I can meet with them afterwards and talk about it. Somebody who comes to every few shows, kind of like a consultant stand-up. But as far as having twelve people pitch on my stand-up, I wouldn't want that.

The 'Bob Hope' model hasn't entirely vanished however. Many comedians also make money writing material for other comics to use on television, especially on panel shows, but also if a lot of new jokes are required in a hurry. Jo Caulfield used to write for Graham Norton.

JO CAULFIELD

Oh, it was an amazing job writing for Graham Norton, a beautiful job. I did it because I knew Graham before. His first series, I did the warm-up and they had trouble finding writers and then they said, 'Well, Jo knows the show, why don't we give her a go'. It was male writers and they were writing too gay, you know, just far too gay. Graham would say sometimes, 'can we just not have it end with "and then I fucked him up the arse", that's all I ask. Not every joke. If you can't find a punchline then I'll say it, but we have to save it.'

The panel show is a relatively new venue for stand-up comedians, but for many a very important one. Phill Jupitus has been on *Never Mind the Buzzcocks* since it started in 1996 and he doesn't like to over-prepare.

PHILL JUPITUS

Phill Jupitus is a British stand-up comedian who began his performing career as Porky the Poet on the London stand-up poetry circuit. After a spell as press officer for the Housemartins, he began hosting a radio show and became a familiar face in London stand-up and improv clubs. He has been a regular panellist on the pop music quiz *Never Mind the Buzzcocks* since its start in 1996 and he also acts, notably playing leading roles in *Hairspray* and *Spamalot* in the West End.

I sort of don't want to do my homework. I'll just turn up on the night. Trust me. We did a rehearsal yesterday for *Would I Lie To You?* and upfront I said to the producer, 'Look, I'm going to seem incredibly dull and uninterested in the rehearsal, please don't think that when the show happens that that's what I'm going to do, it's just that I have no time for rehearsal. It's not part of my process.'

When you do a panel show, the recordings take between an hour and a half and three hours. You don't know how long it's going to take. Sometimes it's incredibly quick. The quickest panel show I've ever been on was hosted by Terry Wogan. He's so fucking good at his job, that's why it was so quick. He's been hosting for years and there wasn't a single retake. It's one of the loveliest things I've ever heard a floor manager say, this guy, I can see him now, he said, 'I've just got to check with the gallery'. He looked around and with a smile on his face, he said, 'There will be no retakes, Terry'. It's one of the coolest things ever said on the floor. Terry Wogan is one of the three Tories I forgive, the other two being my parents.

I used to panic too much. You'd worry about getting jokes in. You'd think, 'Oh I've got to get jokes in'. I asked the producers on *Buzzcocks* to send me stuff upfront and the more I agonized and worked on *Buzzcocks*, the worse I was in every sense. I tried too hard in the early years. I was too loud. There wasn't enough light and shade. I was too needy, frankly.

I think that now I arrive on the night, and it's very much about what happens in the room. You sit in that room with five people you've not really met before, probably. More often than not, there's one or two you have maybe worked with, but it's strangers. You sit in a room with five strangers and you have to create an entertainment. And if you are pressured by that then you'll never get it off. And my job on *Buzzcocks* is just to calm down.

Figure 3 Phill Jupitus © Idil Sukan/Draw HQ

The form of the act can also dictate the extent to which the performer is reciting a script. A stand-up comedian is usually a soloist, but in the case of double acts such as Richard Herring when he worked with Stewart Lee, a different approach may be required. Herring explains.

RICHARD HERRING

When we used to do double-act stuff in the 1990s, we scripted it pretty heavily. We would mess around in the double act and change stuff on stage. We always did. There was an element of ad-libbing and things would develop, but when I came back to stand-up [after a nine-year break], it was very much trying to work out exactly what I should say and learn a script. I would actually watch comedians and, ultimately, my aim would be to go on stage with nothing and talk for an hour and it will all be funny or enough of it would be funny. So I have got to that stage where I feel comfortable about going on without a script, but it's nice to have a script to fall back on.

For many, stand-up comedy is a live art form and it feels anathema to begin the process by sitting and writing.

HARLAND WILLIAMS

Canadian/American Harland Williams is an actor (*Dumb and Dumber, There's Something About Mary*), musician and radio personality as well as a stand-up comedian. He also writes and illustrates books for children. He has a bi-weekly podcast called *The Harland Highway*.

I always write on stage. I will conceptualize things when I'm walking around or lying in bed or making love or whatever. Then once I'm on stage, I will have a nugget or a premise in my head and then I will let the words kind of come out on stage. Then, each time I do it, I will refine it a bit or I will just keep it in my head. I don't like putting anything down or recording things because then it becomes serious.

> To me, comedy is like a hornet's nest. If you could picture my head as a hornet's nest and all the hornets inside my skull are jokes flying around in mad circles. Every now and then, one flies out of the little hole and goes out into the world. I'm sure there's a few that got away but I usually somehow manage to keep everything in the hive.

The idea of having a mind full of ideas is just the starting point for some comics.

JIM JEFFERIES

I've never written any jokes down on paper. I mostly tell stories. If I'm at a bar with my friends and I tell a story about what happened and I see everyone laugh, I make a mental note. Then I tell the story on stage as it happened. The next time I go back, I tell it again with the embellishments and what needs to be taken out, what needs to be put in. Normally I don't go and do comedy nights where people go and try out new material. I'm normally on stage between an hour and an hour and a half, so I sort of wedge it in the forty-minute mark for five minutes because I know it's bookended by two good jokes.

Adam Bloom has strong feelings about the need for writing comedy to be an active process.

ADAM BLOOM

I never sit down to write. I do the writing while walking down the street and then on stage. I just have a pen and paper. I have an hour of bullet points, but you can fit it on the back of a large stamp. With a small, thin pen. And that hasn't changed at all since I first started. I don't believe the spoken word should be written down. Because you then do an impression of how you think you speak and then learn it and then do a bad impression of yourself on stage. So you're becoming a bad act in real life.

Robin Ince's system is even more chaotic.

ROBIN INCE

I've learnt basically I don't write shows, I write thousands of notes. I have notes everywhere. They're sometimes three words, and they're sometimes a sentence, and sometimes the whole back of a postcard, and I have them almost every night and I try out these ideas. I've never found it very easy to sit down and write. I know some people actually write their sets. I know some people's notebooks are full of jokes that they've written. When I'm found dead, suffocated under however many thousands of postcards, it will actually be a selection of non-sequiturs and apparent code-words. The jokes are never written down.

Daniel Sloss has found a way to keep the energy of a live performance while not having to do all of his writing in public.

DANIEL SLOSS

Daniel Sloss is a Scottish comedian who began performing and writing comedy professionally while still in his teens. In 2010, at the age of 19, he became the youngest comedian to perform a solo season in London's West End. On TV he has appeared on *Michael McIntyre's Comedy Roadshow*, *8 Out of 10 Cats*, *Russell Howard's Good News* and many others.

I write a lot of jokes in the shower. I don't sing. I'm tone deaf. I just rant about stuff. I'm like 'Oh, that's quite amazing. I could turn that into a bit.' It's a weird job stand-up comedy, just random – oh, that's really funny. I need to write that down somewhere. iPhone, either Dictaphone or the notepad and then just writing down keywords. So there's some really weird stuff in there.

I'm pretty sure I managed to get a five-minute routine and the keywords were just 'duck rape'. If anyone ever went through my phone, they would be really weirded out. Also the little voice memos which I leave myself are just – only to me. So I'm not going, 'Well, I think it would be funny if we had a joke. It would turn out this was what was going on. But it really wasn't'. So I just record into my phone, saying, 'I hate when people do this and I hope they all die.' Then I listen to it and go, 'Oh, yeah, I remember that. God, I'm an angry person.'

Many comedians bemoan the fact that they can't just turn on a tap and have material flow out.

JO CAULFIELD

I wish I had a foolproof process. I have lots of different sorts of processes. Sometimes just sitting and trying to do something. Sitting at a computer. But that very rarely works for me. Also then I write in a very odd way, in that I don't talk like I write. I sort of write like it's a Dickensian novel or something. I tend to have an idea and think 'I think there's something in this' and then do it on stage. And I record it, and that's when my brain will work out the right way to say it. The pressure of people staring at you, and your brain is in a heightened state anyway, just makes the words come out right. The more you do it, the more you know how to get in that state. I almost feel like it's nothing to do with me. I'm not conscious of it, I'm not doing anything. It's just coming out and I will say a word and after I will go 'oh! That was exactly the right word that conjures up this image and it made it go in a different direction', but at the time I'm not conscious of that.

I mean, there are certain rules and you go 'well, what is going to be the punchline that will end in maybe people clapping. I'll move that line around because maybe that's the stronger one.' You do that kind of work on it once it's come out on stage and then I'll look at it and copy up what I say.

Sofie Hagen finds that she doesn't so much write material on stage as backstage.

SOFIE HAGEN

> Danish comedian Sofie Hagen has been hugely successful since moving to the UK in 2013, winning the Chortle Best Newcomer award and appearing on Alan Davies' *Aprés-Ski* on the BBC thanks to her joke-writing and insatiable amiability.

The five minutes before I have to go on stage are the most productive minutes for me ever. I just go through what I'm going to say, then my mind goes 'you can say this and this and this' because I'm more comfortable when I'm not on stage. When I'm on stage, it's very rare that I'm comfortable enough to just kind of riff, so the five minutes before I go on stage, that's when my brain goes 'here we go and here's all the thoughts and ideas and whatever'.

I think that it's because there's no pressure, because I am not currently saying it but it still has the pressure of, you have to say it in a bit. You want to be funny. If I sit at home and write, there's too many thoughts going, 'you're not good enough, why would you say this?' and then nothing funny comes out of it. I know you can get past it if you write, say, twenty minutes and then maybe something will come of it. I'm not doing that, should do that. But the five minutes before I gig is just the right amount of pressure and lack thereof and that's when it's fun and I'm kind of excited about going on, I want to say all these things.

For Sam Wills, aka The Boy With Tape On His Face, the challenge of 'writing' material is somewhat flipped by the fact that his act doesn't involve any speech.

SAM WILLS

Sam Wills is better known as The Boy With Tape On His Face. This innovative prop comic performs with a strip of black gaffer tape across his mouth and his act consists almost entirely of involving audience volunteers in elaborate creations in which everyday household objects are repurposed to create amazing tableaux. Originally from New Zealand, he now lives in London.

I have an interesting technique where I don't write anything for a long time. I store up a lot of props and various bits and pieces and then I get locked in a room. My wife puts me away in a room for about six weeks and I go slightly crazy. I play in a room for six weeks and muck around, then eventually come out of there with a show. I'm not 100 per cent certain how it works.

My wife has to put up with a lot of the bad stuff. I run ideas past her. If she laughs instantly, I know it's funny. If I have to explain the joke several times, then I know I'm flogging a dead horse. There've been routines which I've convinced myself they are funny. I'm sure at some point I will find exactly what's funny about them. She's the one who says, 'You need to let it go. Drop it.'

I think when it comes to the audience interaction, that's when it's trickier. Because sometimes it's the timing of sets. I have an idea and I think, 'Roughly, that will be four minutes long'. In reality, when I bring somebody up on stage, they bring a world of chaos to it. Then I realize, 'Okay, this is now a ten-minute bit'.

Sofie Hagen faced a different problem when she first came to the UK – how to translate her Danish act into English and now sometimes the other way around.

SOFIE HAGEN

I did two years in Danish, nothing else, and then I moved here and I've done it for a few years in English and it's almost the same amount of time you have to spend learning because it's so different. Most stand-up is in the words and in the way of phrasing sentences, so I found that it's harder to make a joke funny in Danish because in English you have about four times as many words as we have in Danish, so when I have to do a sentence in Danish it will probably be fourteen words and that could be three words in English, it's quicker to get to the point.

I think more immediately in Danish, because it's my real language so most stuff will come out Danish. I'll just speak and all of the little tag lines and stuff will come out, then I translate it back again and then I will inevitably use that one. It's a great way of working.

Not writing a script keeps your comedy fresh and alive, but not having a permanent record can create problems for you later on.

MOSHE KASHER

Moshe Kasher is an American stand-up comedian who was born to deaf parents and brought up in Oakland, California. After performing comedy for almost ten years, he broke through in 2009 when he was named Best of the Fest at Aspen and Best New Comic by iTunes. He also writes books and plays and acts occasionally. He hosts the podcast *The Champs* with Neal Brennan.

I've never written anything down. I don't have anything written down anywhere. Once in a while, if I have a big show, I will write down the set list. But I don't have them archived anywhere and I don't take notes. I was looking at my phone the other day at one of these old set lists and there's one on here called 'Going "uh" to a girl'. I don't know what that joke is. So it's gone.

To avoid this, most comics have some kind of system to track and record new material as it emerges. Some just write phrases or bullet points. Others have a more elaborate mechanism. One-liner comic Gary Delaney learned the importance of this the hard way.

GARY DELANEY

I'm very organized now. I didn't use to be. I didn't even have a computer until about four years ago because I couldn't afford one. So I just had bits and bobs of this, the memory stick, and bits of paper and stuff on my family's computer. All of that stuff is lost. So all of that first six or seven years of my career, there's no real record of that apart from scraps of printed-out paper that I have got in a box in the office.

What I was doing for a recent show was just going through and digging out a hard copy of when I had really early new material nights that I've done. Looking for things. You think, 'Well, that was a good idea for a joke but I didn't have the skill to pull it off in those days'. So I will take the kernel of the idea. I will rewrite it and I will try it again. Because as a comic, with only two years under my belt, I wasn't doing that idea justice. So that's what you do when you haven't got new ideas. You can plunge into your old ideas and try and fix them.

Gary Delaney talked us through his joke-creation process in some detail.

GARY DELANEY

I start off – and a lot of comics nowadays, instead of what used to be their notepads, just use their phones. You have a shortcut on your desktop to add your voice record function or your notepad thing now and you collect up your core ideas – which are usually just phrases for me, something you can build on. So you start off with those initial ideas because it's very hard to sit down with a blank bit of paper and go, right, I'm going to come up with twenty jokes on that.

Then, when I've booked myself into a new material night – and I've made that credible commitment – usually that day, I have to sit down and turn these loose phrases and things into proper jokes and do all the boring legwork on it. It's really just trying it, seeing if it fits, moving it around. Does it work with a two? Does it work with a three? Should that be at the end? Should I put the cliché at the beginning? Just starting it and just trying all these different things until eventually it fits and then saying it until it sounds – it has that right sort of bippity-boppity rhythm on the mouth and sounds pleasing.

So once I've done that and then I write them up, I usually do it as round numbers. So I will go somewhere with twenty or thirty jokes and obviously Sod's law dictates that. I don't think I'm any better than random at choosing which of my jokes are going to be successful. Nearly always if I love a joke, that's the kiss of death for anyone. It will die.

If I've got twenty-nine jokes, I will put down any old bollocks to make it up to thirty so it's a round number. Inevitably, that will be the one that works. Why thirty? That's just the OCD. I would have difficulty standing out there to do twenty-nine jokes.

So you go out there and you try them, literally reading them out. Then there's probably two more stages of writing that occur on the stage. One is, sometimes you're up there and – especially if it's a bit hard – you look at what you've got on the paper and you panic. You look at it and you go, 'That is not funny enough to say out loud'. You go, 'As I start this sentence, I've got to find a funnier end to it because that's not enough'. You have to very quickly say out loud something better than what you've got written down there, to save your embarrassment. A lot of jokes get fixed that way. You look at it and you go, 'I can't read it out in front of these people. Now, I'm here. I'm too embarrassed. That's shit.'

That's why I think performing is a great discipline for writing. It's easy when you're writing for other people to say, 'that's good enough'. The thing is, good enough isn't good enough. Not when you're doing it for yourself on a Friday night in front of 300 drunks who don't really like you and the last guy nailed it. Good enough isn't good enough then.

So you look at it and you madly improvise something better. Then when you go through and you play back the tape – because you tape these gigs obviously – you will often see whether consciously or subconsciously that you said something different and better to what you've got on the paper. Sometimes that's just editing on the fly and sometimes that's just because we speak different to how we write. So you go and rewrite it the way you speak even if that's wrong and that becomes the joke. I go through my jokes and I would generally – on a typical new material night, a third will do really well, a third will do okay and a third will die.

So I take that third that have done really well and the third that have done okay, I might rewrite and try again. The third that have done really well, I will then progress them to the next level and try them somewhere else, a bigger show – like more high-profile but still new material. More likely you drop them in a midweek gig, some little gig. You pick which are the best three. You'll drop them in on a little Wednesday gig where it's not really that crucial, dropping them in the middle where it's not really going to harm my career if they bombed.

Generally you start dropping those in and I, personally, find the same sort of ratio again. Once I've dropped them in, and they're being measured against the proper jokes, then they're judged far more harshly. So once again, of that collection, a third will succeed, a third will be OK and a third will fail.

So I will take that third of the original third and then I will start dropping those in at more high pressure. You could drop them in on a Friday night or whatever. Once again, about a third will succeed and a third will do OK and a third will fail.

So I end up with like a ninth of my original set, something like that. It's quite often lower. It's probably a ninth now but here it used to be lower.

Another excellent way to develop your material is to work with other comics, to bounce around ideas and see things from a slightly different angle. This can often grease the wheels of your mind when things are particularly gridlocked and hard to take apart.

DANIEL SLOSS

There's this Canadian comic who is a genius called Tom Stade who lives in the UK, five doors down from me. I was a huge fan of him and I found out I lived near him. He said, 'Oh, you should come around and do some writing with me'. And then like two weeks later, he's asking, 'Why have you not come around and written with me?' I was like, 'Oh, I didn't know you were serious'.

He's one of the reasons my stand-up has changed so much, because he's an outstanding writer. My way of writing before was very much that I would get a routine and I would make it very punchy and stuff but then I would always be cutting it down. I would be trimming all the fats. Whereas Tom is very much like, 'Oh, no, make it longer'. He takes a minute and then turns it into a twenty-five-minute routine after a month. It's amazing. Explore every single avenue because that way, you're never going to do the same topic ever again.

Since we started, I've just been very lucky with the way that Tom has helped me with my writing. It really, really reignited the passion. I have jokes that I love doing. I really, really enjoy them. I get excited when I get to the bit where I just perform them and when it gets the laughs, you know, it just feels amazing.

Once you have a solid set, introducing new material can be hard.

MARCUS BRIGSTOCKE

I was a cracking good comic. And I was so bored. It was so dreary. Because I had a great twenty and a great thirty. And that's a real problem.

> When it's that good and it's bullet-proof, I mean like late-show
> bullet-proof, then it's great. Then it makes it really hard, and really bad
> and upsetting and lonely to run new material in and let it be shit for that
> amount of time – a couple of minutes out of your thirty.

These days many comedians are also blogging and podcasting, both
of which can generate material as well as providing another way of
publicizing gigs and DVD releases.

MOSHE KASHER

I think for me, the cool thing about podcasts is that they take their own
shape. You don't know what they are. You sit down. You start doing it and
all of a sudden, you got all these inside jokes. Like, on the podcast[1] – our
motto or whatever is now, 'You're fucking with the champs'. All of the
people that listen to us, they say, 'I fucked with the champs'. That's what
they say.

Now we didn't orchestrate that. It was a thing that just sort of
happened organically. You fuck with the champs, ladies and gentlemen.
Now, anybody that comes to one of my shows who listens to the podcast
says, 'I fucked with the champs', and it's like a thing.

Having an instant platform with such a low barrier of entry is fantastic
for audience-hungry comedians at every level. However, Robin Ince
isn't at all sure that podcasting is a blessing for the rest of us.

ROBIN INCE

Well, they've given the means of production to the proletariat with
the internet, haven't they? It's a Marxist dream! Unfortunately it turns
out that all the proletariat wanted to do is make podcasts and so now

---

[1] *The Champs*, with Neal Brennan.

it turns out that they're only listened to by the people who made the podcasts.

You could make a documentary now. You don't have to have very much for a camera and you're able to go out and make a documentary, and I think that's fantastic. Rather than sit around and wonder why someone else has got something that you felt was something that should have gone to you, well just go out and make something. Make your short film. Make a feature film. Think about Shane Meadows and Paddy Considine when they'd have a weekend off, and they'd go, 'let's just make a short film on the moors. Don't know what the plot will be, but let's just go out there and start filming.'

And there might not be a market for it. But it doesn't matter. You've made your art. And it always goes down to that cliché. You do it because you must.

Richard Herring was one of comedy podcasting's pioneers and has three or four active podcast series at any one time. As a comedian who had TV success early on but didn't sustain it, he finds the freedom that outlets like podcasting provide extremely liberating.

RICHARD HERRING

What I think is great about it, and what I really love about it, is just you have the autonomy to create basically a radio show (or a TV show if you've got the resources to do that), that you can put out with no audience interfering in it and you can have an idea. I think for a while, after I'd done *Time Gentlemen Please*, which was a sitcom with Al Murray, I was sort of sitting back and waiting for people to get in touch with me. And they weren't really coming to me for stuff and then I realized that actually you've got to get out there and do it yourself. So that's probably the reason I went back into stand-up. But also, I've got lots of ideas and people don't want them.

So to do a radio show, you could have an idea, then someone has got to decide they want to make it. That takes a few months and then suddenly you're going to make a pilot. So it can take two years before you get it on and then they will tell you, 'You can't do this joke. You can't do this joke. You can't do this. Are you sure you want to do this?'

I think people initially were going to worry about the fact that no one is paying for any of this. How are you going to make money? It wasn't really the issue for me. I wanted to get my stuff out there and as it has happened, I think it's really great because it means that you've garnered new fans who then come to see your live shows or buy your DVDs. So it does work as a financial model.

When I started off, the idea of doing my own radio show was appealing, except you had to get the radio show. But now you can sit in your attic and record something and put it out and people hopefully will find and discover and listen to it. So it's great just getting stuff out there. You're getting new fans. I think it's very intimate. It's very like stand-up because it's autonomous and immediate. I like all that and that's what I really love about stand-up now.

So doing something where I play myself at snooker in my basement and commentate on it – there's nowhere in the world that that would be broadcast. No one would put that out. If you went and pitched that everywhere in the whole universe, I think no one – even an infinite universe, no one would commission that.

While Richard Herring was developing his podcasts in the UK, Todd Glass was pioneering in America.

TODD GLASS

Before I did mine, I just knew Jimmy Pardo. I know other people had podcasts. But in the comedic community, Jimmy Pardo was the first person that we all knew to have a podcast and when I did his, it was unbelievable. It was just great.

I'm always afraid when I say the same thing a lot, people will say, 'You said that on every show'. But you have a different audience. I do like the clarity of this because it explains why podcasting is so addictive to a lot of people. Podcasting is so simple. It's taking radio and giving it the purity of stand-up. So why wouldn't it be great? No editor, no director. The reason stand-up is so great is because it's the vehicle. But it also can be fucking god-awful. You go and see someone and it's atrocious. Well, it's an open mic night. They're only doing three minutes. But you don't have to run your stand-up by anybody. So you get bad. But then you get fucking the best of the best. It's the same with podcasting.

The stand-up comedian is the ultimate writer-performer, and podcasting is an ideal medium for that kind of talent. Other internet outlets are more geared to the writing side of the equation. One-liner specialist Gary Delaney finds Twitter is an ideal medium for him and has been on it from the very beginning.

GARY DELANEY

When I first started on Twitter, there was hardly anyone who put jokes on it in those days. It was really easy to stand out. It was great. I only had a few hundred followers with just a few comedy gigs and stuff on there. Twitter wasn't that big and you could try a joke out and it would – if it worked, you would drop it in your club set the next day.

After a year or two, that just became not viable any more because Twitter got too big. I mean now I've got like 50,000 followers, some of whom would come to gigs. So you can't really use it as a testing group. Also just the quality of people on Twitter deteriorating as the number of them rose.

At that time, 2008, 2009, I didn't have a huge amount of writing work and professional work – so I was quite happy just to use it, put stuff up and just raise my profile and it did help me get work. I got followed by lots of producers and what happens is, people who I used to work with in clubs, who are now famous, go and retweet your joke to their half a million or million followers, which includes lots of industry people. Then they start following you and then work comes through. But again I think I got kind of lucky. I think people who are trying to follow that route on Twitter now, the route that I did, are finding that road much more congested and much harder.

Because it was an open path in the days that I joined, I got loads of benefit from it. But now – I mean in my show a couple of years ago, it was in a room half the size and I probably finished every day talking to six or seven people on Twitter. 'Oh, great show', 'thanks so much'. They followed me on there. Now, I'm getting one or two a day in a room twice the size.

So, Twitter can be a promotional tool, a means of connecting with an audience and strengthening the relationship built on stage, it can be a test-bed for new ideas, or it can also be a medium all its own.

NAT LUURTSEMA

I think we churn through a lot more jokes and a lot more material on Twitter now that otherwise we would've inflicted on an audience. It's a good road tester. Tom Craine uses it to see if a subject interests people, and I think that's a better way of doing it than a refined, honed joke. There's definitely halfway between too witty to waste on normal conversations but not good enough to put it on stage. Jigsaw always do that to each other. 'Is this a joke or a tweet?'

Some of the comedians who flocked to Twitter a few years ago have now pulled back.

PHILL JUPITUS

One of the things that used to happen a lot on Twitter is that you'd say something funny and the response would be, 'Someone's already said that, you cunt'. Immediately, almost immediately – 'That's not funny. That's already been said.' Just constantly. And the thing is, if you say it in a room full of people and you create the notion or idea yourself and you follow that idea, then no one is going to think of the idea before you do, and that's why I like live or being in a room in front of people. And also because when you're 6'4" and you weigh 20 stone and you're in a bit of a bad mood, people are less likely to call you a cunt to your face.

Moshe Kasher is on Twitter as well as podcasting but isn't convinced of the benefits.

MOSHE KASHER

The closeness you get to the audience is a bit weird. A lot of the mystery is gone, definitely. I don't know if that's a problem, because I've never been into like the mysterious shadowy figure. But there are people who are like that. How weird would it be if Dave Chappelle was tweeting all the time and doing a podcast and coming out after the show and then being like, 'Hey, what's up everybody?' You know what I mean? You want Chappelle and Louie to be mysterious. 'Where did they go?'

But at the same time, I think like building intimate relationships with fans is cool because they're really your fans.

Even Gary Delaney has found that Twitter has a significant hidden downside.

GARY DELANEY

You have to write quite a lot and that's kind of why I put myself in this position – to do this show to make myself write more. I had to do things to force myself to come up with some stuff because I had a lovely set. I built up quite anonymously a really nice sort of really good solid twenty-minute set round clubs that worked really well.

Then the internet crashed it and I did bits on the telly and I just burned it. It just didn't have that impact any more. So I'm just looking to replace everything. I think you can never outrun that treadmill. You're only ever going to have a smattering of things that are really good bankers and are new before they start to tail off. So it's the nature.

Rather than moaning about things, I try and use Twitter to my own publicity advantage and get stuff out of it, and I do to a degree.

But genuinely, I think if the internet didn't exist, I would be a much richer man. Well, I wouldn't necessarily have gotten the breaks I got because I wouldn't have come to the industry's attention. But I would still have a really solid gold set that could all go around clubs and rip it each night without people going, 'Oh, yeah, I know that one, I know that one', and be able to drop things, because I would still have every golden joke that I've written, rather than having to chuck them away after a while.

Others are put off by the mere idea of an entertainer having a prominent internet presence. Social networking sites connect people on a very personal level. Is that really want audiences want – let alone performers?

HARLAND WILLIAMS

I think part of the mystery of show business is that space between the public and the people providing the entertainment. I find guys like Jack Nicholson and Marlon Brando and Clint Eastwood – there's a mystique to those people and I almost don't know if I would want to meet them because I think it's the mystique that's just as alluring as the content that they provide. It's hard in this world these days to have mystique about another human being.

People can reach out to me and – I don't want to sound like an ass, but I don't reach back to them as much. I do communicate to a degree but it's all through machines. I don't personally phone people or personally tweet people but I try to keep it on a mass scale because I think it's important just to keep that divide. I think it's what keeps people kind of intrigued and enthralled. At least that's how I feel. So I'm basing it on that. I wouldn't want people to know about every little detail of my life.

Mark Watson, by contrast, is virtually a Twittervangelist.

MARK WATSON

I was in it quite early and not in the way people talk about being early adopters. It was just before it became enormous, I think, before they had endorsed it and all that. It must have been about five or six years ago I went on it. There are quite clear drawbacks to it. Like, a lot of people are nuts. That's the main drawback with everything to do with the internet.

In Twitter, you are uniquely in touch with those people – or most of the time they're in touch with me. But beneath all the nonsense, I think Twitter is kind of a miracle thing really. It's essentially a conversation between everyone in the world perpetually. People don't understand it. They always caricature it by saying, 'oh, it's just "I had this for lunch"'. It's true that boring people are boring on Twitter. But interesting people are interesting on it, too.

Gary Delaney has found that Twitter can also lead to problems with plagiarism.

GARY DELANEY

I try not to let it wind me up too much nowadays, but it used to be the case that if comics had a great set, they could carry on doing it until they did it on the telly. It's why people did those sets for years. But if you're a one-liner comic, that isn't the case any more.

I did a thing in a show where I tracked which of my jokes appeared on Google the most. The most popular at that time was Old Macdonald had Tourette's, which ended up on 666,350 listings.

There's a lovely little joke I wrote in January 2011 and I thought 'that's a funny joke but it's quite obscure. It will never work in clubs.' So I thought I would just throw it away on Twitter because Twitter audiences are generally cleverer than club audiences. It was a nice little joke. The joke was, I got a new job playing the triangle in a reggae band, and ting. Lovely little gag. And it was clear from the action on Twitter that it was a funnier joke than I thought. I thought, well I've made a mistake there. So let's try that in clubs. So I started doing that in clubs and it would go really well. It was a clean banker, which is a really valuable thing. Anyone can have a rude banker but to have a clean banker is great. That's what you need for telly and things as well.

So a very valuable joke. And then, come 2013, it just stopped working. The reason it stopped working was because about six months later, loads of variants on that joke just emerged all over the internet. It's absolutely swamped. I've even seen them on texts. I've seen them on Twitter and just this huge amount of them. If you put it into Google, it brings up 22 million hits now. I'm sure not all of those are actual versions of the joke but as many as I clicked down through are. There are loads of different variants on it. I heard a DJ on Radio 2 who did one of them the other day. So I thought well, that's probably the best clean joke in this Edinburgh show and I had to drop it before I actually got to Edinburgh.

That is the nature. So it gets to the point where I know that a joke, even if I don't do it on telly, is going to get burned within a couple of years. A shame, really, if you write a brand new joke that gets a woof. It will get a woof around three months and then the reaction will start to tail off because it's like enough critical mass of your audience have seen it on a text or whatever.

So you get three months' use out of it – and then it will still work but it will never work again as well as it did. Now I just put leftover jokes on Twitter. Things that I think are funny but I don't think will ever work in clubs, I put up on there.

Even silent clown The Boy With Tape On His Face, Sam Wills, isn't immune from joke theft, although his act is certainly Twitter-proof.

SAM WILLS

I've heard of a guy in a London club who stood on stage and decided to mime out 'Endless Love' using his hands and not oven gloves. So it's like, okay, you're blatantly ripping off this whole section. There's a guy in Benidorm who calls himself 'The Man With Tape On His Face.' A tribute act who's done fifty minutes of my material. I'll probably kneecap him if I saw him.

Tribute acts do exist, obviously, but it's a strange one. You've just got to question the moral intellect of the man. Really? You're going to do this? Are you really blatantly ripping off my show? He clearly knows I'm not happy about it because we've asked him to stop doing it. He was just posting stuff to Facebook and my wonderful fans would contact me and go, 'Did you know about this guy?'

I don't know about the legality of it. Technically it's a choreographed routine like a dance and whatnot. I suppose when you make something a tribute, it is a tribute. But for me, I don't know. It's confusing when I have people contacting me saying, 'My parents saw you in Benidorm'. No, they didn't.

Moshe Kasher doesn't find the same problem.

MOSHE KASHER

I don't really believe in joke thieves. But even if they do exist, no one can steal my jokes because nobody can tell my jokes because they're for me. Who's going to steal my jokes about my deaf mother and my Hasidic dad and how I became a man?

Deborah Frances-White talks to Paul Provenza

New Yorker Paul Provenza began his stand-up comedy career at the famous Improv comedy club. He also worked as an actor in TV shows and off-Broadway and in 2005 he directed the movie *The Aristocrats* with magician Penn Jillette, in which dozens of comedians perform their version of the same joke. In 2011, he developed the live show *Set List* with Troy Conrad, in which stand-ups are faced with a list of topics they have never seen before and have to improvise a routine around them. After several runs at comedy festivals across the world, a television version was filmed for Sky Atlantic in the UK.

DEBORAH FRANCES-WHITE: You seem to create alternative spaces for comedians to play in – Set List *being an example of that. Why do you feel the need to do that? How do you come up with those places and ideas?*

PAUL PROVENZA: I think the genesis of that comes from a certain dissonance that I feel between the creative impulse to do stand-up and the urgency that some people feel to be in that world. The creative impulse is very, very dissonant with the reality of the business and the industry. And I think that over many, many years I found myself missing the purity of that original impulse and I found myself wishing that I could feel what I felt in the very early days more often, where it wasn't about business, it wasn't about contractual obligations, it wasn't about figuring out how to navigate the industry or a 'career'.

I started very young, about the age of 16. And when I started out, what I found was a world that was like the island of misfit toys. I found this world of people who were either dysfunctional or alienated or who just felt themselves outside in some way. The great thing about stand-ups is the more eccentric, the more idiosyncratic, the odder and the more outside you are, the more appreciated you often are. And so what is normally a liability in life becomes your currency. And that's revelatory and that's life-affirming. And that does shift and change the way you exist in the world.

Why do you think that becomes harder to do as you go on?

Because the nature of making a living in anything changes the purity of it. Doug Stanhope once told me the way he looks at it is that anybody who tells jokes for money is a whore, basically. He says that the real true moments of comedy are when you crack a joke with the guy stacking the shelves in the supermarket at 3.00 am. He's not expecting it and you change his day for him. You don't then ask him to buy a t-shirt for ten bucks; you don't ask him to buy a CD because he liked your joke. It just happened and it's who you are, and it made a great impact on somebody and it changed their day.

As soon as you add any sort of commerce into the equation, everything has to change. I wanted to get back to doing stand-up just for stand-up's sake, just because I wanted to feel those pure things again, those unfettered joys again. That's why I went over to the UK and started working where I had no profile, where I didn't have to reinvent myself if I was going to go through any sort of transition. I just felt like I was in a new world and I could be whoever I wanted to be right then and there.

Do you think Set List *does that? Does it allow comedians to reinvent themselves in the moment, for the night?*

Yes, it's very much about the moment, which is the real beauty of comedy. What *Set List* allows to happen is letting-go. It allows you to just be anyone and anything that is possible and when people do well in *Set List*, it's because they've let go of everything else they normally do. It may come out sounding exactly *like* something they normally do, but they got there by letting go of that.

Doing *Set List* is a rather existential experience, because it calls upon everything you've ever learned, everything you've ever seen, everything you've ever experienced. Whereas when we're normally doing stand-up, we're writing with a strong sense of our character, our point of view, technique, craft, wondering how we get the audience to go with us in this direction or that direction. There's a lot of work involved. When you're doing *Set List*, it happens to you. It captures what was great about the first times people were on stage. It's like losing your virginity. You only get that experience once. And *Set List* comes the closest to that again.

I wanted to ask you about how the show has developed. When I first saw it, the topics used to be really interesting juxtapositions of things, but recently when I've seen it, all the topics have been very provocative.

First of all, you need to know that we do have an internal structure in *Set List* and this is through a great deal of talk and experience of doing the show between myself and Barbara Romen, my co-producer, and Troy Conrad who created the original concept. Because it's about taking people out of their comfort zones, we realized that a lot of performers were actually comfortable being out of their comfort zones in terms of technique or style or structure.

We needed to step the game up, so we decided that it would be really fun to take people out of their other kind of comfort zone. So, sometimes what we'll do is to make a preposterous statement like, 'My defence of school shootings', so that we force the comedian to go outside their comfort zone in talking about that kind of subject matter. 'Why I'm pro-Hitler.' We put people in a position where they now have to justify a preposterous statement that's out of the social and sociological comfort zone, out of the morality comfort zone.

And that creates a lot of very funny things, and what it also did was to create another layer to play with, which is the audience being very aware that this is outside morality and so it gives us the opportunity to play with that meta-aspect of comedy. Because comedy lives in this place where most art has difficulty being.

It gives them creative permission. Not permission like, 'You're actually a racist so now, have at it'. It's permission to go to those places where an audience understands that you're being forced to go into this place, so you're given a pass. They know that you're just taking on a challenge and it's an uncomfortable challenge.

But when we put together a set list, let's say there are five topics in a set, we will go out of our way to try and make sure that they're like holes on a golf course. They need different clubs; you need to take a different kind of swing. Some of them have traps in them. All those kinds of things, so that if a comic is getting comfortable, and starts to find a comfort zone within the *Set List* process, we force them out of it over and over and over again.

Are the topics tailored to the comedians you have on the bill?

Not really, it's more random than that. And a lot of people don't believe it – some people think it's crafted for each comedian or whatever. That's only a tiny percentage of it. It may go something like, 'Oh here's an amazing topic, would I love to see what Paul Foot can do with this! Let's give it to Paul Foot.' That's about the extent of how it's crafted for any given comedian.

That's one of the reasons I think why the show works as well as it does – because it's *from* comedians *to* comedians. So we have an intuitive sense of what's going to be challenging, or what's not going to be challenging, or where the dead ends are. We will often find ourselves rejecting topics because we go, 'Well, look, you can go five different directions here but every one of them is a dead end'. And then sometimes, we'll say, 'You know what, let's give that one to Kyle Kinane, because he never hits a dead end, and I'd like to see where this goes beyond what I can imagine'.

Do comedians sometimes report that they've taken something they've riffed at Set List *and put it into their act?*

Yes, very often actually. I know of a number of occasions where people have told me that. In fact, Drew Carey told me he actually started playing around with *Set List* when he was writing a new act and he said a number of pieces that came up in *Set List* he was able to take and turn into something meaningful.

Who's the best at it?

Oh boy. There is no single best because so many people are so good at it for different reasons, but there are some people who are amazing to watch. Wil Anderson is absolutely stunning to watch because his way of doing it is a sort of shotgun – but he's not just randomly throwing pellets out there, he just keeps going and going and going, it's constant verbiage, you can barely hear him take a breath and he just moves and moves and moves. And sometimes it surprises you because he's actually been very, very focused, he's just seduced you along the way.

And sometimes you can tell that he's randomly, aimlessly shooting until he hits something and figures out where he's going. But mostly, what is really remarkable about watching him do it is that he is completely fearless and almost never stops.

In your acting training, I'm sure you've come across this idea that actors will often think about a line before they deliver it, which means they are now on the line as opposed to being in the moment. It's one of the things that's so great about the screwball comedies – the dialogue happens so fast that nobody has any time to get ahead of it, so they're actually in the moment. That's what Wil does. He's truly in the moment because he's not giving himself a second to mull anything over, he just goes with the impulse and it doesn't matter where the impulse takes him. And he ultimately will drive it somewhere else. It's fascinating to watch.

In contrast is Matt Kirshen, who is very slow and deliberate in what he does and when you watch him do it, you can actually see him *blueprint and construct* frameworks! I've told a number of young comics, 'You want to learn how to write stand-up? Watch Matt Kirshen do *Set List*.' Because you can actually see him create the rough idea and then you can see him go back and reinforce the connection he's made, because that needs to be a little stronger. It's unbelievable. So everybody who excels at it excels in their own way.

Robin Williams talked about it on a chat show. It almost feels like a format that allows everyone to be Robin Williams for a few minutes. How did you get him involved in it, and what was his attitude towards it?

He actually got involved in it because he came to see it at Sketchfest in San Francisco. That's the thing about Robin, if something was interesting, he'd show up. So he came to see *Set List* and just loved it. He couldn't wait to jump up. He would thank us after doing *Set List*, he would say, 'Oh, I needed that so much, thank you so much for letting me do this', because what it did for him is interesting. He comes off his own reference points, but within Robin's mind it's a finite universe. And what *Set List* did was to open that up to the infinite. That was really challenging for him and on a creative level, just completely inspiring, because he would never think of the things that would show up on his set list. He would never have those reference points. He would always be within some world of his own.

On his YouTube episode, he gets one topic: Crucifixion After-party. And he turned it into a little scene and it was brilliant. But it was devoid of anything you've ever seen Robin do before. There were no stock characters, there was nothing that was in his wheelhouse. He did the drunk guy at the party who hears that – 'What, the stone moved?' It was all these ellipsis laughs where he didn't actually write a punchline – the audience just connected all the dots. Just wonderful. He loved that. In private he would criticize himself, he would say, 'I feel bad, I keep going up and doing characters, but all the other people on the bill are so good as themselves that I had to go a different way'.

When we were editing the Sky show that he did, I would be watching it and watching it going, 'What is it that's different about Robin?' And I realized that, for me, it was that I was only seeing 90 per cent confidence instead of 100 per cent confidence. That's wonderful, absolutely wonderful.

The only rule of *Set List* is: 'If you've said it before, don't say it here.' It's more an encouragement to be in the moment. But there is no right or wrong with *Set List*, it's just: be in the moment. Here are ideas, do whatever you want with them. If you want to take them literally, take them literally. If you want to take them conceptually, take them conceptually. If you want to twist them around into something else, do whatever. Whatever moves you creatively. The only rule is don't do material you've done before – that's it!

What was the driving creative force behind The Aristocrats?

The real impulse behind that was actually jazz. Penn Jillette and I had always found the Aristocrats joke hilarious. We'd both heard a number of people tell it. We'd say, 'When so-and-so did it, he did this'; 'When so-and-so did it, she did that'. We always thought it would be kind of amusing to just get a bunch of different people doing the Aristocrats. We talked about it for years as the kind of thing we would like to do and somehow through a series of events it ended up actually happening.

It happened partly because Penn started to get deeply into jazz, and we started talking about how in music there are standards that everybody can come along and make their own. Who does the definitive version? Well, you have a baseline on which to judge them – you have the original. And we thought, you know, comedy doesn't really have that – except the one thing that we knew of which *was* like that, was the Aristocrats. So – what if we treat this like it was a jazz standard and we want everyone to do their own iteration of it?

And when you see Emo Philips do it, it sounds like something Emo Philips wrote! When you see Bill Maher do it, it sounds like a Bill Maher joke. And we thought that was fascinating, how it's about the singer and not the song. That's what was behind that.

What advice would you have for a young comedian, about to do their first gig and feeling terrified?

I would tell them that's exactly what you should be feeling. It really is all about being in the moment. You know, we talk about comedy as being about telling the truth but that's a very particular use of the word. Because obviously, this didn't happen to me today on the way to the show. But it's about a bigger truth, which is being real and being authentic. I think that's the most meaningful thing that I've learned and the most meaningful thing I could say to anybody else. But it's not something you can hear and register and go, 'Got it, flick on switch "authenticity"'. That's something that everybody has to process and filter through their own beings.

But I think it is all about authenticity. Even the comedians who hide behind characters – I don't mean 'hide' in any pejorative sense, I mean the comedians who wear a mask or who are playing a character of some sort. They're all really authentic. It's something that's genuine, it's real for them.

Sarah Silverman is a great example because she's such a distinctive and clear character, but a lot of people aren't even aware that she's doing a character. They take it at face value. She will take points of view that are just awful and really dark – but what she's doing is telling the truth about ignorance, and the truth about self-centredness and the truth about unselfconsciousness. And that's very authentic for her, because if you ever meet her, you'll know that she's about as real a person as there is.

Do you sometimes see comics who you think aren't being authentic?

Here's the thing that's important to remember about comedy – again, I'd like to use a music analogy here: there are chart-toppers, there are boy bands, there are bar bands that just do covers, people who play weddings and they just play all the standards. All those things are true for comedians as well. Not every comedian you see is breaking the boundaries or working in an artful fashion. Some of them are just in commerce. Some of them are just selling a packaged good time, fast food, whatever the case may be. And I'm not judging anybody, but those distinctions are clear.

And it's important to remember that, that there are so many comedians out there that when you catch them at a club, you really just saw the comedy equivalent of a bar band. And that's what they set out to do, that's what they meant to do. Maybe some of those people will transition into real artists, maybe some of them are passionate enough about being artists that that's their manifesto right from the get-go. But, you know, if your *Pet Sounds* album goes nowhere, you've still got to make a living.

People have very weird perceptions of comedy in general. Comedy is the only art form I know of where the recipient gets to determine its existence. 'I didn't laugh at that, that's not comedy.' Nobody sees a shitty painting and goes, 'That's not a painting'. Somehow we feel we can do that with comedy. The response to it is what defines it, and there's no other art form like that.

Chapter 3
Persona

Developing your material into an act and how the 'you on stage' is not the 'you in Starbucks'.

DEBORAH FRANCES-WHITE: The easiest way to think about a stand-up persona is to think about a caricature. A caricaturist takes the most recognizable feature of a face and exaggerates or exploits it. That's how most people find their approach to stand-up. They turn the volume up on an authentic part of themselves. If in life they're vague and rambling, they play this up on stage. If they have a tendency to dress like a dandy, they evolve this to the point of theatricality when they're behind a mic. They let out their inner school teacher, curmudgeon or party animal.

Like boyfriends, some people try out a few personas before they find 'the one'. I remember hearing that Graham Norton was told early on he'd have to decide whether he was going to go 'pink' or 'green' – that is, gay or Irish – because when you're doing clubs, it's thought helpful to have 'a thing'. Are you the posh one, the camp one, the political one, the surreal one or the Australian one? I guess if you only have five to ten minutes, then having a memorable hook can be useful. So use it if you think it makes life easier, but if you feel this reduces your possibilities, just be yourself with more energy.

When I say have 'more energy' I don't mean leap around the stage (unless that's your natural physicality dialled up). I mean you need to radiate some kind of energy to draw people to you. Tim Minchin has spoken about changing his image – hair and guy-liner – because if you want people to look at you, you have to be interesting to look at. Some people create energy through stillness, some through ebullience and some through focus, but all great performers have an energy and purpose to their performance – you just have to find the right one for you.

The question you have to ask yourself now is not what you are going to say, but what your attitude is to what you're going to say. If you're talking about libraries closing, are you curious or furious? You could do the same joke both ways and it would read very differently. If you're examining whether there's a god, are you agnostic or caustic? More broadly, what is your world view? I was once in a tour bus with the hilarious David Quirk, who always seemed to me like a man-genue. He turned to us and said, wide-eyed, 'I don't see myself as a comedian really. I just live life and report back.' A lot of his comedy comes from his naïve wondering perspective on the world. Also in the bus was Russell Kane. Much of his best-loved material came from a rather sophisticated, intellectual, literature-loving view of the world. The audience loved watching one after the other because the juxtaposition was so terrific.

In truth, you are probably drawn to stand-up because you are overly opinionated, a little weird or live in your own world. Capitalize on that. You'll be fine.

STEPHEN K AMOS

Sometimes you see a comic who has got good writing skills but not good performance skills and it takes a while to kind of marry those two things together. There's a new stand-up – well, he's not new any more. He's quite a big star in England now. But when he started, he was quite young and very, very good-looking. He kind of had this persona being quite high status and sort of Jerry-Seinfeld-esque. I just said to him at the club I saw him at, 'The audience that you're performing to are at least ten years older than you. That persona doesn't really work because you haven't brought anything to the table that's going to make them engage with you. You come across as quite an aloof young man.' I saw him about two, three weeks later and his style had completely changed. He's much more upbeat and he's a huge success. Whether he took on board what I said, I don't know. But it was a pleasure to see.

Judah Friedlander discovered for himself where his comedy niche lay very early on.

JUDAH FRIEDLANDER

There was this one club. It was basically like an open mic-type place but they would have a real audience there. I noticed at the time it seemed like every comic was always trying to bond with the audience. I decided to take the opposite approach. I can't relate to the audience at all because I'm just so superior to them. There's nothing I have in common with these people. I was doing all these jokes about these ridiculous athletic achievements and records I've broken. Then I thought one day it would be cool to make a hat that said 'World Champion' but not of what. This hat served two ways. One, it's like who's this ridiculous guy bragging about being world champion and then it doesn't say of what? But that actually drew the audience in because they're looking at the hat and they're like, 'Oh, he's world champion. What is he world champion of?'

So my act on some level, I'm also making fun of people who are so self-involved and arrogant. Then in the past several years, the world champion thing has even gone in a different direction where he's no longer a bragger. He actually is a real life super-hero role model. Everything he's saying, when he talks about scoring fifty goals in one game for Brazil and he was the goalkeeper, he's not bragging. He's just humbly stating some facts that happened that day, to see if he can bond with the audience. But there's still no connection.

So it's almost like he's a lonely hero, trying to make a connection, but he still can't because he's just so superior even though he's not bragging. It's just the way it is.

It's inevitable that a young comedian's developing stage persona will be influenced by current tastes and fashions in stand-up comedy. This presents an interesting dilemma: do you copy what works and risk being seen as an imitator with no original voice, or do you do your own thing and risk alienating a crowd that has come to see what everyone else is doing?

MOSHE KASHER

I was always comfortable on stage. When I first started, partially because of my material, but partially just because of the way I look – and partially because the people that I roll with, I was very much in the alternative scene, whatever that means. But when I first started in the alt scene, there was a little bit of a frowning on performance. The vibe was like very much like, 'I'm just barely here, man. I almost abhor even doing stand-up.' There were a lot of comics like that, but I was always a big performer and I sometimes felt like frowned upon.

Quite a few young comedians start out by seeing a performer and thinking 'I want to be just like that!' Over time, your own style will emerge from behind this, but you may still want to emulate your hero's success. Alex Edelman remembers watching a young Louis CK.

ALEX EDELMAN

Alex Edelman is a New York and London-based comedian who has lived in Boston, LA and Jerusalem. His show *Millennial* won the Best Newcomer Award at the 2014 Edinburgh Fringe. According to the *Guardian*, with 'technical flair and a precocious authority, Edelman's comedy manages to capture the voice of Generation Y'.

When I started in Boston, Louis CK was a Boston guy and he was beloved in Boston and I idolized him. He was just this guy who was kind of goofy and silly. He hadn't really changed his act yet, but it was clearly there and there was something so brilliant about him. He's been around for a long time. He started when he was around 17 in Boston. He was in Boston for a long time, then he was in New York. And then he was writing for Conan, and writing for SNL and directing Chris Rock movies. The career that I aspired to when I was starting was Louis CK's career before he had *Louie* and this universal acclaim. It's so funny, because I would still settle for Louis's career before he became this enormous thing. When you start you're just a mix of all the people that you want to be – and inexperienced. And then when you get better you're a much more blended mix of all the people you want to be – and some experience. So the ingredients in that smoothie never really change; they just become more refined.

Stand-up comedians tend not to talk about putting on a mask, they talk about discovering who they really are – even if that process involves actively creating something that does not already appear to be there. Eventually, inspiration, material, routine and persona start to become one.

ADAM BLOOM

When you write a joke and then tell it, the audiences laugh – or even more importantly to me, comics come up to you and say, 'That's great'. Then you realize what's unique about you. So suddenly, it's like women who show off their legs over their boobs or vice versa because they know that's a thing about them that people will find most – we all know what our best features are.

I would be going out there, showing off my legs, not realizing it's my boobs that were getting the attention. Then when you realize that your brain can do something that most people's brains can't, you focus on that. There's no point telling detailed stories about the fear of getting caught wanking by your mum if everyone has that fear.

> What you've got is a perspective on the world that others haven't got, which allows you to look at something and pull a joke out of nowhere, like a magician pulling a coin out the air. Where did that joke come from? All they're looking at was a wall.

Discovering what material fits your persona is just as important as discovering what material you can actually generate.

JO CAULFIELD

I think it was when Jordan first appeared on the scene and Jodie Marsh. All of a sudden there were these very sexualized women flogging sexuality and I thought, 'Oh my god, I thought we had gone beyond this', and it seemed like we were going back. I do remember trying to do a sort of feminist rant and saying how wearing a push-up bra actually doesn't make you powerful. The audience just didn't take it from me at all. In kind of a nice way, they just sort of waited until I went back to my other stuff. Now I realize I wasn't good enough to be funny about it – because you have to be funny about it. No one wants you to preach at them. You do this terrible thing where you go, 'everyone's going to agree with my opinion anyway', so what is the point of saying it unless I can be funny about it? I thought, 'oh that's interesting that they wouldn't go with me and also I don't have the skill to have that opinion and also make it funny and interesting'.

Personally I am much more political than audiences think I am but I'm not funny about it, I'm too angry. I don't find it funny. I sometimes find it annoying that people can be funny about it because I think it's so important. That's not a way for me to go because I would just be raging and going 'no, it's not funny. Stop laughing. This is really serious!'

Different comedians use the physical space of the stage in different ways. Some stand behind the mic, never removing it from its stand. Others use the mic and the stand as a prop, whirling them around their heads, threatening to bring down the lights.

ZOE LYONS

> Zoe Lyons began her comedy career in 2004, winning the Funny Women competition, and was nominated for an Edinburgh Comedy Award in 2007. She is a regular panellist on British TV and radio comedy shows.

I am very physical on stage. I wasn't when I first started. One of the very first gigs I ever did, I went to the mic stand to do my set and the cord was wrapped around the stand but there wasn't enough give in it for me to move properly. I basically did the gig hunched over this foot-long bit of cord, because I was too nervous to even take it out of the stand.

Now I lark about like an absolute loon. It was my partner who said to me that I should be more physical on stage because it's how I am in real life. It is a bit undignified. But you know what? It's what I do and it makes me laugh. It's what comes naturally and that I think that is what you're trying to achieve on stage.

Vocal energy makes a huge difference as well.

RICH HALL

> Having started out as a street performer, acerbic Rich Hall was a sketch comedian on American TV in the 1980s but achieved enormous success in the UK in the 2000s, first with his Perrier Award-winning, country music-singing character Otis Lee Crenshaw, and then on TV panel shows such as *QI* and *Have I Got News For You*, and his own programmes for BBC4.

> I was very loud because I was used to not having a mic. I was used to having to improvise and having to deal with all kinds of interruptions like the police stopping my show. Plus, I went on really late the first time I went on in the club. So I didn't need to use the mic. The mic was there. I don't need a mic. I'm going to talk loud and there are only ten people here. So I think the other comedians thought that was a bit crazy. It was a pretty good first impression.

Sometimes a costume becomes an integral part of this persona. And the clothes that you choose can influence the way the audience perceives you without you calling attention to them verbally.

NAT LUURTSEMA

Nowadays I'm higher status on stage. I make self-deprecating jokes, but I have to go out there higher status. It was only when I started working with Jigsaw that I realized how much fun it is to be high status. How much fun it is to dress up and look as good as you can look and strut on out and then you can then rip yourself down because you still don't look weak. You've gone out looking like you're in charge.

For me, the female comedian's uniform was always skinny jeans with a sort of smock-type maternity big t-shirt over the top and then maybe a cardigan over the top of that just in case you were verging on slutty. For me, about three years ago when I started with Jigsaw, I pulled on a pair of skin-tight leather trousers with zips and high heels. The response I got gave me so much more to play with. Previously, I was making myself invisible.

I dress up usually in my everyday life. I dress to look as good as I can look. Then I'd be like, 'Oh, I have a gig this evening', and I'd go home and frump up in the sort of outfit that if I walk into a pub no one looks twice at me. Why on earth was I doing that?

While the appeal of a comedian's lifestyle may be imagined as involving writing in your underwear by day and wearing sneakers and jeans on stage at night (take that, evil corporate boss-lord!), getting your appearance right can make a big difference to the success of your act.

GARY DELANEY

In the early days, I would just perform in jeans and t-shirt and trainers. Somebody would shout out 'student' before I even said hello. I've had to deal with that as my very first thing. One of the older comedians – I think it was Keith Dover – said to me, 'Look, I know you don't want to have the uniform and wear a jacket and a shirt and all that sort of stuff. But you need to buy yourself that opening thirty seconds, that little bit of initial respect to get your first couple of jokes out and get your laughs. So swallow your pride a bit and do it even if you don't want to. You don't have to wear a jacket. Just wear a shirt. Just wear a relatively smart shirt and just black jeans that look like trousers. Just so you look half respectable.'

When you start out, there's a danger that your comedy persona may be a mask for you to hide behind, rather than a more direct route to your inner life.

ROBIN INCE

I think there is a reason that a few stand-ups started off as character acts – or even Mark Watson doing a Welsh accent. Some of that is kind of masking your vulnerability, because you're putting on a front – you're not actually being you.

Then you will see comics going on – someone like Josie Long – and they are directly representing their belief of what the world is, what the world looks like and who they are. And I think that can be more damaging to you, because when an audience hate you – and these things will happen – then they are hating *you*, they're not hating your manufactured persona. They're not hating the joke you wrote merely to provoke them into laughter but with no other purpose than that. They're not seeing merely a flaw in the factory that you're using to create your jokes. They're seeing you and they're going, 'I tell you what, I don't like you'.

And I tell you what, as social animals, there's no way… I mean, it gets easier as time goes on. I think it gets easier as you're more and more yourself on stage. The one battle you have is to be as good as possible for yourself, and to deliver everything in what you think is the right way. But every now and then there will be an audience who just go, 'No, you're not for us, mate'.

Forcing laughter out of another human being is a weird thing to do when you take a step back and consider it.

CONAN O'BRIEN

Simpsons writer and Groundlings improviser Conan O'Brien was not the obvious choice to take over *Late Night* after David Letterman decided to leave, but he quickly made the show his own and has remained one of America's favourite talk show hosts ever since, while continuing to write, produce and act.

I've always thought of laughter as coming from our reptile brains somewhere, because it's actually some weird bodily process. It's an art form where we're dealing with ideas and language but the response you're looking to create is like trying to get people to sneeze or hiccup … And if they're not sneezing and hiccupping, it means you've *failed.*[1]

As a new comedian, it can be hard initially to see how big the gap is between funny in the pub and funny on the stage.

---

[1] Taken from *Satiristas*, op. cit.

TOM WRIGGLESWORTH

Every comic probably does this: tries to second-guess what people find funny. You end up then in a world of very similar type comedians and very similar topics and slants and takes on things. Then you realize that's probably not what makes you laugh when you're just with your friends and you slowly gain the confidence and get to a finding-your-voice moment where you just think, 'This is how I'm funny when I'm at home. If I can turn it up a bit when I'm on stage, that'll be fine.'

I couldn't tell you exactly when it happened, but when a gig goes wrong is usually the blueprint for that sort of birth, isn't it? It all goes wrong and you just fall back on yourself and then you build out of that and you end up being the comedian you probably should be or definitely want to be.

Jim Jefferies says that it was coming to the Edinburgh Festival Fringe which solidified his comedy 'voice'.

JIM JEFFERIES

Before that, I was only doing twenty minutes. Then when you throw yourself in the deep end, you have to do an hour and you realize, I've got to pad this out. I learned how to tell stories, which I didn't really do before. I did little jokes. Then I found out I was really good at telling little stories. Not only was I good at telling stories, but I told stories that were twenty minutes long. Most comics tell a story three or four minutes long. I told these long-winded stories. I remember coming back from Edinburgh and I was doing club sets that was one joke for twenty minutes, thinking, 'this is something different, I haven't seen any other guy doing this'.

I don't think about it while I'm on stage, but I have realized over the years – more since I've been recording DVDs and can watch myself back – that there are certain walks I've done or faces I've pulled that people have found funny. In my HBO special, there's a little run that my dad does when he chases after me and he sees I'm holding a vibrator. Now that run has been put into two or three other jokes in the next specials because I know that people physically find me funny when I do that. I've never been a real physical comic but I think a lot of people underestimate the power of moving while on stage. I'm not talking about Dane Cook where you're pacing back and forth and doing all the actions. I wander around and I sit down for a bit, then I go stand and lean on a speaker. It keeps the brain ticking. I think that's important.

Other comedians tell stories about a mentor figure who eventually set them on the right path.

TODD GLASS

I learned how to make audiences laugh pretty quickly. But you also want to have other comedians think you're funny. Not every comedian has to think you're funny, but you certainly like to make the ones that you respect and like laugh. Then you want to make audiences laugh. For me, it took a long time. Maybe because I was young.

I'd been doing comedy maybe five, six years when I was working with this comedian. I was making him laugh offstage. I knew it. I was really getting him to laugh and then he said to me very affectionately, in a very kind way, he goes, 'It wasn't the worst. It was just what it was.' We were hanging out the next day again because he was from out of town and I was from Philly. So he says, 'What are you doing up there?' I knew what he meant.

He says, 'You're so funny!' In that moment, I knew that if you're not funny, you can't learn to be funny. You're fucked! No one can tell you, 'You should learn to have funny bones!' You can't. You have funny bones or you don't. So I was honoured as opposed to offended and also knew that he was being genuine. He said, 'You have funny bones. You aren't bringing them up to that stage though.'

Josie Long got advice from one of her comedy heroes on her first-ever tour.

JOSIE LONG[2]

> Josie Long began her stand up career as a teenager, winning the BBC New Comedy Award at 16. In 2006 she won the Edinburgh Comedy Award for Best Newcomer, and has since had three nominations for the main prize. She has toured numerous shows, as well as appearing regularly on TV and radio, including appearances on *The Culture Show*, *8 out of 10 Cats* and *Have I Got News For You*.

I did it with Stewart Lee where I supported him. He was really generous with looking after me and giving me a lot of advice but not in a way that was ever, ever preachy or unasked for. It was really helpful. I felt really emboldened, because the stuff I was doing then was really weird and I hadn't yet worked out any ways to kind of link it to my life very well or anything like that.

So it was always really out there and there would be times when I would just die so hard – like there was this one time in Sheffield where I died really badly and then somebody was standing at the back and they said, 'This is as bad as Ted Chippington'. And then Stew came up to me after. He was like, 'I was so proud of you! I was just really pleased that it was like Ted Chippington.' It was good. It made me more defiantly weird.

So, all of these choices – what to write about, what form the material should take, how the elements form a greater whole, and how the comedian relates to the audience – combine to create a persona, create an identity which hopefully will resonate with an audience,

---

[2] Taken from an interview Marsha Shandur did with Josie in 2010 as part of the 'Marsha Meets…' podcast series for Xfm.

relaxing them enough to make them laugh, provoking them enough to remember the experience. But ultimately, except in the case of overt character comedians like Al Murray's The Pub Landlord, this creation is an expression of the comedian's own identity.

Gary Delaney began by reciting gags in a deadpan fashion, but quickly realized the limitations of this particular comic identity.

GARY DELANEY

Too inflexible. You will die in a low-energy room. It doesn't suit opening, it's too constrictive on longer sets and other people did it better than me. So that ended. I started just trying to be a lot more myself on stage and I always giggle at my own jokes now and that's just because I spent so many years desperately trying to be like Bill Wyman at a Stones gig, that when that cracked, it was really liberating. I really want to try and be not artificial.

Telling one-liners – it's an artificial way to speak. People don't talk like that. So the audience – when trying to work out that comic's persona, their stage persona – they're trying to answer the question, 'Why is this guy talking like this?' That's why people have these personas. Most one-liner guys have a really strict nailed-on persona and I probably would have tried to if I had joined the industry earlier. But that's why there are lots of variants on what I call the spaceman persona, the weird guy, or Jimmy Carr's high status-type thing.

I thought I would just want to be a guy who's ambled up there and is like 'Hey, here are these jokes I've written. I hope you think they're funny.' And just really try and strip it down and not be slick and just be myself wandering out there with a bunch of jokes. That's my plan. It's really different to everything else that has gone before. It's a bit more honest.

When I started, I dabbled a little bit and then I lost my bottle and stopped for years. When I came back, it gave me a bit of distance to look back on what I was doing and think, 'Hang on, you were shit at everything apart from one-liners'. That's why people talk about your comedy voice, your style, your persona. When you're a new comic, people bang on about it like it's a tremendously important thing. You have to find it and people try all these different things to find it. I think that's all bollocks. I don't think you do find your comedy voice or your style. It finds you, because it's the thing that you can do. You keep on trying things. You find the thing that you can do and you repeat that. I tried to be wacky. I loved all the wacky guys, all the Simon Munnerys and whatnot. It turns out that wasn't me. I wasn't good at it. It wasn't my skill. If it turned out that my skill had been talking to the audience or being a big actor or whatever it would have been, then I would have gone that way. So I think, as long as you're keeping what works, you don't need to worry about voice and style and all that crap and that's a lot of nonsense that people are taught.

Some people bang on about the importance of timing. Bollocks! Comedy is just a very complicated thing and it's hard for people to understand, so people latch on to timing as if that explains everything. Timing is really simple. Don't speak too fast. Do a little pause before the funny bit. There you go. That's it. How difficult is that? That's everything you need to know. No need to overcomplicate things.

Whether you find your comic identity, or whether – as Gary Delaney insists – it finds you, many comedians speak of the liberation they experience when they finally know who they are on stage.

DANIEL SLOSS

It's a very easy thing to say, but be yourself for the love of god. You don't realize how much you will enjoy actually being yourself. I used to write gags that weren't me. There was still good material, but now, I'm actually saying what I'm thinking and I'm just more natural. It's just so much more fun. It's just a genuine joy to do. So take as much advice as you can get from other comics, but don't try and *be* other comics.

That's what I used to do. I would watch a comic I love, like Ed Byrne or Glenn Wool or Louis CK, and then I would want to try doing comedy like them. I would write those certain jokes but then those weren't me. They were good but it was very forced.

As private thoughts start to become public and an offstage persona merges with an onstage one, there are some parts of the comedian's identity which gradually become inescapable. God knows, ethnic minority comedians have historically had to face racist audiences. But for homosexual comedians, life is even more complicated. Mario Cantone attempted to elide the issue of his sexual orientation early in his career.

MARIO CANTONE

Mario Cantone is a stand-up comedian and impressionist best known for his role as Anthony, the gay wedding planner, in *Sex and the City* and as the resident gay man on *Chappelle's Show*.

I wasn't talking about my love life on stage. I still don't talk about my love life. I wasn't talking about being gay but I wasn't lying and I did female impressions. So if they didn't know, you knew. But I was in the mainstream comedy rooms and I wasn't totally out to the audience but I certainly didn't fucking lie.

But I wasn't doing like, don't you hate it when your girlfriend… never, never, never, never, never. But most of my audience is straight. It's women and straight couples and straight men, much more than gay men unfortunately.

When I'm put in front of a gay audience, like in a benefit or they're forced to see me, it's tremendous but they just don't come out. I don't know why not. They like women. They like Kathy Griffin who I love too. They love Margaret Cho who I love too. They love a good drag queen which I love too. So I get that, but it's – I'm probably one of the first mainstream gay comedians to come around in the States.

Stephen K Amos came out in 2006, after five years on the circuit.

STEPHEN K AMOS

I had just finished a tour in Australia and had come back to London over Christmas. The news was on the telly in the background. They were talking about a body that was found in Clapham Common, somebody who was killed in a homophobic attack, so I glanced up. They flashed a picture of this person and it was somebody that I knew and it just put a lump in my throat and tears in my eyes. I was just thinking, 'Oh my god'. I took for granted that we live in London, which is a very permissive society. It's very much a place where you can express yourself to a certain extent. I thought, 'If this is still happening in London, then I need to say something about it because people make assumptions about me all the time'.

Most people assumed up until then that I was just this typical six foot two strapping black man who probably had groupies and went looking for girls after a gig and all this kind of business – which is further from the truth because that's not my style, I don't look for anybody after a gig. So I decided to say something in my next show that acknowledges and expresses who I am. It was really well received, which I wasn't expecting – maybe I was being naïve. Even though people who know me, my inner circle, my friends, I never hide anything from them. Everyone knows exactly what I'm about.

It came to me at the right time. If that incident hadn't happened, I'm not sure if I'd have done that then. Because I was having a good time and also I'm very aware of labels and I'm so anti-labels. When I see myself described as 'London black gay comic', that really pisses me off because there's more to me than being from London, being a black man and being gay. That doesn't define me completely. What's in my spirit and my head, that defines me, and what I say is what people should judge me for.

When I started in comedy, apart from Lenny Henry, there weren't any black comics that I could relate to. That's probably why I didn't think comedy was an arena for me. The stuff we were watching on TV was the 1970s and early 1980s comics which was all about mother-in-law and racist, homophobic jokes. Why would a gay or a black person ever step into a comedy club when that's what you see on TV?

In 2014, the BBC announced that their male-dominated comedy panel shows such as *Have I Got News For You* and *Never Mind the Buzzcocks* would be required to feature at least one woman in every episode. This caused not a little controversy. We asked regular panel show performer Marcus Brigstocke what a woman would have to do to earn her place and not invite accusations of tokenism.

MARCUS BRIGSTOCKE

Simple, they would have to be one of the boys. One of the lads. My thing with the panel shows and the issue about putting women on it, i.e. you must have a woman on each panel show, to me is arse about face. It is not so much a question of there are three boys and one girl, or four boys and no girl, it's a question of are we making programmes in which funny people, regardless of who they are, can flourish, or are we making programmes in which a certain type of quite testosterone-led comedy can flourish and everything else struggles? And I would say that the production of shows that suit fairly pushy, aggressive young men is totally out of whack. It is not a question of having a woman on the shows, but a question of having shows in which women and whoever are well served by the programme.

Jo Caulfield also had a strong reaction to the announcement.

JO CAULFIELD

I think the BBC handled it very badly recently. You can't just say, 'We're going to book more women'. I do think there are loads of men I know who I think are very talented who can't get on telly for whatever reason, because it's a very arbitrary business. I think, in our business, I do think you have to be careful about saying 'it's because I'm female'; sometimes it's because you aren't good enough and sometimes it's because they're not lucky and sometimes it's because they didn't have the right hair. It's because of all sorts of reasons.

It's not just institutionalized sexism. I think the same thing about people who went to university. I didn't go to university so I feel there's a certain type of person that the BBC are comfortable with because they're like them. They feel like not my kind of people.

One of them said something about, talking about nicking something out of a hotel room and I said, 'I would never do that, take a robe or something, because I worked in housekeeping and you don't know, they might have to pay for it'. They went, 'Why did you work in housekeeping?' Well, for money! They thought that was absurd, they thought maybe it was a project or something. No, I was 18 and I needed the job!

Sara Pascoe is immensely struck at the different attitude towards women in the comedy community.

SARA PASCOE

I really didn't identify as a female particularly before comedy. I really just felt like a person. But then, when I started stand-up, what was odd is that every day I arrived at work I was told I was a woman.

There's a very famous comedian who I did a radio thing with last year. I'd never met him before and I was really excited to meet him. Just before he went on he said, 'I always like it when we have a woman here', and my hackles just rose and I said, 'What do you mean – a woman?' And he said, 'Oh, it's just, er, it just brings a different energy. Less testosterone-y, more conversational.' And I hated him. He'd never seen me do stand-up, and he had made a judgement on my gender. And then I was very, very aggressive on the show and it worked out well in the end. Every time he spoke, I jumped in because I thought, 'I'm not having you say that to a girl ever again'.

I have met him since and I said to him, 'I found it really patronizing what you said'. And he said, 'I was trying to make you feel comfortable'. I said, 'I know you were, but your assumption was that I wouldn't be able to bring it because I was a girl you hadn't heard of'.

People saying, 'I don't find that person funny', that's fine. But I don't want to have another agenda on top of it. I don't represent all women. I can't. I don't want that responsibility. If I'm shit, I want it to be because I am shit. I don't want it to be: 'On behalf of all women, I've let everyone down.'

Josie Long realized that it's hard for judgement *not* to affect you.

JOSIE LONG[3]

People our age and younger are brought up to believe that we're on a level playing field. Then as an adult you're suddenly brought up to date with the reality of how much you're going to be affected by sexism. It's just such a shock.

I think the problem is first, having to accept that it's not yet [a level playing field] and secondly, having to accept that it does affect *you*. That's what was really hard because I always thought, 'Oh, I'm different! I will be all right!' But actually, it's not. People are still going to marginalize me and be rude to me and patronize me and then if I try and talk about it, they're going to say I'm moaning.

I thought about it the other day and I thought, I've been doing this solidly since I was 21 years old. Which [at the time of this interview was] eleven years. In that time, probably once every – I would say on average once a day, but just to be conservative, say 300 times a year – I've had somebody say to me, 'There aren't any funny women are there?', or 'Well, women aren't as funny as men', or 'I don't like women comedians', or even 'Oh, I like you but I don't normally like women'. Anything like that. Some sort of hint that for some reason they're judging men versus women in the arena of comedy – which is ridiculous.

Then I thought, if I add that up, that's 3,300 times that I have been in some way undermined throughout my career, that my male counterparts have never ever had. That's a *lot* of knocks that you have to take.

---

[3]Taken from an interview Marsha Shandur did with Josie in 2010 as part of the 'Marsha Meets…' podcast series for Xfm.

To begin with, you don't notice it. Then after a while, you sort of feel like it's your fault and it's only now that I'm definitely an adult and that I'm more confident than I was, that – actually it's just starting to really grind me down now and really get to me. Even talking about now, I can imagine some comedy nerds – especially ones that really can't bear me – reading this being like, 'I just don't think that's true'. But the truth of my experience is I have experienced that much that my friends have not. That's stressful.

Comedians from other countries have different stories to tell.

SOFIE HAGEN

I just want to be good. You have to accept TV like it's the inevitable thing that you have to do eventually because it makes you. That's how you get out. That's how you make people see you – but it's not my goal. I did TV in Denmark right before I left, a week before I moved here permanently. I did two minutes of stand-up, on TV.

After that people started calling me about doing reality TV in Denmark. Because in Denmark I am one of four female comics, so they just put you on TV right away and everyone wants you and everyone wants you to do all these things because you need them. And I just didn't want to do it and it was going way too fast. I just wanted to get good, but there's not a lot of opportunities to get good. Then I came here and all of a sudden I am in a place where I can gig two or three times a night every day of the week and I can get really good.

I think if I have to be out there and take stage time away from someone, I'm going to have to be the best at it because otherwise it's not fair. So I have to work really hard at getting good. I know that because I'm Danish and female, there is a chance that I will be pushed forward for TV work I am not necessarily ready to do. Because I'm sort of a novelty and it's a selling point. So I need to at least be really good, or it's not fair. I don't want to sell myself on anything but the fact that I'm good at jokes.

I got an email from a show, some radio panel show I'm doing and it was a long script, almost. And in certain places they'd forgotten to type my name so they'd used the name of the girl they originally booked. There were three other girls' names in this thing because the first girl said no and they had to change all the names, but then they didn't change one, then the next girl said no too, so they changed it again. So I could see they were all girls, and it wasn't a girl-specific show, it could have been a guy, I could just see they'd gone, 'Oh that girl can't do it, so get a new girl in'; they hadn't thought, 'But then ask a guy who's available'.

For some, the club scene seems much narrower in scope than it was at the birth of alternative comedy.

JENNY ECLAIR

You would have a mime act, you would have a poet, somebody singing a song, people like John Hegley were around in those days with the Popticians. It was quite fluid. Now it's had to sort of narrow itself down to a point where everyone thought – fucking hell this is really boring isn't it? It's just young white men in suits live at the Apollo.

When I started, it was a kind of playground for oddballs and there wasn't a class thing there that I sometimes see in television. There was this alternative playing field that I think was very level, that was very well committed – certainly no restrictions to being a woman. That came later.

I don't think they realized they didn't like women comics until halfway through the Eighties and they sort of went – what are these women doing?

Festivals are arguably a more even playing field.

Figure 4 Sofie Hagen © Idil Sukan/Draw HQ

MARCUS BRIGSTOCKE

The Edinburgh Festival is a place where anyone with an idea can take a show, set their own agenda, do their show and have it be brilliant. There are still issues about who will go and see female comics. But it's not the same as the circuit. On the circuit, most of the female comics I've ever worked with usually spend five minutes of their twenty-minute set heaving the audience and the agenda of the room into a place where they can then do what they need to do.

I only started noticing that when I changed my comedy to much more political stuff and I had to spend five minutes heaving the room into the direction I wanted to take it. So I played Jongleurs for years and loved it. I thought it was brilliant. I worked really regularly and did European politics at Jongleurs, Thursday, Friday, Saturday night. I did European politics, single European currency, the integration of the European nations without just being Euro-racist, and it worked. The audiences really liked it and it played. There was nothing ever wrong with Jongleurs, there was plenty wrong with the comperes. It became, for some reason, acceptable while I was on the circuit – because I don't think it was acceptable when I started – for a compere to go out and find a table with three women on it and one bloke and ask, 'How much?' *Really?* They're all hookers? Because that's the only way *that* could possibly have happened? Amazing!

The comperes became weak because there were so many comedy clubs and there weren't enough good comperes to go around. Compering takes much more skill than anybody realizes. Like people will go up to a compere after a really good show at a comedy club and go, 'I actually liked you, mate, and thought you were nearly as funny as the real comics – you should have a go at that'. No one realizes the skill that takes. But those aggressive comperes' agendas are terribly masculine and very testosterone-led and that didn't equip women well on the circuit for it to be a pleasant experience. When you've got to give up 25 per cent of your allocated time on stage fixing the room before you can try what you wanted to do, you feel a bit cheated, a bit ripped off, and that's the launch pad – but Edinburgh's different, Edinburgh's great for that.

Sara Pascoe is frustrated with how being female is often the most notable thing about a woman comedian.

SARA PASCOE

If you do comedy courses, some comedy courses say, 'If you are non-white, if you are a woman, if you have a disability, if you're fat – you have to mention that first or the audience will wonder when you're going to bring it up'. And I think that's completely wrong. We're 51 per cent of the population. We're more representative than men. Our experiences are more representative, very slightly. So it should never be, 'I'm a sub-culture'.

Some people seem to think that men are talking for people, and women are being pigeonholed as talking only for women. So then, when someone makes a sweeping statement about how women have more women in the audience, you think – what? You don't go to the men's shows and go, 'oh look, it's 80 per cent men – because he slags off women for an hour'. Because men talk for everybody and that's the thing that's still there.

Someone said once said about Sarah Millican that it's a shame she didn't talk about feminism because she was so popular. I felt she did the *most* feminist thing possible, which was to go into an all-male environment and be better than everyone. She was unfollowable. When she was an opener or she was a middle spot she did better than every single man on the bill. There is nothing more feminist.

In Edinburgh, there's a lot of guys who now think having a feminist angle is hack! It's weird how quickly that happened, in two years. Having-a-feminist-bit is the new having-a-sad-bit. You know like how comedy shows used to end with a bit of music and 'then my dad died' – that whole cliché? And what's so annoying about that is the idea that a movement about human rights has become hack! That's what drives it all back and people become scared of talking about their experience again.

Jenny Eclair talks about life offstage too.

JENNY ECLAIR

I have spent years in dressing rooms, thinking, 'Oh! I wish there was another girl here', just years! I felt so uncomfortable sometimes because I have always been a yakker. You know when you are in a dressing room and going lalalalala and because men are often shy and disguise it with this cynical, laid-back, not speaking and making you feel like shit, making you feel stupid, like some weird child that's got overexcited.

Anyway, that is so long ago it doesn't affect me any more, but I used to get such anxiety on car trips with comics, because if you were doing the Red Wedge Tour you'd be put in a small van, there would be twelve of you or whatever, and the knot in my stomach of waiting and thinking – can I say something funny now? Have I got the line? Can I get it in without stumbling over it and it sounding funny? Here's the gap… here's the gap… you know, all that sort of shit.

Once I heard a discussion about women on panel games and the female producer of *Have I Got News For You* was on, and I was at home and I just had this wave of fury go through my body – it was probably hormonal – and I thought for fuck's sake, she is on this programme saying that women turn her down, that she can't get anyone on – nobody will come on, women are too scared, it is so difficult to get women who are prepared to come on. So I tweeted that I'd never been asked. Jane Garvey, god love her, Jane said, 'I've just had a tweet from Jenny Eclair, saying she's never been asked. Thirty years being a stand-up comedian and she's never once been asked to do *Have I Got News For You*, what do you say to that?' She said, 'Well um, well um, well um, yes that's probably true, if she says that, it's probably true, but the thing is, well, what I have to say to that is Jenny Eclair is not a lot of people's cup of tea.'

At this point I was at home, I was so embarrassed, I was absolutely mortified to be in my own skin, I didn't know quite what to do with myself, there was quite a lot of Twitter activity after it but mostly very nice towards me. But it was basically like being told to my face – we actually don't like you, so we're not going to have you on, and do you know I think that's fair enough, I think that's fair enough.

Deborah Frances-White talks to Marcus Brigstocke

DEBORAH FRANCES-WHITE: Does performing at comedy clubs for years change your relationship with an audience, do you think?

MARCUS BRIGSTOCKE: If you come at it from the club sensibility, while you still like your audience – don't get me wrong – *they* are a thing to pull down, they are a challenge to overcome. Whereas, with the Edinburgh Festival experience, it's not at all that they are a hurdle to be leapt over, but they are absolutely integral to the show, and they are what informs it and makes it joyful. That changes after you leave the comedy circuit. That changed for me. You start to do your own tour shows and people are there to see you. You need to shake some of that fight out of you.

I supported Bill Bailey on tour when I was quite a new comic. Bill was amazing. I would go and watch him every night. He is properly a master craftsman. And he said to me, 'You've got to stop swearing, mate. You swear so much, you don't need to. Every time you swear it bounces back off the walls in the theatre and ricochets around the room. It's not the same as the clubs.' And I tried, but I couldn't do it at the time. It took me until years later to write my show, full of swearing and start to pluck out the bits that were informed by the comedy circuit, because it is just that bit more aggressive.

Do you think comedians rely on swearing too much?

Of course, swearing is funny and good and useful and powerful and excellent. But yes, we rely on it much too much.

I'm writing a show for Radio 4 at the moment, and it just can't happen and it's really tricky. Not that I swear a lot – I try to use my swearing effectively, in the right place. To me, it's like seasoning. But sometimes a sentence will never be as funny without 'motherfucker' at the end of it.

There are sentences in which swearing makes it funny, there's no two ways about that. But there's too much reliance on it. That also comes back to women in comedy. Here's an excellent broad strokes generalization: people – boys and girls – don't like to hear women swearing as much as they do men. I would say that is a fact, whether it is politically correct or not.

I would say it is a trend, not a fact. It can't be a fact.

Then if the trend is true, it is a fact for now.

But I don't think every woman doesn't like to hear women swearing as much as men. I would say it is a trend. So for a chunky part of the audience it might be true.

But that will affect the rest of the audience, and therefore it is true. It doesn't matter, in a sense, as a detail because the bigger picture is so much more interesting – which is, how easy is it for men and women to laugh at women who are being funny. And I think at the moment, it is still more challenging from the get-go for a woman stand-up to succeed on stage. That's embedded in absolutely deeply entrenched gender roles that are observed willingly and unwillingly every single day.

I know what you mean and that might be a trend. But if you came to see my show at Leicester Square Theatre, it's 400 seats and 70 per cent of my audience were women. I come out, they automatically feel they have a rapport with me. I play very high status if I banter with guys. It's no struggle.

Absolutely. Don't get me wrong. None of the generalizations that I make there, that I would stand by, can be proved or disproved by the relative success of very funny women.

It's more than just being female. What I play is a charming, high status female. What happens is a lot of the traditionally male comic personas are aggressive high status. You get a Rich Hall or an Al Murray – both amazing comedians – they basically say, 'You're a bunch of losers, you will shut the fuck up, and listen to me'. If you're picked on by Rich Hall or Al Murray, that's kind of a compliment. They can't lower your status without raising it by giving you attention. But they're still incredibly high status and in charge of the audience.

Conversely, Paul Foot has quite low status. It's clowning. Clowning is often very low status. I would say more men than not, on a traditional British club circuit, would play high status. And American guys who end up on Letterman doing a slot will play high status to the audience. 'I'm the school teacher here, you will all shut up.' They take down the heckler. They demonstrate they can take down the bully in the playground.

Women often come out to be a bit more low status maybe because they feel it's more endearing. A high status, defensive woman can be seen as very challenging. That's what Sheryl Sandberg talks about in Lean In: *'If a man does it, it's ambitious, if a woman does it, it's aggressive.' I think one reason why Sarah Millican is so popular, apart from her incredibly hard work and talent, is that she plays charming, high status. 'So, I'm in charge of this room, I like you and I want to raise your status, I don't want to lower it.' That's a wonderful thing to do to an audience.*

That's key. I think the most enjoyable comedy for me, and the most skilful, is high-low. It's both at once. Bill Bailey is a really good example of this. Bill deliberately makes it look like he doesn't know what he is doing. Rich Hall in a different way is high-low. Rich comes out like big barking dog, but then he's baffled by the world, he's like a little boy, so there's this high-low confusion. 'What is this? I don't understand! Somebody explain.' But where it is different and more challenging for women – if you disregard the right and wrong of the patriarchy – patriarchy exists. Masculinity is dominant right now. So high-low is much harder to achieve for a woman.

Sara Pascoe is high-low.

Yes, I think every decent comic is high-low.

What an enormous generalization that is – every decent comic is high-low?!

Definitely. Name a decent comic and I'll explain to you how they are high-low, if you don't know.

Okay, well I'm obviously going to try and think of one who is not high-low.

Go for it. Not going to work. I'm a comedian and proving facts is my job.

Alright: Louis CK. I would say Louis CK is high.

You've never seen him then? Seen how he dresses? If he even dresses.

Yes, I've seen him live.

Metaphorically there is egg on his shirt. Because I'd heard Louis CK. I'd never watched him, oddly, until last year. And I watched him, and he obviously just walked on stage and started talking. The only reason I say that anybody who is any good is high-low is that, in order to perform comedy, you have to be high status. You are standing on a stage. You have to own the room. And then, you can only do it by expressing or exposing some kind of vulnerability. Now with the shows I've done with you,[4] you are engineering the show in which the vulnerability is played out by us. But you are still putting the show together.

Yes, it's my construct. But it was done deliberately to get improvisers to show vulnerability.

It's the best stuff, and so that's why I say it's high-low. If you take a comic who gives the impression of high-high, say Brendon Burns, he is at his least effective when he plays high-high. He's at his most effective when he is like, 'Fuck you, fucking thing…' and then mutters to himself because he can't understand the world or cope with it. Oh, there's the little childish thing. There's the person going, 'Love me, please, because I'm confused in the same way you are'. The most didactic comedians are, at their highest status, sharing their

---

[4] *Voices In Your Head* – a show in which Deborah directs improvised performances from a lighting booth as an invisible voice.

very lowest status by saying, 'I don't get this, guys'. Sometimes, if you take Jerry Seinfeld – and it's harder to tell because he's a joke-slinger, but he's even going lower status than the audience because he's asking questions of the audience that they understand – but he seems not to.

I did about seven years where I wore a corduroy suit on stage and became convinced I couldn't do comedy unless I was wearing it. In part, it gave me a great opening line that I knew would always get a laugh, and once you get the first laugh, you're away.

What's your corduroy suit opening line?

Good evening ladies and gentlemen, I realize a lot of people are looking at me now and thinking, 'A supply teacher has wandered onto the stage'. I confirmed the thing that no one was thinking and then they felt clever because they understood the thing that was said.

That's a sort of Derren Brown thing.

It all is. It all is. Without wishing to spoil it – that's the last thing I want to do because I love it so much. And it was high-low. I wouldn't say I ripped it off, but I was influenced by Bill Bailey's thing of making it look like I didn't know what I was doing. I fiddled with the mic. I know how a mic works. I know how to reset the height of a microphone stand, I know how to use a microphone. But I would fumble it every time. I probably moved a thousand microphone stands in the first year of comedy, and every time I pretended.

I want to put something to you, Marcus, because you have now convinced me that every comedian is high-low in a way. I think – the audience assume you're high because you're tall, middle-class, a bit posh, intimidating. Not that you are intimidating in real life, but there are some men and women in the audience who might be intimidated by you, just because of our assumptions that you seem well-educated, nice-looking and tall.

And attractive – distractingly attractive.

Right. Sure. So, because you are distractingly attractive, we make assumptions about you. To you, it is very useful to show that you don't know how to use the microphone, because that lowers your status a little bit. For me, because I am a woman, I need to come out and take the mic immediately and look like I know what I'm doing, because the assumption might be, 'Oh she's not going to be very good', and if I come out and own the stage and can work the mic, they'll go, 'Oh she does know what she's doing'. I always put my weight on my front foot, as if I am coming towards the audience.

I quite agree. I quite agree. And I've seen lots of people fumble with the microphone, and it would do men many more favours than it would ever do women. I totally agree. The female stand-ups I've seen, there is a tension in the room. Sometimes acknowledged in a very unhelpful way by the compere – 'I'm going to introduce a woman now, but don't worry'. I've heard those exact words said, it's so depressing.

There was an article in the Independent *today. The headline was 'What's the biggest problem with women artists? None of them can actually paint, says Georg Baselitz'. That painter's toxic opinion was granted a headline as if it had merit. If he'd said 'Asians can't paint' or 'Jews can't sculpt' the headline would be 'Respected Artist Ends Career'. My rant was about the views being aired as if they are contro-versial or titillating in a national newspaper. And the women around me being so intensely clever, wonderfully creative, outstandingly talented and incredible, in every way. I am surrounded by such extraordinary women at the moment. They just don't stop coming. As human beings we all have our own inadequacies and failings, but as over 50 per cent of the population we've got it covered, don't fucking tell us we can't paint or we can't banter. Women can fucking banter. Don't tell me I can't banter well enough for a panel show or a chat show.*

This is what I'm talking about. I am talking about something that is not engineered just as a boys-only playground. Women go out together, sometimes girls and boys.

You never see that on the telly. You never see two women being funny together.

The point is you don't need the comedic version of *Loose Women* to prove that. You just need shows that feel the same as the pub you go to with your mates. Boys and girls, you piss around, you have a laugh.

Do the Right Thing *has just answered that question. Listen to Danielle Ward's podcast. She is the host and writes her material. Margaret Cabourn-Smith is a team captain. Michael Legge is a team captain. They have two guests – they have always had 50/50 men and women guests. Women feel totally welcome. It is not a hostile environment. It is hilarious. It is hysterical. I went to see it recorded live in Edinburgh. The audience were beside themselves.*

And it just answers the question. If you create an environment that's anything less than hostile and testing, women will be as funny as men every single time. During the recent controversy about getting more women on BBC panel shows, I saw people saying on Facebook and Twitter that women tend to be funnier on radio than they are on television. Do they think women lose their ability to be funny when a camera is put on them? Really?

It's absolutely a symptom of why I still like making radio comedy. There's not enough money in it to attract the same kind of arseholes. The people making radio comedy do it because they love comedy. There are some who pass through on their way to telly and that's fine, but there are a great number of truly excellent radio comedy producers and they make radio comedy because they love it, and they get paid bugger all, and they work longer hours – and I don't mean longer hours dealing with some pointless circular argument about how it's going to look or should this or that happen.

The trouble with television is it makes too many shows that don't just exclude women, they exclude anyone who's not a certain sort of club comic. Lots of comedians don't find them pleasant or fun. Not just women. Lots of men, too. I only really understood what women combat when I started doing political material on the circuit. I realized you have to spend the first five minutes winning the audience around, because they put up a barrier. It was then that I realized that that's what women have to do at nearly every circuit gig.

That's why they need high status behaviour.

High-low. Every decent comedian is high-low.

Figure 5 Marcus Brigstocke © Idil Sukan/Draw HQ

Chapter 4
Structuring your Set

How does a joke become a routine? Segues, runners and call-backs.

DEBORAH FRANCES-WHITE: Once you've got your material and your persona on some kind of roll, it's time to put the moving parts together into something resembling a routine. While there's something delightful about watching someone who looks like they're just chatting to the audience and it's all off the cuff, the reality is there is often a great deal of structure, thought, time and planning involved in making comedy look effortless. There's a reason that Jerry Seinfeld's material about airplane nuts is a classic and your Uncle Jerry's hilarious holiday story is actually mind-numbingly dull: Seinfeld did the work to get the bit right.

Assuming you're not the kind of comic who is going to deliver a series of one-liners, it might be useful to think of your set as a story. Is this story about your take on the world? Is it about what bugs you? Is it about what delights you? Is it about why you get out of bed in the morning or why you can't be arsed? Think about why the audience would want to spend five or ten of their valuable drinking minutes listening to your thoughts.

You might use a framing device to link your ideas together. Could your frustration with fire extinguishers be part of a morning-from-hell story that also includes your fear of your child's history teacher? Could you join these ideas so the narrative conflates the two incidents?

Do you have a more rhetorical device, like reasons you want to live to over a hundred? (Even as I type that idea I hate it, but you might be able to make it work. It sounds hack to me.) If you're not going to make your set all part of one story, you might want to create segues or bridging devices. These are easy to write. You have some material about walking your dog in the park and some material about how you're addicted to Facebook. What links these? You put a picture of your dog on Facebook with some kind of punchline – and you're in. Some comics don't worry about them. They just finish a bit that has a big laugh and then change topics like this:

'So… that's why my dog's called Dolly Parton.'

Laugh.

'Facebook. You heard of it? I'm a big fan.'

This can work if you're very high status, because you're in charge of the conversation. You can just switch topics without apology. It can also be fun to watch a very low status comedian bumble through a routine. She might get to the end of her Dolly Parton dog bit and look confused, almost unsure as to why the audience is laughing, act as if she's forgotten what she was talking about and then suddenly discover a wonderful memory of her Facebook addiction. More like:

'So that's my dog… Dolly Parton…'

Laugh.

'That's what I call her now. Well, everyone does, I guess.'

Laugh. Confusion. Memory.

'Did you know Facebook can be like a really dangerous addiction? Like crystal meth or *Mad Men*?'

Laugh. Confusion.

'It's not funny.'

While you can ditch segues if they don't work for you, call-backs – or reincorporations – are a comedian's best friend. I remember friends of mine, who had regular non-comedy jobs, discussing going to see Eddie Izzard. Eddie had a routine in which he questioned the branding of Caesar dog food. He thought it was an irrelevant name and that they should rename it 'Mister Dog'. About an hour later, when the audience had completely forgotten about that, he did a bit about being a time traveller in ancient Rome and saying, 'Take me to your leader … Mister Dog'. My friends were effusive about how brilliant it was and one of them said, 'It made me feel clever, because he'd made the joke so long ago – but I'd remembered it'. I think that's at the heart of the widespread, never-ending success of call-backs – they surprise your punters and make them feel clever, all at the same time.

You can look for symmetry in your material to see where call-backs might be begging to happen. You may decide if you put Facebook addiction up front, then when you're in the park with your dog, you can be Facebooking pictures of her and adding status updates about her bone-burying and each one will get you an extra moment of joy with the audience.

When I was writing my second *How to Get Almost Anyone to Want to Sleep With You* show, I remember noticing that I had a bit about predictive text accidentally changing the message 'I have the keys' to 'I hate the Jews' and that I had another separate line about Nazis. All I had to do was put the Nazis up front and then bring them out again after the accidental 'I hate the Jews'. It's so delightful when that happens that you feel like taking a week off, but you can always create opportunities for call-backs if they don't leap out at you. You can be brutal and think, 'How can I wedge Dolly Parton the dog into this bit on my dad's weird-flavoured ice creams?' Something might occur to you. If it doesn't on the page, it might on the stage. Once you train your brain to think that way, it will find its own call-backs.

Ultimately, whether you use a story framing device, segues or call-backs does not matter as much as your set sounding like it all comes from you. If everything you're saying is truthful, it will feel of a piece. That doesn't mean it has to be factual – it means it has to somehow truly express the world as you see it, rather than copy the style of a comedian you admire or one who is easy to imitate.

If you are doing a longer show then you probably will have to think about how your material serves a theme or tells a story. But your first five- and ten-minute sets only need to be your observations or what's obvious to you – and the more truthful they are, the more they will shape themselves into a routine that flows in a way that means the audience will stick with you, 'get' you, and want to hear more from you.

ORNY ADAMS

When you're building a routine, it's placement of jokes. And that's why it's so important to me when on stage at a gala that this goes here and this goes there. There are many times that a joke alone, independently, doesn't get a big laugh but you place it in the right time with a routine, it does. I have jokes that I know need to be up top. I have jokes that need to be when the audience is a little bit tired. That's how great composers, Mozart and Beethoven, they knew when their audience was going to drift a little and get tired. They knew that they would eat a big meal, sit down, and go listen to their music. And they knew – and then they'd add the singing, right? And then they bring it back down. And it's peaceful again. So they knew. And it's the same way with jokes.

While Orny Adams has a full orchestra to create a symphony with his set, one-liner comics like Gary Delaney only have a single instrument – but they still need to work it like Jimi Hendrix.

GARY DELANEY

I have heard and I think my experience backs it up, that fourteen minutes is the audience tolerance for one-liners in a monotone before you have to change flavour. Sometimes I will try and drop in, not exactly a story, but at least a longer joke to change the pace a little bit. If I have to, I will talk to the audience. That's very much a last resort. I used it all the time when I didn't have enough jokes and I was much better at it in those days because I had to do it every night to pad out a twenty. As soon as I had more jokes, I stopped doing it.

> So other things being equal, every one-liner will get slightly less reaction than the last because of diminishing returns. Not a problem when you do a couple of dozen but by the time you get up to 150 or whatever, it starts to become a real problem. That's why you start mixing up the pace and stuff.
>
> One of the tricks that I use was to gradually get ruder and ruder, partly because that gives the illusion that you're going somewhere. It gives that dynamic and you get a bigger woof off something that's horrific and about your mum or whatever it is.

While the reaction of the audience can often give you a great many clues as to the best order for your material, some comedians find that the best place for working these things out is actually on stage.

MOSHE KASHER

Sometimes, I'll accidentally tell a joke. I did this joke about being transgendered. And it ends with me saying I'm a man or whatever. That's the end of the joke and then I segued it into, 'But the question is, how did I become a man?' Then the bulk of my current hour show is a very long story about how I became a man. So that bridge happened that night and I thought, 'Well, that's a perfect place for that joke to go'. I do the transgender joke there and then I say, 'But the question is, how did I become a man?' and then it leads into this other thing which gives the 'That's how I became a man' line at the end a bigger payoff. That just happened that night.

But until you're more comfortable with being on stage and performing, it might be easier to start off by following Neal Brennan's lead.

NEAL BRENNAN

While I'm writing I just try to put it in a tone of speech and then unpacking the thought in a – mathematical is not exactly the right word, but in a structured way. Then you try and find the order. I've been writing some material about women that's just five observations and so I'm wondering, 'What am I trying to say and then how can I find the right order?' It's just about all the illusions that women have to put on and then sort of parsing out the jokes based on that. Then the final joke is like about wearing heels – but that's the best joke. So it's like all right, well, you're going to go last. You're going to be our big closer.

For Neal Brennan, it's obvious that the best joke should come at the end, and in the case of a sequence of jokes about one subject, that's probably correct. But considering a ten- or twenty-minute set, there's also a strong school of thought which advocates for opening with your best joke, so the audience immediately knows you have the power to make them laugh.

GARY DELANEY

I used to be a big believer in 'start with your biggest joke' and I did for years. I started with a lovely little joke I had which was, I like to annoy my Israeli flatmate by giving him any post that's just addressed to the occupier. That was my best gag and again it was that rare thing: a clean banker. I used that for a year. I mean, I only dropped that a couple of years ago. I still occasionally bring it back in a club on a hard night.

I was at Jongleurs, Southampton one weekend. I went out on a Friday and I opened on that and it just bombed and I thought, 'Oh fuck, hang on. I've opened on my funniest joke and that has died. Nothing in the next niineteen-and-a-half minutes is as funny as that', and I lost my bottle. I just fell to pieces. I thought, 'Oh, I've killed it. I've killed my career.' So on Saturday, they rang me up and moved me to Portsmouth because I wasn't doing very well.

So I came to Portsmouth, which is actually a harder club, and I walked out just thinking, 'this is my last time ever on this stage, I don't give a fuck'. I had a great one because I just didn't care. It was like the pressure was all completely off.

Here's Nat Luurtsema's take on the same issue.

NAT LUURTSEMA

I used to start with my best joke, and I think it was Gary Delaney who told me, 'it's kind of wasted because they're not listening. They're just getting used to you so actually it's a real shame to bat it out there and get nothing for it', and I just went out with something. I've never really had that killer opener. I've got a good one at the moment but it is a bit wasted because they're just sort of taking you in and they're just like 'what sort of person are you?'

Right now I just sort of go in and it's kind of deliberately mundane. The trousers I wear are really tight trousers. 'Trousers a bit tight? Maybe. A bit tight. I find if I drop something I don't own it any more', and then I just let that sink in and bit by bit they start laughing.

Putting your jokes in order is all well and good, but once you graduate to longer shows (or even doing shows of your own), it's important to be able to move elegantly from one topic to another and have all of your material work together as a whole.

TODD GLASS

I don't really think much about routining. I guess I chunk stuff up together. OK, that belongs there. Decide where it goes. But you know what? I think the longer you do comedy, the less I have segues because I realized the connecting line is your perspective.

So whether you're talking about having a dinner party or a cute dog you saw at the dog park, it all goes together because it's all really your perspective on whatever you're talking about. So everything sort of fits together. I don't really have segues as much as I used to. In the beginning of my career, everything was about, 'How do I get from that topic to that topic?' Then I thought, 'Well, hopefully a joke will get a big laugh'. You will take a drink of water and you will go, 'I was at Subway the other day'. It's almost adorable when I see a comedian that still overly segues the bits together.

And as we said at the beginning, another crucial element, especially in a longer show, is the call-back – referencing an element from earlier in the show which the audience feels good for remembering. This tops and tails your act with a bookending and creates a circularity to your composition – a bit like being given airline nuts at the end of a Jerry Seinfeld show.

ADAM BLOOM

My call-backs are not written backwards. They're written forward. I've got a routine I like. I come up with an idea I could tag onto that and go back to it. But I don't think, 'I'm writing this bit. I have to call back to that.' So even my call-backs are improvised while walking down the street or on the stage. There's one Edinburgh show I did that was themed. So then, I *had* to write it because I can't just pull out an hour of stuff on anger management, but also a theme show has to have some kind of arc.

With stand-up, you can think, these bits work at the beginning, these bits work at the middle, these bits work at the end. That's a show. An hour of a person talking to me isn't a show.

Some call-backs are less deliberately pre-planned artifice and more happenstance, such as for Stephen K Amos.

STEPHEN K AMOS

When you find your voice, you find your rhythm. I see that so many times particularly when you go on stage. The audience gets into your rhythm. So sometimes, I've actually messed up a joke, but the audience have laughed because they're in the rhythm of your sound and your style – that's why there is an art to it.

But in terms of writing witty call-backs – that happens for me organically. The more I do the show, the more different things come in. I always mix up the order as well. I don't ever want to be stale and stagnant so I try to keep it fresh to myself. Then you find something else happens and something else happens. And you think, 'Oh my god, I could actually link back to that'. I used to do a joke and, after having done the joke for a year, I did it once and something just came to me which makes the joke ten times better. I thought, 'Why on earth didn't I think of that?' and it just wouldn't have happened for me if I'd tried to write it.

While Bloom and Amos enjoy the way performing feeds into their future routines, other comedians like Jim Jefferies are far more pre-planned and prepared with their routine structures.

JIM JEFFERIES

If you watch the DVDs, you can see it's the same structure in every one. It starts out small jokes, small jokes, something about my life and where I want to go, problems with religion, sex jokes, big story.

These are five subjects I can write on all day, so it's always a new lot of jokes on those subjects. They're the realms I work in. I never go off into fantasy or anything surreal. If anything, I take the religious stuff out sometimes and put an extra story in there. Me talking about myself and my life, I can write those all day. Sex jokes, they can be replaced with another story. But I always end with my life and a big story and little tiny jokes at the front to warm up.

Little tiny jokes are the ones you write when you're actually shooting the shit with your friends. I have a lot of friends who aren't comedians. It's difficult when your friends are comedians and you're shooting the shit because then who owns what? When they're not comedians, they're so happy for you to use even half a line that they put into it, so that's alright.

Sara Pascoe has a particular technique for generating a solid and satisfying routine and, for her, structure is enormously important.

SARA PASCOE

Say, for instance, you've got a story that's about a dog in a park. What you always have to ask in terms of structure is, where are my 'outs'? So I can talk about something else and come back to the park. Like Russian dolls, tucking one routine inside another routine strengthens both routines.

So the idea would be: there's a routine about a dog in a park. And then, because you're talking about an animal, you might mention a trip to a zoo. Or how you're a vegetarian and you can segue off into that. Or you might talk about how there's a lot of crime in your neighbourhood. There are things you could put inside the routine that's about something funnier than dogs in the park. So actually, that routine ends up being seven minutes with three different stories inside it. Always reminding you – 'Oh, anyway, I was in the park, and then this dog did this'.

Sometimes I might put an asterisk next to something, going 'you're definitely going to have to write something about sandwiches', even if it's just two lines that will be really funny inside this bit. And other times, you go, 'I've never had anywhere to put this line but now it can go in here'.

People's brains love patterns. So there's nothing more satisfying than someone coming back to a story or referring back to something you've mentioned earlier, or finishing a joke five minutes after you started that joke. The longer you can make an audience wait for it, the more satisfying it's going to be – and also the more work an audience's brain has to do. That's why structure's really important.

And some people's shows are really, really satisfying and you walk away and you think you've seen something which has been crafted. And other people's shows are really funny and very observational, but it's like fast food. You walk out and actually you've not had to do any work at all.

As you will have noticed, comedians bring a lot of preparation to making this look effortless, and as such, there are a few ways you can best prepare yourself for your first foray onto the stage. Sometimes you will need a prompt to help you remember what comes next.

HANNIBAL BURESS

Sometimes I will just put on – if it's a headline or so, I'm doing an hour, hour and thirty minutes, I will put a set list on the stage monitor, on the stage. So the audience can't see it but I can look at it without it distracting. So it doesn't look like I'm just looking at a notebook. But it's right there. It's in my vision and so that's how I can remember some newer ideas.

It's tougher especially once you get kind of locked into an hour. Sometimes it's hard to find space for the newer material unless you really make yourself do it or have to remind yourself to write it down on paper.

Other people just say the new material aloud offstage until it starts to stick – but be careful who you say it to!

Figure 6 Hannibal Buress © Idil Sukan/Draw HQ

SARA PASCOE

Saying something three or four times puts it into your brain. So, rather than having a piece of paper on stage, tell it to three people – especially if it's a funny thing that happened. By the time you've told it to three people, in a way it's become an anecdote already so it's halfway towards becoming material, so that can be helpful. It's something comedians don't like about each other when they realize, 'Oh someone's trying out material on me'. But you can't help it. You have to see if a couple of people are interested or think it's funny before you then go to an audience with it.

While many comics just learn their material by rote, Gary Delaney has a more detailed method of remembering his routine.

GARY DELANEY

I don't actually have a great memory. So I would have a set broken into thirds and I have all the thirds broken into triangles and just try and have a sort of loosely visual selection, so I know that a cluster of jokes would always go together. So, if I remember the signature joke, I remember the two or three that normally follow it and the set would be broken into a third. So I know that in the first third, there would be ten or twelve clusters of jokes identified by their signature jokes. So I can think, right, well I've got ten clusters here and I pick my clusters. That would normally be the first cluster and whatnot.

The beginning of shows are much easier and viable. It's very easy to get a joke to work in the first five minutes. It's very difficult to get a joke to work in the last five minutes. Something that slays at two minutes in may well die at eighteen.

So I did it like that, but then that memory system started to collapse because I did too many things with that system. That was what I used when I did my last bit of the show. Mentally, you have a little bit of the end of one thing and bring it on to the start of the next thing.

But those systems weren't sophisticated enough. So I'm currently using memory palaces or I think the loci method, to give it its proper name. I find it fascinating. I read a book on it recently and the Greeks and the Romans had the memory palaces. All their academics had it because they had to learn everything. They didn't have printing presses.

The human memory is a visual memory. It's a caveman's memory. Words and numbers are all recent. We're not used to them yet. Our brains haven't adapted. Our brain was designed to get you from your cave to the hunting ground, past a bit of marshy ground – not over there because there's tigers, and back to your cave and left at the river. So you learn spaces. People learn spaces and images much more quickly than anything else. The most commonly used one is your house.

My show is based in my house and I have a series of mental images from when I wake up. The first thing, you want to wake up in the morning. I'm woken up by a loud noise and that loud noise is Blur on my pillow playing 'Song 2'. Then next to that, there's some screens and this huge pocket with an inhaler and a mobile phone in there. Then there's a poster for my show and then there's a coffin with the number 19 written on it. Then – this is on the bedside table now – there's Joe Pasquale and he's sniffing helium out of a canister and he's being squirted with a flamethrower. Next to them in the window is a pole dancer with quite large breasts dancing on a pole. Next to her is a man watching the pole dancer and he's in the process of being mugged. Next along is an Indian restaurant. It's the same pole dancer and this time, she's having a curry. Then in the door to my bathroom window, there's a dwarf and then there's two little girls in the bath. There's a bowl of pasta on a little chair just by the table. There is a huge medicine bottle on the bathmat. Outside the window is whales and there is a picture of a bridge and there's loads of devils jumping off the top of it.

In the shower itself, there is Benny Hill running up to some woman in his over-the-top manner but then actually ripping off her clothes. On the bedroom windowsill is a Belgian eating a waffle. On the little wooden thing next to that, we have medicines. On top of that is a twelve-year-old bottle of scotch that looks like a child. Underneath that is Jimmy Savile. Next to that, there are five zombies all trying to use the toilet. In the bathroom mirror, there are two images reflected at me. One is a man with a bar through his head. Next image along is Nelson from the Simpsons pointing out of the mirror and going, 'Ha-ha!'

Then you turn around and you go into the bedroom. In the mirror in there, there is a man with swimming goggles on and he lifts up the swimming goggles and piss comes out. Then you open up the cupboard door. At the top half of the cupboard, there's somebody in a wheelchair and they're on fire and they're jumping through a hoop. Underneath them is a disabled parking space and in the next one along, there is a small child who's dead on the floor and he has got one armband on and he drowned. Next door to them is Tony Hart who has a felt tip for his penis.

Next door to them – you open the door and a load of moths fly out. Next door to that is a dead Princess Diana on the floor. Next door to that is a fridge and the door opens. There is a sausage in there. It looks like Albert Einstein. Next door to that is a big Hoover that has swallowed James Dyson and you can see his arms and legs sticking out the Hoover. Next door to that is the front door with the bedroom and that's covered in spunk.

That's the first ten minutes of my show.

Deborah Frances-White talks to Sarah Millican

In 2008, Sarah Millican's show about her recent divorce won the comedy award for Best Newcomer at the Edinburgh Fringe. Since then she has made regular appearances on British television and won thousands of fans for her sharp observations, combined with her warm and friendly approach. Her own stand-up show, *The Sarah Millican Television Programme* began airing in March 2012.

You're a big name act now, do you ever use a support act?

I didn't up until very recently. I didn't have a support for the first two tours and for the first ninety dates of the third one. And then, after chatting to other comics who used a support, I considered it for the first time. I still wanted to do a ninety-minute show and I'm friendly enough to not feel the need to have the audience warmed up before I go on. But I was knackered and fancied some help. So, I picked a few comics that ticked three boxes. Can they do the job well? Will my audience like them? Do I enjoy their company? And so for the last fifty dates of my most recent tour, *Home Bird*, I had a friend there providing support on and off the stage. Off stage was just as important. Someone to have breakfast with, go stationery shopping in a strange town with, forage for post-show chips with. In the show, I'd go on and introduce them, it's only decent, and they'd do fifteen to twenty minutes and bring me on. So I still got to do my 90-minute show and we were done by 10.15 p.m. which means it's early enough that people in the audience can get buses and things.

You're the loveliest comedian ever, thinking of your audience's transport needs!

Well, you know, a lot of the people that are my core fan base will have bought tickets a year ago for these shows, so it's a lot of prep involved for them and that's why I never put tour tickets on sale for something that I haven't started writing, because I don't think the audience should be more prepared for this tour than I am. Everyone's like, 'Right, well Brenda can probably come in and look after the bairns, we could probably get a cab there…' and I'm still like, 'I don't know what it's about!' I can't do that, so I have to start writing it before the tickets go on sale so at least I know that I've done more work than they have.

Yeah, maybe the minimum requirement is that you are slightly more prepared than your audience.

Even if it's a year and a half away, I still have to have started writing it before I put the tickets on sale, it's a rule I have. On my last tour I used to tell them what time it was going to finish, cause I love knowing what time things are going to finish. When I go to the cinema the first thing I do is find out how long the film is, so that I know what time it's going to finish, cause I like to know when the fun is going to end and I get to go home, because I like going home.

When you were a support act, did you find it harder because the audience had come to see someone else?

I supported Reginald D Hunter, and when you're a support I think it is harder, because they don't want you – they actively don't want you! There's disappointment when you come out. But because they don't want you, and they also don't know you, they don't know anything about you, so you can sometimes absolutely hammer it…

So it's the Susan Boyle effect – no one's expecting you to be any good.

Yeah, it's a bit of a surprise when they're expecting you to be not as good. You might not be as good as the person they've come to see, but the person who is on the tour poster has generated expectations, whereas you have not, if you're support. I've taken that with me – winning them over.

　My argument is now that 50 per cent of my audience absolutely love me and 50 per cent have been brought by the people who absolutely love me, so they potentially don't like me at all, so they have to be won over. And what you hope is that the people who were brought come back as a fan and bring somebody else.

Is it more satisfying to win new people over than it is to please the fans?

I think they're two different things, I think you want to create more fans but equally the most important ones are the ones that are already fans, because you have to keep them happy. If I only ever play to the same amount of people – it's about 200,000 on my tour – if I play to that, then I have an audience for every tour. I don't have to hit the dizzy heights of the Peter Kays and the Michael McIntyres and the arenas.

Did you always feel like that or did you get to a certain level where you felt you'd rather have proper loyal fans than just loads and loads of people going to a stadium?

That's why the tour is so long. I could do arenas, but it's just not for me. I don't think comedy works in arenas. I don't even think bands work in arenas, if I'm honest. I would see a band, and watch the screen and the screen was out of sync with the singing, so I was like, 'well, I may as well be on my fucking sofa'. It suits more animated comics – I don't take the mic out of the stand, I don't move from my spot, so theatres are much better for me. I mean, some of the theatres I still do are a good size and some of them feel much bigger than they are because of just the shape of the building. But I always get people to cheer as soon as I come out. I say, 'the people at the back give us a cheer', and I include everybody so they know that I know that they're there.

I'm not a big star when I go on stage, I don't feel. I don't walk out and have my arms wide and I'm not high status in the slightest. I know some people are and it absolutely suits them and it's exactly what they should be doing. But I walk on, I'm quite mousey and quite normal. I think people think that I could live next door. I look a bit like your aunty, a bit like your neighbour. There's not a massive difference from what I'm like on stage, to what I'm like off stage. I'm obviously less funny off stage.

You're obviously very successful, but do you still feel you have higher to climb, or are you happy where you are?

I have never predicted my success, I've always just taken what I've got. My ultimate aim was to pay my bills, with 'funny money' – that's what I call it. So I wanted to pay my bills, by being a comedian and writing jokes and performing jokes. Because my last two tours sold about roughly the same amount, I thought, 'alright, well this is where I am, and that's absolutely fine', because I don't want to compromise what I do in order to gain twice as many fans. I don't want to go, 'maybe the swearing keeps people away, so let's get rid of the swearing'. I really like fucking swearing. I don't think you should dilute what you do in order to be more popular.

No, and ironically you would probably lose people, because you would lose something true about yourself. I don't think it would work in the long term, I think it would only work in the very short term.

Often when a new comic starts, you see them and you think, 'Oh you already know who you are'. And then they lose it and they scrabble around for a while and sound a little bit like Stewart Lee or a little bit like Frank Skinner or whoever it is. I had my voice early on, I think, because I hadn't really seen that much comedy. I'd seen comedy on the telly, but I'd only really seen three tour shows of people. I'd never been to a comedy club before, until I stood on stage in one, so I didn't have that kind of morphing into somebody I admired, because I'd not watched it enough.

How did you know you wanted to do it if you hadn't been around it?

I used to write, I had a column in the free paper for a while, where I wrote film reviews that were funny. I tried to make them funny because it was a free paper. I reckoned that most of the readers of a free paper maybe can't afford newspapers, so therefore it's unlikely that they're going to go to the cinema, so I need to make that column funny in itself.

Then I wrote short films and short plays and things and they always had a funny angle. There was a night at Live Theatre in Newcastle where you could send in five to ten pages of whatever you were working on and they'd pick the best ones and they did a live reading with some actors and the audience came and the audience voted on which one they liked. Now I was never working on anything big but I used to just write five pages and send it in – just a conversation between two people – and invariably I won because it was funny.

So I wrote things like that and then when I got divorced I just thought, 'I can do anything I like now!' I was faffing around at work in the civil service on the computer on my lunch break and just saw this workshop for people who'd written but not performed and I went along and lovely Kate Fox, who is a stand-up poet, was running the course. I went along and it was all performance poets and me. And then at the end of the night there was a little performance and I just read the monologue that I'd written about my divorce. I did it for two minutes and it got some laughs and it was quite sad in places because it was never meant to be stand-up. I remember going to the ladies' loo afterwards and jumping up and down, because I felt like I'd achieved something I'd never done before. I felt like I'd ticked something off my list. And then six months later I rang Kate Fox back, who'd run the course, and said, 'I think I want to try doing stand-up', and she said, 'I know'. She'd been waiting, so she got me my first gig and that's how I started.

Were you scared at first or did you enjoy it right away?

I was terrified, but I had such adrenaline when I came off stage. It felt like I'd sort of overcome something that I'd always panicked about. I'd done it and I'd done it well, and that's what it felt like. It wasn't necessarily about making people laugh. The first gig that I did was five minutes at a really rough pub in Newcastle and that was when I came off stage and thought 'Ooooh!', because they, they didn't laugh for the first two and a half minutes and then this huge laugh, just from one extreme to the other. And I thought, 'Well, *he* might not love me but all of these people do!' It was entirely addictive.

And do you still get that? Do you feel more alive on stage than off?

I feel more comfortable on stage than off… which is quite weird isn't it? Maybe it's not weird if you consider it's my job. For a long time I didn't really have a home life when I was doing stand-up. It wasn't balanced in the slightest. I think in your first few years of doing stand-up you do throw everything at it, because you have to. You have to work really hard. You have to be constantly scribbling and travelling around the country and trying to impress or trying to get into new clubs, and constantly trying to get better and improve. Being able to play any room, I suppose, was always my ultimate goal.

I think now that I have a balance I often feel quite alive at home, which is nice. It's more balanced. But I still consider it a job. I love it. I find the travel is the job, the bit on stage I'd happily do for nothing – but the travel, I think the travel is the bit that you really get paid for.

You have a reputation for working very hard. People always say, 'Oh yeah, Sarah Millican writes all day and then she performs at night. She's writing all the time.'

I think if I spent half of the time that I spend doing admin, writing instead, I would have a lot more material. I sort of scribble all of the time. 'Writing all of the time' – that sounds like I'm in front of the computer and just churning out gold and I'm not, I have a notebook.

Are you sure you want to blow that myth for people?

I am happy to blow that myth because it's untrue, and I don't think anybody does that. In the early days when I was working, I would get into work earlier while the cleaner was Hoovering around, before anybody else started work, because I didn't have a computer at home. I would write for an hour and then I would clock into work and then I would do my job, and then I'd go home and do an hour of writing before I did anything else. I wish I did that now. I guess when you've still got your job you work a lot harder because you want to get out of your job.

I always think that middle-y bit where you're on the cusp of leaving your work but you're not quite there yet is quite probably the time you work hardest because you're working two jobs. I scribble constantly so I have a notebook and anything funny that pops in my head goes in there, because I always think, 'Oh I'll remember that tomorrow', and you never do.

It's awful, isn't it, when you know you have something good and then it's just gone.

It's gone and you always think that was probably amazing, but realistically probably one out of ten was amazing and the other nine were a bit alright or slightly shit. So I scribble constantly and then I do new material nights an awful lot. I do gigs where I do an hour of new material, and it's not an hour different every time because I sort of churn it and tweak it and make changes. But I panic on those days of those new material gigs. And then I record it, and then I don't always listen back, but I try to listen back whenever I can, and tweak it. So that is basically the beginnings of writing an hour-and-a-half show. I never sit down and do nine hours of writing in a day, though I do sort of always scribble.

Do you ever try and brainstorm things or are you always just writing down lines?

It's stuff that I'm inspired by. I'm never going to sit down and go, 'I'm going to write one joke about trees, or jokes about cheese'. What's more likely is that I'll come out with something funny in a conversation or I'll have a funny thought, or I'll hear a funny thing and have a funny response and I'll make a note of that and then that might develop into something much bigger, or it might stay just a short bit that gets added into something else.

I never actually sit down with a topic and write, and I never do topical stuff. I get really annoyed by topical stuff, because I think it must be so awful to have a brilliant joke that in a fortnight's time can't be used! My jokes, from the beginning of me writing something, I might be with these for four years, by the time I've written them, worked them up, tried them out, taken them on tour, made a DVD, promoted the DVD – that could be three or four years. I can't have something that is completely irrelevant after two weeks!

So it's mainly inspiration from your own life?

Somebody once said to me, 'you're really lucky because all of your family are really funny', like all I really do is record my family. I hope there's a little bit more to it than that!

Yes, it's identifying the funny, creating the turn of phrase…

Being able to see the funny in something, being able to have the conversation with somebody and take it away and shape it and hone it and add little bits to make it slightly better. Make that into a story that sounds still real. Everything I do is based on truth so it sounds still real and it is still real, but it may have been tweaked. My dad will come and see me and he'll say, 'Oh that was funny, that conversation we had', and I'll say, 'No, I've made it slightly funnier, Dad. You were funny but I've made you funnier.'

You actually did the bit of work that takes it from 'funny round the dinner table' to 'funny on stage'.

Exactly, and that's why I think people respond well because they often think, 'Oh, we're just like you', and you think, 'You are in so many ways, but also I have this knack for being able to sharpen things, polish them, shape them and make them funnier'.

How did you take on the clubs? Did you find any resistance from the audience who were used to acts that were a little bit harsher or a little bit more high status?

Not that I particularly noticed. It might have been that the resistance was there but I was so focused on what I was doing. I think you win them over by being really funny, quickly. I got some advice from Graham, who was the sound man at Jongleurs. I went out and didn't do very well. It was alright, it was alright, it wasn't a death, but it wasn't good and he said, 'Your first joke was too long, you need a really short joke so they go "oh, she's funny" and they relax'. The next night I just moved a couple of things around, I did a really short joke first and then they laughed, and they relaxed and then I had them and it was fine. He was totally right and I love things like that – where it's something that I should've known and I should have worked that out. Thank god, thank fuck, thank god for Graham…

When you're working on a TV show, you're not also on stage every night are you?

No. There is a lot of preparation, a lot of writing, but for the TV series I do try everything out on a stage. Ninety-nine per cent of the jokes that are written for the TV series get tried out once or sometimes twice, so even though I am still doing the writing part of the TV series, I still am very much trying out things two, three, four times a week and then when we do the recordings…

Most people don't do that, that's very unusual…

No, and I'm so horrified by that! I'll try things out, jokes I don't know are funny yet – because, face it, you don't know until you say it in front of an audience. You think it might be, but you don't know and you try that out in front of an audience with cameras watching you – that is horrific to me.

I remember one of the times I did *Mock The Week*, when you get up to do your bit of stand-up in the middle, Hugh Dennis tapped me on the arm and he went, 'Remember, this part is your job' and you think, 'Yeah, that's true'. All the rest of it, listening to the people and trying to bounce off them, that's all quite scary and quite new, but the bit where you stand in front of a microphone in front of an audience, it's the easy bit, you know.

That was so sweet of Hugh Dennis. Do you find in general there is an inclusive environment on panel shows?

I find so, yes. I feel more comfortable in the company of comedians. I feel like I'm really myself with my family and with comedians.

Do you have a sense that there's something inside of you that drives you to perform?

I think I'm a little bit needy for an audience. I used to do a little bit of performance-based stuff at home when I was little. Never at school, because I was quiet as a mouse at school, but I used to do a little bit of tap-dancing in front of my mum and dad even though I never learnt how to tap-dance. I used to write poems, I used to stand behind the curtain and read them to my mum but behind the curtain because I was embarrassed, so I was probably quite irritating as a child.

It sounds like you were a miniature Victoria Wood…

I've always liked being told 'well done', I've always craved that. That's why I did well at school because I liked getting good grades and that's like somebody saying 'you're good at that'. Originally stand-up was therapy for me. One hundred per cent it was therapy, just me getting straight out of a divorce and going out on a stage. It was very raw and I'm surprised that I didn't crash and burn more than I did. I think partly it's that when somebody first says to you that you're funny and funny enough to be on a stage, why wouldn't you always do that? It's the best job in the world, that's why I do it, because I've found something I'm good at and I'm not really very good at many things.

I'm sure that's not true. It's really a combination of having found your voice, having a very likeable persona, but writing really, really, really good jokes. I hear people being bitchy about people a lot, as comedians are. But people never say that about you, they never, never say, 'Oh, she didn't work hard enough'.

When I won the Newcomer award, Jo Caulfield (who I love) said to me, 'Well done, you've done the driving'. I always think if somebody looks at my career and thinks, 'god, I wish I had that' and 'how did she get that?', I'd love them to have a go at it for a month to see if they could do it, because I think a lot of people really want success, but aren't willing to put in the work. Gary[1] always described comedy as like riding a bull – as in, it will throw people off who don't work hard enough, but you cling on, you keep trying, keep trying and keep trying and if you're good enough you'll get there.

Have you ever died, properly died?

Oh god yes, of course. I did one in Soho and it was just silent. It was all stag dos and it was just complete silence and then somebody shouted 'next' and I came off stage and I was mortified. I just walked straight out and I was in tears, but not like floods of tears, but I was upset. I remember ringing Gary and he said, 'Oh, what happened?' I said, 'Nobody laughed, I said my jokes and nobody laughed', and he said, 'Did anybody shout that you were shit?' I said, 'Nobody shouted I was shit, but they said "next"'. He said, 'Did anyone throw anything at you?' and I said, 'No'. He said, 'Did anybody follow you out to the

---

[1] Delaney, whom Sarah married in 2013, and whose thoughts on comedy are found elsewhere throughout this book.

car park to tell you they thought you were shit?' and I said, 'No'. And he said, 'That's not a proper death', and I was like, 'Ah, at least let me have this!'

It's the right thing to say, it's not like 'no you were great'…

Yeah exactly, it's like, 'Oh, it can get a lot worse than that, love!'

I have my rule, my 11 o'clock rule that I instil on myself and anybody else who ever whinges about having a bad gig. By 11 o'clock the next day, I have to get rid of it. If I'm angry at myself or pissed off at the audience or confused about what I did wrong after a hard gig, by 11 o'clock the next morning I have to shake it off, because I probably have a gig that night and if I go in thinking 'I'm shit', I will die. Equally if I have a brilliant gig I have to get rid of all the smugness by 11 o'clock the next day because if I go into a gig that night thinking 'I'm amazing', I will die – so there is literally no win!

Although today I woke up late, because I didn't get home till 4 o'clock because I had to drive back from Newcastle last night, so I allowed myself an extension on my rule. I gave myself until 11 o'clock tonight to be smug which has never been done before, but I made a DVD so I extended it… It's my rule, I can do what I like.

PART TWO

Performance

Chapter 5
Getting Started

Open mic spots. Learning to die before learning to fly.

DEBORAH FRANCES-WHITE: Just do it. Just get a gig. Get on stage. Go to an open mic. The first gig is terrifying and elating at the same time. Most people have a great first gig because the first time an audience laughs at one of your jokes, it's a euphoric experience. Enthusiasm mixed with vulnerability is appealing to the audience. There's very little riding on it – just doing it is the achievement. Laughs are a bonus.

The second gig is usually just as terrifying but not as good. You might be a little cocky, which is much less appealing to the audience when you're not very competent. If the first gig went well, there's pressure on the second gig to be just as good, and if it isn't you'll feel depressed. You will want to dwell on that, which means by the time you get to the third gig, you'll have stayed awake all night, brainwashing yourself that you're not good enough.

This is a terrible strategy. Instead, decide you are not going to do one gig, you are going to do six gigs. The first six gigs are scary. The seventh starts to get fun. Get your first six gigs done as quickly as possible. Your aim is not to be good at stand-up comedy. Why would you be good at it? It would be weird if you were – you've never done it. Your aim is to do six gigs of any quality whatsoever. That way, you can't fail as long as you stay on stage for the full five minutes. During those six gigs, you're going to collect data. What happens if you talk really fast? What happens if you take your time, getting to the stage and taking the mic out of the stand? What kind of gig do you have if you go out to die? How do the audience react if you pretend to be an incredibly confident, experienced comedian?

Experiment, rather than 'trying to be good at stand-up'. This is a job where trying your hardest is not your best strategy. Go for quantity. Record the gigs on your phone. Listen back. If a joke didn't get a laugh on the first gig, are you going to ditch it or try a new strategy on the second gig? You could change the expression. Rephrase it. Pause before or after the punchline. If it still doesn't work, can you try it again with a new strategy?

I remember seeing a documentary about Eddie Izzard, in which he talked about having a map of London on the wall. He had different coloured pins in the map for places he'd gigged, done badly, and done well. His aim was to get every pin in the map to storming. That's a great plan because it separates the process from the ego. It assumes success is something that is about having lots of goes and noting successful strategies and seeking to recreate them and then reinvent them. It's no wonder he's seen as one of the world's greatest comedians.

There's no question that some people with a lot of intuitive ability for imaginative ideas and performance have given up stand-up because they feared failure or couldn't live with bad gigs. It's also true that there are many great working comics whose skills are almost entirely learned. Don't give up because you're not as good as you will be in six months or a year. Don't stop because you're frustrated that you're a comedian with five weeks' experience, not five years' experience.

The only way to not be in fear of your first gig is to have done your first gig. This time next year, you can either be someone who's still talking about doing stand-up or you can be a comedian with a year of experience under your belt. They are your choices. Get your first six gigs done as soon as you can, so you can start enjoying yourself.

Get any stage time you can. Volunteer to do presentations at work. Do karaoke – sober. Go to improvisation workshops. Do an acting class. Sign up for a stand-up workshop. Do anything to get comfortable on stage. Anything you do often enough becomes normal.

If I had to ride a horse right now, I'd be pretty nervous. That's because I've only ridden a horse three times and the last time I got thrown off. But if I rode a horse every day for a year, it would be hard for me to stay nervous. It would become what I did. Stage time is like that.

It just becomes a place you're comfortable. Performers often feel more comfortable or alive on stage than anywhere else in the world. Once you start to enjoy being on stage, it can become absolutely addictive. I think it's because you will be one of the small minority of human beings who enjoys being looked at by a crowd, so there's a huge power in it.

Every stand-up career, no matter how successful or disastrous, starts with someone asking for an open spot. There are no guarantees that you will become a celebrated stand-up comic if you do those first six gigs. But there is no Louis CK, Joan Rivers, Eddie Izzard or Robin Williams in the world who hasn't done them. There is no Billy Connolly, Sarah Millican or Lenny Bruce who hasn't died and decided to go back out there again.

The truth is, most people are astounded you're doing it at all. So just do it. You know you want to or you'd have skipped this part of the book.

JENNY ECLAIR

The thing is, I wanted to be an actress. I didn't know I wanted to be a stand-up comic because I didn't know such a thing existed because I was born 142 years ago and when we were on the ark. I didn't have television. I lived abroad when I was small because my dad was in the army so we did quite a lot of travelling around and between four and eight I was in Berlin.

And then later on, when I came back to this country, I saw the thing that made me laugh first, independently of my father telling very rude poo and fart jokes which he was very, very good at, and then I saw Fanny Cradock being abusive to her husband on the television in a cookery show and I thought it was one of the funniest things I'd ever seen in my entire life – but I didn't know that that was a job. There was nothing to indicate in the 1960s and 70s that female individuals could stand up behind a microphone and tell jokes and because I'd never been to a club I'd never seen it happen.

Lacking suitable role models, some comedians create the role for themselves out of whole cloth. Others may be hanging around comedy clubs for a long time before venturing on stage themselves.

GARY DELANEY

I think it's a universal truth that most comics who start comedy aren't so much inspired by watching somebody great and thinking, 'I would like to be like that', as watching somebody shit and thinking, 'I can do better than that'.

An old college friend of mine, Martin, dabbled in stand-up and I wrote quite a lot of his jokes. I got a nice little vicarious thrill from him getting up and doing them. I had written this joke about nurses and I told Martin, 'That's a killer joke. That's the best joke. You have to do that. That will slay! They will love that.' The joke was: I read that when a man dies, the man's body leaks – everything relaxes. The body leaks fluid from the penis and the anus. So when a man dies in a hospital, it's part of a nurse's job to tie a knot at the end of his penis and put a cork up his anus. The way I see it, there's two very clear lessons you can learn from that. One, never go out with a nurse or two, go out with a nurse.

I gave Martin that joke. And he did it a couple of times, but told me, 'I'm not doing that joke any more. It doesn't work. It's not funny.' I said, 'Well, you're doing it wrong.' So obviously the only answer was do it myself then. He was trying to give me a gentle kick.

Others have been turned off comedy in the past and so don't even consider stand-up as a vehicle for their creativity, or an outlet for their desire to perform.

SARA PASCOE

I found stand-up by accident and for ages I didn't take it seriously. I thought comedy was very silly. If you'd asked me at 20, when I was at university, about comedy in general as a genre, I would have said it's very lazy, it's very easy, it's very rude, and it's pumping sewage into the world. It's not a good thing. It's people being nasty. And then I was trying to be an actor and I remember going to see an open mic night. And I didn't think anyone was very good. I thought they were all very bad and I gave them all notes afterwards because I didn't know that's something that you didn't do. 'The reason I didn't laugh at your thing about evening primrose is because actually it takes six weeks to work.' Things like that. Then I was looking back and wondering, 'Why did no one like me?'

As part of the stand-up comedy boom, becoming a stand-up comedian started to seem more like a plausible career. To cater for the many eager young faces who want to make a living standing behind a mic, some people began offering stand-up comedy courses. Greg Davies started his career at one of London's best known and most respected.

GREG DAVIES

I did the Amused Moose course with Logan Murray. For me, personally, I would never have done comedy if I hadn't done that course. Because it felt like a very brave thing to do and I think that Logan Murray is very skilled at helping you tease out which weapons you have in your arsenal that you can exploit in public.

So it was very useful in that regard. But in terms of what do I think of comedy courses: no one is going to go on a course for weeks or months and then actually be funny – because you have to put the hard yards in.

I think a really good comedian needs to have spent years and years needing to make people laugh, and *then* I think they need to start comedy, and then ten years from that point they might be a half-decent stand-up.

On the course I got encouraged to exploit the physicality that I already had and the skills that I had long since developed. I got encouraged to exploit those in a thoughtful way. Logan just encouraged us to find our voice. Comedy is truth, isn't it? It has to come from a real place. It has to come from you ultimately and he's very good at encouraging you to find what that is. So that's what I took from it.

For many, being funny is something which has been a feature of their personal life forever and at some stage it occurs to them to attempt being funny professionally. Jo Caulfield, however, discovered the beginnings of her comedy voice in another setting entirely.

JO CAULFIELD

I know I enjoyed making people laugh. I always think that's more what it is with comics, that we just get more of a kick and it's more of a drug to us than other people. Other people just make their friends laugh and then go home. When I was a waitress, I was a very funny waitress. I knew I would make money from tips if I was funny and I would often be funny by being rude to people. I would go home saying, 'What I said at table 20, that was really good'.

And so, at some point, you have to make the transition from being funny with friends or customers to being funny on stage. You aren't quite at the 'professional' stage yet – but you are now in public, with all the attendant pressures and expectations that come with that shift.

HARLAND WILLIAMS

My first show was just an amateur night in Toronto. You phone in and the first fifteen people through get a spot. I tried for about a month and a half and I never got in and then one day, they picked up the phone and said, 'Hello'. I said, 'I want to do the amateur night'. 'All right. You're number 12. See you tonight.' Boom!

Then my heart was racing all day in panic mode. I was terrified. I planned it out. It was five minutes' worth of fat mother jokes. I decided to go with an easy premise and my strategy was just to feel what it would be like to be on stage in front of people getting laughs. So it went well. The first one went well enough that I went back.

Amateur or 'open mic' nights, where anyone can stand up and have a go, are where many comedians face a real audience for the very first time. Here's Gary Delaney's first gig story.

GARY DELANEY

I booked it in on 14 February 1997 at the Comedy Brew House. I kind of tend to disregard that little abortive stage in my career because I didn't really know what I was doing – I officially say I started in 2000 but I didn't. I dabbled in 1997.

I was completely oblivious to the fact it was Valentine's Day and that was obviously why there was a spot in the bill because nobody wanted to work there. I think I dragged down the girl I was seeing at the time as well. What a treat for her. I didn't sleep for three nights beforehand but I had written lots and lots of jokes and I remember just lying in the bath before work, just running through stuff in my head.

I booked it to do my first gig. In my head, it was a great gig. I have no doubt that if I watched it now, I would wince and curl up with embarrassment, but they laughed a few times and at the end, I got off stage thinking, 'This is the best thing ever. This is what I want to do with my life.' I just lay awake in bed that night thinking, 'Oh my god, this is amazing. I found my thing.'

Not everyone's first gig filled them with quite so much joy at the time.

ALEX EDELMAN

I did my first open mic a few weeks before my fifteenth birthday. I was terrible. The story would have been much more appealing if I had been good at it. If I had been this beloved underground figure, this toddler, who was doing really well at something that adults struggle with – that would have been a really powerful thing. But that was not the case. It was just me bombing in a pizza restaurant on a Tuesday and then roller-blading home in utter shame. I told my parents I was at the library but I think they knew I was somewhere else, they're not dumb people.

If I had done well the first time I did stand-up, I don't know if I would have stuck with it. I think the single greatest boon to my stand-up is that I have a massive chip on my shoulder. It's a fear of failure, a fear of not performing as well as my peers. I'm not professionally jealous of anybody but I feel like if there was someone who was working harder than me, well I wouldn't feel good about it.

The more you perform, the more you unlock a little bit more of your own potential. That's such a motivational speaker thing to say, but it really is true. I think the fear of failure and the fear of not being great should be the most powerful driving emotion. I don't understand people who go on stage and they're doing stuff that's just uninspired. They're doing the same thing week after week in front of an audience that's not getting it and doesn't think it's funny – and they're not changing a thing. How is your fear of failing not more developed? I don't understand it.

Rich Hall transitioned from being a street performer to a stand-up comedian and his first gig included some later comedy royalty.

RICH HALL

I was a street performer. I got crowds together and with a film camera with no film in it. But I'd pretend that I was filming a low-budget movie and I needed crowd scenes so I would get people to act out scenes. I had scripts and I passed them out and then I'd get a big loud hailer, put it right in people's faces and yell, 'Cut!' Berate them and tell them to do it again; I was kind of directing a movie that didn't exist. Then I would pass a bucket around at the end.

People would say, 'You should go to New York. You should go to LA. You should try to get on at the Comedy Store or the Improv in New York.' In the back of my head I figured I would and then finally, I did.

Like all comedians, I stood in line to get an open spot at some of the clubs in New York. My first time on was at the Comic Strip in New York. Jerry Seinfeld was the host. Larry David was on. George Wallace was on. There were quite a lot of people who later on we would recognize as great comedians.

I knew when I was in that room and went on that time that this is probably what I needed to be doing.

Many comedians have the first formative experience at a very young age. Judah Friedlander was only 19.

JUDAH FRIEDLANDER

I was living in New York but I was down in DC, Maryland visiting my folks and I went to an open mic. I'd been writing jokes for about three years and I was 19 when I finally started telling them on stage.

I was very introverted. I finally did it and it was an open mic night and I was supposed to do five minutes. I had to get there at about 5 or 6 p.m. I didn't go on until around 11 p.m. and right before I go on stage, the host says, 'I'm cutting you to three minutes', because the audience was starting to leave a lot. Then I remember I got a couple of laughs but it just felt warm and it felt like home. It just felt like, 'All right, this is the right place to be'.

I never really felt nervous doing it. The second time I did stand-up was six months later. I didn't realize you were supposed to go out every night. I had no clue how the business worked. I thought the guys you saw on TV doing stand-up, like the guys who are on Letterman or Carson, had maybe done it ten times before and literally Letterman or Carson saw them at a club and were like, 'Let's give this kid a shot'. I had no idea how it worked.

Among comedians we interviewed, Judah Friedlander was far from the youngest to start. Nathan Caton's first gig was when he was only 14.

NATHAN CATON

It was in my local church. It was a talent show. And I got dared to do some comedy. 'Yeah, I'll do it.' You know teenagers. 'Yeah, I can do anything.'

I did some jokes about my grandma, some jokes about people in the church, and then I did a spoof of like the Lord's Prayer. I was just taking the piss, but it went down well. Nobody said, 'You're going to hell for that, Nathan'. No, they liked it. They were cool. They're like, 'Don't worry. He's 14. We'll allow his sacrilege.' If I was 19 then they would be like, 'Yeah, you're going to Lucifer'. And then I did my first real gig in the comedy club when I was 19 and then that's when I started gigging properly.

At 14 years old it was lovely. At 19 years old I was bombed down to earth. I died. It wasn't technically my fault. OK. Excuses: it was in a rubbish little bar in our street. There were only about twelve to fifteen people there. Half of them were the other acts. There was an area behind me where there were people playing pool and it was like: a curtain; laugh area; then people playing pool. So if you weren't enjoying my jokes, you could watch people playing pool. And then it didn't help that my material was kind of rubbish. I was a cocky 19-year-old and I was doing jokes about a 19-year-old boy charming a girl in the club. But the weird thing was even though I died, I liked getting on stage.

There's something about being on stage and being able to just chat rubbish – it felt liberating. So I went back for more and I continued gigging on the circuit until, by the time I finished university, about 21, 22, I was making a decent enough wage that I was kind of labour fit. And

I was still living at home so it made sense. I just went to comedy full-time.

I studied architectural technology. There's not a lot of architects who go, 'You know what? I could do jokes.' They're quite boring people. I'm probably the only architect-turned-comedian. 'Hey, buildings. Hello? Hello? Oh gosh, tough crowd.'

For some comics, like Adam Bloom, their first time on stage can be one of the best moments of their lives.

ADAM BLOOM

My first show was a bit of beginner's luck. I was getting no laughs at the beginning, then I got heckled and dealt with it. Then something went a bit wrong with a prop I was using and I improvised out of it. I suppose the crowd loved me for struggling and being a fighter. Then it gradually stared to build. This magic happened and it kind of whirlwinded into this storming gig. It was like, oh my god, this helicopter that wouldn't start, then just suddenly took off without me almost.

It was the best part of my life. It really was. It was amazing. It lasted fifteen minutes.

Jo Caulfield also found that the stage initially was a very welcoming place.

JO CAULFIELD

I did the Comedy Cafe, that was the first one I ever did. It was really good, which I think happens to a lot of comics because you're so full of joy and fear and adrenaline that the audience gets something off you. That powers you through. I had sort of worked out what I was going to say but, again, what I had done is remembered things I had said in conversation and I thought, 'That story that I told my friend, I'll do that'. I think it was one of those new act competitions so I won one on the first night. If you won you got 25 quid and you got to come back.

I remember being hugely thrilled and thinking, 'Oh, that's it, this is what I'm going to do'. I remember the comics who were there at the time – some of whom are still going, some who aren't – and who were friendly and nice and it seemed like, 'this is beyond my wildest dreams!' All I wanted to do was to make sure I didn't chicken out. That was my only thought: don't leave before they call your name.

The next week I went back and it wasn't as good. I did different stuff. It took me a while to realize that you really have to learn how to do it. I had no concept of that, of how you went about learning. I think now people see so much more of it so they know the rules. It took me a couple of years to even work out, 'I really need to do this a lot and learn how to do it', rather than just go up and go, 'hopefully this will be just like going to the pub with my friends and I'll think of something funny to say'.

Many comedians look back at their early attempts and cringe a little. Moshe Kasher vividly remembers his first gig – and even his first gag.

MOSHE KASHER

It was in a place called the Luggage Store Gallery. It was a little art gallery and there was a guy there called Tony Sparks who's like the godfather of San Francisco stand-up comedy. He's responsible for more wonderful comedians committing to and continuing comedy and also more god-awful, horrible comedians continuing and committing to stand-up comedy. He's like the mother hen of the San Francisco comedy community and he would always say, 'You know, everybody, this is his first time here. So we got to give him what?' and the audience would shout, 'A lot of love!' 'That's right! A lot of love. Give it up real big for Moshe Kasher!'

So I went on stage and I told my first joke. Now here's a little interesting tidbit. I had an album that just came out on DVD called *Live in Oakland* and I went back to my hometown to record my hour special and on that album is a joke called *Schizophrenic Pride (The First Joke)* because that was the first joke I ever wrote and the first joke I ever performed. I thought it would be kind of cool to do it again because it was kind of a sophisticated joke for a first joke.

My second, third, fourth, fifth and next ninety-nine jokes were just all about farting and burping salami and things like that. But that first joke was sophisticated enough that I retooled it and put it into my first special.

Not everyone who gets bitten by the stand-up bug was a precocious child, always starring in the school play.

SOFIE HAGEN

I didn't want to do it. I just wrote. I liked writing the jokes, I thought that was fun. I loved reading about it, I loved watching the stand-up every night of the week and then they forced me to do it, cause they said, 'We can tell that you want to do it', and I was like, 'No, no, no – I just want to hang out with comedians and go to all the open mics and read all the books and watch documentaries, but I don't need to do it'. And then one of the comedians told me, 'You have a spot next Tuesday', then I just had to do it. I went home and I just wrote sixteen pages of jokes – which I haven't done since. I still have them, it's terrible.

I remember going to poetry nights because I wanted to study the rhythm they used, because that's words as well. I met up with my actress friend and I was like, 'Teach me how to use my body language'. I don't think I have ever prepared that hard for a spot ever since I did that one. I had five comedians look through my sixteen pages of jokes to pick the ones that weren't terrible. I would never do that today.

Andrew Maxwell also vividly remembers the material which made up his early stand-up performances.

ANDREW MAXWELL

My first gig I did was a comedy competition MC'd by Barry Murphy. The paid headline was Ardal O'Hanlon. It was a nightclub down the docks in Dublin that's long gone. There were six of us on and I joined fifth. I just blanked out. Somebody heckled me and I blanked out. It all went very badly. I came joint last with a man who did an act called Neville Sphincter, What An Arsehole.

I used to talk about biscuits, broken biscuits. You know, the discount packs of biscuits. I used to do the inner monologue of broken biscuits, their sad stories, how they've been broken. Also deconstructing Scooby-Doo and stuff like that. I used to be introduced as Andrew Maxwell and the Amazing Didgeridoo, because I could do an uncanny didgeridoo impression. I can still do it.

Some comics take to the stage like the proverbial duck to water.

MOSHE KASHER

I was always very comfortable on stage. Like super, super, super comfortable to a detrimental degree. From the very beginning. So that my friends in the beginning were like, 'Hey, man, we get it. You're good on stage. How about you write some jokes? Write more jokes.' Because I was loose. I want to be loose and just play with the format. But I was new. So it had intermittent success.

And once there, you have tremendous freedom, unmatched by almost any other branch of the performing arts.

MARCUS BRIGSTOCKE

Young comics talk about finding your voice; I didn't know when I started that that's what you're supposed to do, whereas new comics do now. I didn't. What I found was, I tried to go to drama school and I didn't get in, and a friend of mine set me up, and I did my first gig, and it clicked, and I went, 'I can perform whenever I want now'. And that's why I loved comedy, and why I still love it. I could find a gig tonight if I wanted, and go and do it.

The point is you can perform whenever you want. That's why I started doing it. And then I found the other little gifts in it; you can perform whenever you want, and you can say whatever you want. The only tiny condition attached to that is that if you say a thing that nobody wants to hear at all, then you'll be saying it on your own. But that's a pretty small condition.

Marsha Shandur talks to Stewart Lee

Stewart Lee shot to fame in the 1990s as part of a double act with Richard Herring. The two were writers on seminal radio comedy *On The Hour* (birthplace of Alan Partridge) before getting their own radio and TV shows with the BBC. Lee returned to stand-up in 2004 and has since recorded three series of his BBC TV show *Comedy Vehicle*. His slow, deadpan, repetitive style is thought to have influenced a number of other young comedians in the UK. He also co-wrote and co-directed the hit show *Jerry Springer: The Opera*.

MARSHA SHANDUR: *So you just finished the third series of* Comedy Vehicle.

STEWART LEE: Well, I finished recording it at Christmas. It's now June and then I toured. Basically I had a little window between recording it and it was starting to go out where I thought I could try and make some money out of the stuff, because you can't do it again when it has been on telly.

I'm the sort of person if I do that, they will complain, whereas actually I think with other comics, it's something they want to hear. If they're going to see Micky Flanagan, they probably want to hear the fingering bit and the out-out bit. If they go and see Michael McIntyre, they would probably be really delighted to see the man-drawer bit, whereas with me – I've got the kind of people that likely would be irritated with that and they would go on the internet and complain.

The last time I spoke to you was just after the first series and you thought you weren't going to get a second one.

As far as I knew, it wasn't getting a second series. They left it for about two years and then there was a meeting where me and the producer were going in to see the head of BBC2. I went into the room, into her office, and she had a lot of posters up of frescoes from Renaissance Florence, and a few years previously I had an idea for a story about frescoes and I had gone to Florence and I had read loads about them.

So I just started wildly chatting to the then head of BBC2 about Giotto and people like that. We started the meeting and then the next thing I knew, she had this idea that I could have a second series but it would go out at 11.15 after *Newsnight* in an attempt to create this new kind of spot for entertainment which would be sort of clever entertainment of people that watch news when it's watched.

Do you think it was the frescoes…?

I do, to be honest. Yeah, I mean the whole thing about broadcasting, as you know, is people imagine there's some sort of system at work or meritocracy but most of it is random. So I think that's why the second series happened. There certainly wasn't any enthusiasm for it.

Really?

Yeah. But I mean sometimes your face fits – you know, after the second series, I was told that I should try and become more of a personality and go on more things on BBC2 and that would help. I didn't want to do that because I don't really want to be a personality. I want to be able

Figure 7 Stewart Lee © Idil Sukan/Draw HQ

to do the stand-up and for it not to be compromised by an idea of you as a personality.

Actually in the last few months, I've started to get stopped on the street a lot more. I think it's because in the third series, there are a number of things in it that attach themselves to news stories that have happened in the last few months. People tweet them around to people and then you get this sort of secondary thing where millions of people have seen your stuff. There was a routine about UKIP in it, which I wrote in May last year and I kind of guessed the stuff they were saying about Bulgarian and Romanian immigrants wasn't going to happen. I'm writing this and I'm assuming it's not going to happen because it's going to go out after a point where I can change it and then obviously that didn't happen. Then UKIP did well at the European elections. So that has sort of gone viral. In fact one of the UKIP blokes was on the internet saying that I had written this UKIP routine to exploit anti-UKIP feelings and I had used social media to – I mean I don't have a Twitter account or a Facebook account … It just sort of took off. And then it was a little bit about Gary Barlow's tax evasion as well, that that came into the news and that got Twittered about. These were all things that were written up to twelve months ago. They all just kind of got picked up on after the series had gone out.

Well, the third series, they didn't want to do it either. I mean it was two years of… I was just saying, 'Look, can you just tell me one way or the other? Because I – if you want it, I have to start writing it.' Then it won a BAFTA. And then out of nowhere the BBC said, 'We'll do two more series'. So then I got two and actually I think the third series was better than the second one. I think it's partly because you thought, well, we're in for the long haul here. So you could relax, do it better, do what you wanted to do and not worry about trying to please anyone, which actually gave it a more consistent sort of tone, I think. So that's the history of where it is now. The next one, I will just start doing try-outs for this week, to be honest.

How does it differ in terms of trying stuff out, if you're trying stuff out for the telly or trying stuff out for stand-up shows? Is it the same kind of process?

Not quite, because you're trying to sort of get bits that work as a whole half-hour. For example, in the last series, two of the half-hours just

– they just slipped out like the one about UKIP. I was dropping my kid off at school and we were late so we're in the car. I got back in the car and the Deputy Head of UKIP, Paul Nuttall came on. It was the *Today* programme. It was about May last year, talked absolute load of rubbish for about ten minutes. It was so bad, it was funny. I went home, found it online, listened again, transcribed it and then the whole thing just sort of wrote itself really.

So you actually sat down and transcribed the whole thing?

Yeah, yeah, because it was so funny what he had said and sort of dishonest and un-self-aware and that episode was done in a day. Then I just had to run it in and learn where the pauses were and which bits you could mess around. But basically, the nuts and bolts of it was done. Then there was another half-hour about property in London. I mean that one, I ended up writing about ninety minutes to try and find the right twenty.

How did that come about? Do you remember?

Oh, I just couldn't get it. I had an idea of what it should be about and it just kept going round and round trying different stuff out. There was a period for about two months where there was a fifteen-minute bit in there about hamsters I had as a child. It took ages. It was like pulling teeth and months and months trying to get the right half-hour for that.

What does that look like? Is that you trying out live?

Yeah, live. You know what I do, I do for the series. I do it and I call it 'Work in Progress'. So I did a month in Edinburgh, three months in London, four months around the country and little club gigs of half an hour as well. So I got to do it. We will try out stuff. I will charge £5 less for it than I would for a normal tour.

So what about the actual writing? Are you kind of disciplined?

No, it's really difficult. With stand-up, it's an interesting thing. It's not just writing. Rob Brydon, for example, explained to me that he doesn't do warm-ups but he's not really a stand-up – he's a comic actor who's already beloved by an audience. He has never done the circuit, never done club gigs. But he writes an hour-long funny monologue, learns it because he's an actor, goes out, does it with thousands of people who already like him and then it probably stays the same for the two months. The tour never changes, whereas with stand-up, it's about the form, finding out how things work and changing stuff.

You can't really sit down and just write stand-up because stand-up has to have the illusion of being a spontaneous sort of dialogue. Occasionally, you can slip into very written-sounding bits deliberately for comic effect. But if it sounds too like a monologue, it doesn't really work. It's a night club form. It somehow ended up in theatres but it's like it has got – how to feel like, 'Oh then, I thought this', I mean, and so you can sort of write it but then you have to do it live to break it down. You have to kind of dirty it and scuff it up and take the edges off it so it feels like conversation. You have to forget that you ever wrote it.

How much do you actually write when you're writing?

Well, for a half-hour, I have six pages of A4 typed out and I will try and learn them. Then I will break it down. Then when I come back two minutes later and look at what I initially wrote and it's often there's very little relationship with it because you have to break all the sentences down and it can't sound too written.

I also lately have started to think of myself as a sort of character and the character is a person who is trying to do stand-up and he goes out and he's trying to do a club set basically. He's trying to do a half-hour but he gets distracted either by very serious ideas or by his own anxieties. But he is trying to be an entertainer.

So at the end of the day, the good thing about stand-up is – in a play, why are the people even on stage? Who the hell are they? When a singer-songwriter comes out, what is he talking to you for? Who does he think he is? We know that stand-up is on the stage because he's supposed to be an entertainer. He's supposed to make you laugh for half an hour.

If that character is having some kind of breakdown or going mad or is angry or is so furious, like Jerry Sadowitz, that he can't control the flow of information, that's great. But there is a reason for him or her to be there, which is, there's supposed to be some kind of entertainer at the end of the day. So everything else comes from that.

How did that evolve?

It becomes increasingly conscious. The last big show that I wrote, *Carpet Remnant World*, I must have done that 150 times. And yet, there were bits in there that were genuine moments of breakdown, anger, confusion. However, you can't really do that every night unless you create some kind of separation between you and the person.

On Saturday, I took my kids out for the day around London. As we were coming up on the 149 bus from Shoreditch up to Hackney, a Muslim woman got on in the full kit with just her eyes showing and sat on the seat opposite us on top of a copy of *Awake*, the Jehovah's Witnesses magazine, which had been left there and I just thought, oh yeah, that's it. That's half an hour. It's such a hilarious start to a thing. Like someone from one religion, a religion notoriously touchy about symbols, sitting quite unconsciously with her bottom on the Jehovah's Witnesses newspaper. It's a great way of getting into talking about big ideas but rooted in a small little incident. I mean, I know I can write that in two hours now and it will be half an hour and it will be fine. There are so many funny things about it.

But do you think it's luck? Or do you think it's like the way that people who want to get pregnant see pregnant women everywhere?

I know what you mean. Like people say about religious people, that if you're looking for symbols you see evidence of your belief everywhere. I do think I've been very lucky. I mean, like that UKIP bit that has become the takeaway routine from that series, the one that people talk to you about in the street. If I hadn't driven my kids to school that day, if I hadn't been running late and I hadn't gotten in the car and switched the *Today* programme on and Paul Nuttall hadn't been making such a fool of himself on it, it would never have happened.

As you get more public recognition, are you nervous that you're going to get an audience that's more mainstream?

Well, I keep waiting for it to happen. There was a point a couple of years ago when some people came and they said, 'We always come and see you. Our favourite stand-ups are you…' It was me, Lee Evans, and Michael McIntyre – whereas before it would have been, 'My favourite stand-ups are you, Daniel Kitson and Josie Long'.

But it seems to be all right. The only different thing about the audience is that they get more diverse and it's quite interesting. There seems to be a lot of lads in, which I never had before, and you get the grandparents, their children and their grandchildren on the same show.

There was one awful show in the last London run. It was a matinee. They normally all sell out quickly but this one, for some reason, there were sixty tickets floating about. They'd been returned or something and some blokes who were clearly on a stag weekend, about thirty came. They were obviously on coke and shouted all the way through it. Trying to sort of join in. They kind of ruined it and then sort of couldn't believe that I was selling the merch after – I always do that myself and they were kind of hanging around, trying to show off.

What do you do when someone heckles? How do you deal with it?

I treat it like it's an honest inquiry. But the problem with them is because they're on drugs, they didn't have any sense that they were fucking up or that the people around wanted them to stop or they weren't funny. There's not much you can do about that really.

So what did you do?

Well, just – it just kind of – you can't really do much about that. Arthur Smith always said the comedian should be one drink ahead of the audience, which is really great. He ended up with peritonitis and can never drink again. But you can't really be one drink and several lines of coke ahead of the audience, can you? You can't really second guess what they're going to be coming in on.

Have you done that since you started stand-up?

Yeah, pretty much. But also I'm getting increasingly deaf. So often I can't hear what they say, which is brilliant, because I go, 'Oh. Sorry, what? Sorry, I've got tinnitus in this ear. I'm afraid I can't hear things.' It takes so long to get to the thing, by which time the whole thing has gone really wrong. I don't really mind it. It's just a shame. Sometimes, in some of the long shows where there's obviously some structure to it, there's a bit I need to get through because it's a dramatic moment, or sometimes people get overexcited and ruin those bits.

But I think it's probably because with stand-up, there's an area where sometimes stand-up can move into being a bit like a drama or monologue. There's not much you can't do with stand-up that you could do in a play. You probably get people that have never been to theatre, who never read a book, never watched a film that wasn't just car chases and so they sometimes panic at what they're experiencing and they're frightened of the silence or of the idea. There might be meaning in it. It kind of freaked them out a bit but it's a good Trojan horse, of getting these things through to audiences that would never go to good stuff normally.

So in terms of dealing with the audience, when you first started, how did you get them to shut up?

By being quieter than anyone else.

Really?

Yeah, I think.

Did it always work?

No. Sometimes. Yeah. Be quieter than anyone else and look like you didn't want to be there. Because then, they will go, 'Oh'. Especially now, everything is so noisy, isn't it? And loud and so much – in films, it's so much fast-cutting. It's like white noise to me, whereas when an old film comes on, like the 1960s Italian Westerns, where everything just sits on one shot for ten minutes – that's amazing now. It has all gone the other way, hasn't it?

Then I remember – when I was about 21, Mickey Hutton was a kids' TV bloke who used to also compere at the Comedy Store. I used to do a lot of open spots there. I remember him one night saying to me, 'You need to look like you're enjoying it and engaged with the audience'. I remember thinking even then, no, that's exactly what I don't want to do, because you're all doing that. I don't want to do that.

Do you remember the first open spot you did?

Yes, it was at Acton Banana at the King's Head in Acton in September 1989. It's a pub and I asked them for an open spot and they gave me one the next week. I think now there's about an eighteen-month waiting list. The bill was me, Sean Hughes… He was amazing because – people start to say comedy is the new rock and roll. It was better than that with Sean Hughes. It was like the Wedding Present or something, or the Smiths – it was really indie-ish.

And what was your set like? What did you talk about? Can you remember?

I can tell you exactly. I still do it. It's still the ten minutes that I do when we do benefits and things and it was about religious people knocking at the door. I've had it in the set for when I do club sets for twenty-five years. This gets a bit longer every year because it's so obviously written in the 1980s. It's quite funny to tell people that because then you can use twenty-year out-of-date frames of reference and people find that quite funny.

You do have your people coming to see you, now, don't you?

I think I *did*. But actually, the last tour I had people coming up to me and going, about UKIP. 'I really like that bit. I'm going to vote UKIP. But it was really funny.' I remember a particular guy who had a Thai wife telling me that he was a UKIP voter and this is my wife.

I am aware that, on some level, I look like sort of a parody of what a UKIP person would call the 'metropolitan liberal elite' and I'm quite happy to be viewed as that. I think sometimes I try and be that. At the same time, from the same things I actually think and believe is quite helpful to be able to make this straw man character that is a bit like that.

Why?

Because then they've got a way into it, if you know what I mean. He is a liberal and he does believe in politically correct things. Part of why he does it is because it's one-upmanship. So there's arrogance about it as well. But I don't know. It would be interesting to see what happens.

What was good about the last series is that, the first two series when you go on Twitter and searched your name, the people that hated you and wanted you to be killed, usually their little avatars were symbols of football clubs or of cars or of particular sports-based things or of Union Jacks, right? But this time, it went out the same time as *Match of the Day*. So no nasty people found it by accident. It got twice the amount of viewers but the sort of people that normally hate you were all watching sport. So there was nothing on Twitter from people whose symbol is a football club or a car saying that 'You should be castrated and imprisoned'.

The last time we spoke, you were saying that after doing the series, more people who knew what to expect were coming, which in a way was really good.

But also more people generally. The problem is, if you go to Inverness, not too many people go to Inverness to do stand-up. You go to Inverness. People come out in good faith on a Saturday night and they want to see some comedy. If you just come out to see some comedy, there's a good chance that I'm not giving you what you want.

So the anger from people who didn't like it in Inverness was very extreme. You would look on the internet and they would be saying, 'This man can't do stand-up at all'. And my act, my persona is that I'm too good for you to understand the jokes. 'We did understand the jokes. We just didn't find them funny.' Well, I know that. I'm not mad. I haven't gone around the whole country failing night after night.

So it was the same thing for one year in Edinburgh. I did this big tent in one of the big four venues in a big square and that tent is where the big good thing is on that people like. And so ordinary, decent, working-class Scottish people would book a babysitter on a Friday night to go and see the comedian in the big tent and they would fucking hate it. Then they would feel really angry and they have my sympathy because with the babysitter and going out, it ends up costing them 60 quid, the whole thing, to see a bloke mumbling about boring things. So actually part of it is I take myself out of the places where people are accidentally going to be disappointed.

And yet on the other hand, you get people coming along and they go, 'I had thought I would hate you. I have come with my friend, but I didn't know there was comedy like this and who else is like this?'

Do you have any rules when it comes to controversial subjects? Do you ever censor yourself?

Well, in 2004, about half of the show was about attitudes to 9/11 and attitudes to terrorism and whatever and how the world has been changed by 9/11 and about me pretending not to understand it as a naive British person. They wanted me to do the Aspen Comedy Festival and the people from Aspen went, 'We send all our acts via New York and they do three club gigs to warm up for Aspen'. I mean there's no point, right?

So yeah, on some occasions, you censor yourself. Also, tangentially I've just been on tour doing a John Cage piece – the composer – which is ninety random stories that you have to read out, out of this box, over music. Two of them concerned the death of a child and we were performing in a place where a child had been murdered and I went through the box and I thought, 'I know John Cage says I have to pick these out randomly. But if these come out here, in this room, in this town, people will think you were trying to make some point that you're not.'

So that's the only thing. Sometimes stuff has a localized resonance that it wouldn't otherwise have. Although sometimes that's better. I had a bit where I used stereotypes about Liverpool on the UKIP bloke from Liverpool, in the way that you would use stereotypes about Eastern Europeans. I mean, it's great fun doing it and saying they were all thieves and miserable and stuff. It's really funny to do it.

How did they react?

Well, kind of mock fury, but actually the Liverpool audience get what you're doing.

Before, you've said to me that you don't like getting more people along who get what you're doing...

I don't really. But it does mean you can do some better things.

What like?

Well you can go further with some stuff. I think in stand-up, we need the illusion that it could go wrong or there are genuine bits that could go wrong, like juggling. You have to see the juggler drop the plate, then you buy into it. So as you become more popular, you have to create more problems for yourself in order to try and shake the audience off. So you do that by trying to sing, which they hate, and I'm not very good at it, or by having long things that appear to be going nowhere, or by doing stuff that they don't like, or by doing things that you can't remember. You have to kind of create problems to keep – so there is a risk of it going wrong.

What about ad-libbing?

Well, yeah. You try and create situations where you can ad-lib. But the thing is these days, if you do it – it's mad, right? The thing happened in Ipswich on the tour when the show went off beam for about twenty minutes because something happened in the room, I can't remember what it was. It was about three different people on the go and I was trying to get through this bit and I was starting to get really annoyed with them.

If you make it look too easy, like you're on top of it, people think it's all fake. So actually when something happened in Series 3 in the room and I thought we could keep it in, I turned to the camera and said, 'You know in Series 2 when the bloke got up and I talked to him and you all went on the internet saying that was fake. But it wasn't and this isn't either. This is really happening. Because I'm not going to risk messing this show up and improvising for you all to just say, "oh, it's all fake. It was an act".'

It's quite funny. People I know are saying the same things. It's James Corden's fault because, in his West End show, *One Man Two Guvnors*, there's a fake audience member there every night. Someone is eating a sandwich and he tells them off. He's eating the same sandwich every night.

Do you still do the thing with your posters where you would have different quotes – what was it that you would have?

Yeah, I always put a bad one on, just to sort of show people that the work encouraged a variety of opinions about it and that it was up to them what they thought of it and in a way to keep people out. I had a great quote from a UKIP politician saying it was biased, dishonest, unfunny and something else '– Patricia Something, UKIP'. Which is great, because you think the 70 per cent of the country that hadn't voted for them might go, 'Oh, let's go and see that'. We will see.

So it's kind of a way of trying to control the audience, but also it's great to be able to have a quote saying: 'The best comedian in Britain' – *The Times*. 'The worst comedian in Britain' – *The Sun*. To be able to have those two. They're both true, aren't they? In their own way. I'm not saying I'm the best. I'm probably more likely to be the worst than the best.

Chapter 6

Developing your Comedy

Learning to keep trying

DEBORAH FRANCES-WHITE: If you've been going for a few months, you probably need just enough positive feedback to know that you're not an absolute fantasist. If audiences rarely laugh and you never get rebooked, it may be that this is not for you and you're more of a blogger, a songwriter or a collage-maker. Try other ways of expressing yourself and see if they're more fun. Comedy improvisation is more collaborative, less competitive, and if you have a bad gig at least you've got friends to drink with and/or blame.

However, if more experienced comics are taking an interest in you, even if that's a highly critical interest, you've probably got something. If making audiences laugh is getting easier and more fun over time, you might well be a comedian. If bookers are asking you back, you should probably go and do those gigs until they start to offer you payment of some sort.

In my experience, it's easy to get to the cusp of great things quite quickly. But please be aware, you can be years on the cusp. I once complained about this to my friend Paul Rogan, who replied that I had to understand that on the cusp there were lots of people with sticks shouting, 'Fuck off! This is our cusp!'

I was asked to tour my second solo show around the country and then to Australian comedy festivals, so I just skipped the circuit. Some comedians said I was lucky, because a solo tour is what everyone's after. I sometimes worry that it was an error not to couple this good fortune with the circuit. I didn't know anyone in the industry and no one knew me, so I wasn't asked to do anything other than my own show. And while I got good at entertaining decent-sized theatres, I missed out on knowing how to control a stag night at Jongleurs on a Saturday. It's also possible that if I had that skill, I might have hardened myself in a way that meant I couldn't have written a show like *Half a Can of Worms* about finding my biological family. I guess the best advice is to decide what kind of comic you want to be and then do a lot of prep for that.

The people who become the best, most resilient, authentic comedians probably are the ones who need to be on stage all the time when they're learning their craft. They crave any kind of stage time and see each gig as a way to collect data rather than an opportunity to prove that they are or are not a comedian. They have accepted their fate and they are determined to be the best that they can be.

Ed Wynn, a vaudeville star at the turn of the century (who, it is said, was once knocked unconscious with a pool cue for upstaging W. C. Fields), allegedly said that: 'A comic says funny things, while a comedian says things funny.' You might want to decide which one of those you are and then develop your writing skills or your face-pulling and comedic pausing.

Either way, your ten thousand hours may not all be stage time. It may be writing, thinking, travelling in cars while riffing with comedians, rehearsing in front of a mirror or playing back recordings of your annoying voice or cringing at your fat head on video. Some people keep doing the same things over and over even when it's not working. If you get set in your ways, your ten thousand hours can just be a way to reinforce bad habits and become a performer who is too scared to change. Ask for feedback. Try new material. Keep learning. Keep learning. Keep learning.

If you write twenty killer minutes and never move beyond that, it's like having a perfect, beautiful little baby and putting it in a bonsai pot so it never gets to become a curious, funny, chatty toddler or an enquiring, rambunctious 12-year-old or an independent, scathing teenager. It is wonderful. But you haven't brought it into the world just to admire it and pickle it in aspic. Let it grow. Like a child, it will frustrate you as much as it delights you. There will be days when you shout, 'Why did I ever do this?' It will bring home terrible report cards. It's sweeter when it's asleep. But it will make you laugh and reward and surprise you constantly if you let it.

Your second year of stand-up should feel different from your first. It is probably not enough just to be doing it any more. You will now be only satisfied by doing it well. But when exploration becomes discovery and that becomes opportunity and cash – it will be worth it.

DANIEL SLOSS

It's just great to meet comedy heroes. I'm a huge Glenn Wool fan and I got to hang out with him and he gave me so much advice. Jim Jefferies the other night was just sitting there and I was being like a little sponge. Any information you give me, I'm just going to absorb.

Frankie Boyle told me to stop playing with the microphone stand. I used to swing it and he said, 'Don't do that. You're making an unnecessary barrier between yourself and the audience. Get the microphone standing as correctly as possible.' So that's what I do. I would take it and put it away. One of the best pieces of advice he has given was, don't say anything for the first five seconds when you walk on stage. It's a territorial thing. Instinctively, you just go on stage and you just mark your territory, but not in an aggressive way. You just go out, get on there, take the microphone out. Smile at the audience but don't say anything. Let them feel comfortable in the silence but just very much mark your territory on stage.

Working the comedy circuit almost always means sharing the bill with other comedians, who will offer advice whether it is asked for or not.

NAT LUURTSEMA

I think you know if you're not doing well on the circuit. I think you could be shielded from it if you were just doing one-hour shows in theatres. On the circuit, you know if you've not done well. You hear the laughs you get. You can even do gigs where the laughs are uneven, especially as the opener. That can always be a bit up and down, but then you go backstage and you know how your peers are reviewing you as well. So it's quite hard to be deluded.

I've come back many times and had people say 'you were better last time', or 'you weren't really on it'. I think people are often quite brutally blunt with me, I guess I act like I can take it. Possibly because I was playing bigger clubs quite quickly when I started, I felt I had to act calm so people couldn't tell how new I was. You occasionally meet an open mic-er who endlessly tanks and has done for years and is still going; you're a bit like 'I don't know what coping strategy you've got'.

Of course, not all of the advice given by older comics to younger comics is easy for them to hear.

ORNY ADAMS

One time, I was opening for Seinfeld in Oklahoma City for about probably 3,000 people. Gorgeous theatre. And there was something going on current in the news. I don't remember what it was. I said, 'I'm going to say this upfront'. And Jerry said, 'I wouldn't do that'. But I am who I am and I did and it got a huge applause. Then I did my act and – now I'm smarter, I wouldn't do this – I went for the kill and I got a standing ovation. Not something you should really do if you want to open for somebody, because I ended up not getting many gigs after that.

But I killed, and there's Jerry in the wings and he's got a look on his face and I go, 'He's going to tell me how great I am'. And he looked at me and he said, 'How long have you been doing stand-up?' I said, 'Ten years or so'. And he goes, 'Yeah, I was making the same mistakes at ten years too'. And then he just walked out.

He was right. And that's a smart thing that I've taken with me. And a lot of people I tell that story to say, 'Oh my god! What's wrong with him?' But that was the right thing to say.

I know I can look at a comic and I can see what mistakes they're making. I can say, 'There are three extra words in there. They've overexplained the joke. They move in – they got to take the mic out of the stand. Why is the mic upstage? It should be downstage.' There are a lot of things that you can look at a comic and see. There are a lot of young comics, there are a lot of people that somehow get all their ideas ahead of their art form, whether it's through television or YouTube or something like that. And all of a sudden, they're playing bigger stages. And man, are they getting response.

But I can look at them and I can think, 'Dude, it doesn't have to go like that'. When I was right out of college, I went to see Neil Diamond for some reason. I'm looking at this guy and I like his music but I'm watching him on stage and I'm enamoured. I'm in love with the way he moves. Everything. It was like ballet. And I thought, 'This is a guy that has put in the time'.

Sometimes, asking for advice can itself be a way to move your career forward.

CHRIS HENRY

A former Butlins Redcoat, Chris Henry now hosts and runs *Chris Henry's Comedy Creche* in Glasgow, as well as touring the UK and Canada, being a regular at the Edinburgh Fringe and appearing on BBC Scotland, BBC4 and ITV3.

Speak to people that have made it and are successful and listen to them. Present yourself as the newbie and don't have an ego. As long as you want to do stand-up, you should always be learning new things from other people. Ask them for feedback. Do it because you get advice – but also because it ingratiates you on the circuit. Most people enjoy the flattery of being asked for advice. When you're speaking to someone and saying, 'I really like your stuff and I'd really like your advice', then the next time you meet them, they like you because you've obviously got respect for what they're doing. And it means they're more likely to give you more advice and help you along on the circuit. They'll potentially get you gigs.

So you can make friends by asking what they thought of you. I've had people who have offered me lines and added jokes. Don't be scared of saying, 'Can I take that line?' All comedians have lines in their set that someone else gave them. We don't like to admit it, but we do! And I've had people who've helped me like that, who've then either offered me gigs or recommended me to promoters.

One tool for tracking your progress and improving faster is to tape and watch your gigs afterwards. While the goal is to eventually have as many people watching and enjoying your work as possible, Mark Watson admits that it's rarely much fun watching yourself back on tape.

MARK WATSON

I can't really bear to watch myself that much. Even though the times I have, have always been useful. There's no denying if you've got the guts to watch yourself, you learn stuff. I used to wave my arms around an awful lot on stage. I think I still do. I gesticulate an incredible amount and I was never really aware of that. There's loads of stuff. I hold the mic much too low, from a technical point of view.

There are comics that record every gig on an iPhone or something, listen to it back, make notes for themselves. I really admire that craft. It's just my distaste for the process. No one likes hearing their own voice, I don't think. If I'm not just hearing my own voice but actually watching myself piss about, it makes me feel self-conscious in the same way that getting out of the shower, you might glimpse yourself naked and think, 'Well, I wouldn't want to stare at myself for an hour here'.

Richard Herring finds listening to himself unbearable, but confirms Watson's idea of how valuable it can be for your craft.

RICHARD HERRING

A lot of comedians do record stuff. I can't bear to listen back to anything. I just find myself enormously irritating. I'm not a fan of myself and I don't know how I'm going to listen to all of my podcasts. I just get so annoyed by myself.

I'm on stage for an hour. I'm really concentrating on the show and in that white heat of it sometimes you will create something you haven't even thought of before, something will just come out right. Then there are times you think, 'I wish I had recorded that because I can't remember what I did at all', and sometimes it's gone forever.

It's possible that the need to tape shows, listen to them back and learn from what you hear is much more important for newer comics than for old hands. Maybe, after a while, you're less likely to hear anything new.

TODD BARRY

The quintessential New York comedian's comedian, Todd Barry is hugely respected by his peers but perhaps not quite as famous as his talents deserve, despite roles in *Flight of the Conchords*, Louis CK's sitcom *Louie* and the Oscar-nominated film *The Wrestler*.

I think I was better when I was younger. I think because I was more excited by the sound of my own performing, I would drive forty-five minutes to West Palm Beach, Palm Beach to do my set, tape it on cassette and then listen to the cassette on the way home. I was just excited to hear myself, to hear if it went well.

There are also other ways in which a comedian who has graduated to Edinburgh hours or is touring can get the kind of feedback they need to keep developing, without the horror of regular and detailed self-examination.

STEPHEN K AMOS

The one thing I can't bear doing is watching myself and I know it's a bad thing because you've got to be the one, ultimately, in control. Unless I've got a producer or a director that I absolutely trust, from now on, if I do anything on TV, I will watch myself because I know what I do in the live situation.

When I do try-out gigs, I do tape myself and make notes after. If I'm doing an hour show, particularly up in Edinburgh, I tend to have a director, someone that I've worked with for a long time. I used to have this habit of, whatever the show was called, keeping on saying that. My director asked me, 'Do you know that you say that an awful lot? We've got the message. Just say it once at the top maybe. Maybe once in the middle and maybe once at the end. Ideally just say it once and never again because the show should tell the story.' I hadn't even noticed it, but he picks up on little things like that.

As your comedy career develops, you will hopefully curb bad habits, fine-tune your persona and get more comfortable on the stage. And while there are milestones, such as your first hour-long show, there isn't a standard career path which everyone follows. Some people have a very clear idea of where they want to be and when. Others have a less structured approach to their continuing comedy education.

A lot of comedians we spoke to talked about how their perception of comedy as a career has changed from when they started, and many offered advice for new comedians just starting out.

HARLAND WILLIAMS

Don't just start and say, 'I'm going to do stand-up'. Look down the road before you start. Look to the horizon line and go, 'That's where I want to end up. This is how I want to get there and that's what I want to be.' Because you're going to leave something for the world. I think it's smart for you to know what it is you want to leave and don't just go into it blindly at the beginning, thinking, 'I'm going to get on stage and tell jokes and be a stand-up'. Have a vision for what that whole thing looks like and where it ends. Not that you definitely will get there or you definitely have to go that way, but I don't know, I think it helps a lot if you can envision where it's all going and what you're doing.

My vision was just – it was like I had a road and I could see where I wanted to go and the style that I wanted to present and I knew where I wanted to end up. So all the things that I envisioned on my road have been happening or have happened to me. And I think it had a lot to do with having it mapped out in my head when I started, or before I started.

Jim Jefferies looks back on his early career with some affection, but also some regrets.

JIM JEFFERIES

My career's pretty much gone better than I thought it would, so I guess I've made some right moves. I wish I was perceived as being a lot nicer than I acted when I was young. A lot less cocky. I think I'm a lot less cocky now, but I don't think it matters. I think the damage is already done in many regards.

I try to write as much as possible. I try to write an hour of comedy a year. Otherwise, there's no point and you're only trying to get an occupation to pay the bills.

If you want to have people look at you on DVD and on TV and go on about what a great comic you are, you need to produce at least forty minutes a year, hopefully an hour a year. There are too many guys that think, 'I don't know what happened to my career'. You're doing the same forty for every year. They think, 'I kill wherever I go'. They are. They're ripping the shit out of it every night, but these are new audiences each night. [Building your career] is all about repeat customers.

Go to festivals, because that's where you get noticed by the media. This might sound terrible, but this is how you gauge how much better or worse you are than everybody else. You can tell by ticket sales. You can tell by reviews. You can tell by who everyone is talking about. The only way you get really good is by playing with the good guys.

Richard Herring believes that early success isn't necessarily a good thing for a career.

RICHARD HERRING

When you're a new comedian, you think, 'When can I be on TV? When is this going to happen for me? I'm amazing. Why hasn't anyone realized it?' Even after twenty-five years, I still feel the same sometimes about that and you get anxious – but it's much better not to get discovered early. It's much better just to bide your time and work your way up. I think a lot of people wonder, 'Well, how do I get going?' and 'I don't really want to do stand-up and I don't want to do this. I just want to kind of get going.' You've just got to get on with this. There are so many opportunities to do comedy and you can write whenever you want. You can do podcasts whenever you want if you don't want to actually go to stand-up clubs, but you can also do both.

There are so many opportunities now to get your material out there. But you've just got to keep on working because even if you are great as an 18-year-old – I think me and Stew[1] were not bad as 18-year-olds but we're both a lot better now. I'm very glad that, when we first went

---

[1] Stewart Lee, whom Richard Herring partnered as Lee and Herring on BBC television and radio in the 1990s.

up to Edinburgh, someone didn't see our lunchtime sketch show and go, 'You're going to be on TV. We're going to give you a big contract', because we wouldn't have been equipped to do it.

So if you're sitting and thinking, 'What can I do? How do I do this?', you think, 'Well, anyone can do stand-up comedy'. You can do stand-up comedy to your mum and dad or your mates down the pub or you can rent a room. You can go to a pub. So by questioning it, you're just putting it off. You're procrastinating or putting off the inevitable horrible thing of going to do your first gig. Some people will email me after five gigs saying, 'Well, I've got an amazing set. Can I come and support you?' Well, it's not really how it works.

There is a strong work ethic among comedians. People who have success 'too early' are often scorned, but those who slowly work their way up tend to win the admiration of their peers. And there is a certain sense to that. Stand-up comedy is such a complex blend of writing, performing, improvising and relating – equal parts instinct, craft, inspiration and diligence – that it's almost impossible to master all aspects of it at once. Repetition breeds success.

TODD BARRY

My advice to young comics is to just keep doing it. Don't annoy people. Don't ask for a lot of favours. Don't write to comedians who you don't know and say, 'Can I be on your show?' Don't write and say, 'Will you watch my set? Will you look at my tape? Will you look at my clip?' Don't do that. Just write and don't think about money and agents and shit like that, because you don't know what you're doing yet. Just write material and go on stage every time you can and make that your social life and your life.

For some people it's important for comedians to 'pay your dues', but this doesn't just mean suffering for no reason.

ALEX EDELMAN

I think people make this mistake where they think that paying your dues means you have to deal with a lot of shit. That's a side-effect. Really, it's a layman's term for developing as an artist. It means refining your style, finding what works for you, honing your voice.

You need experience producing something that you're willing to put out in front of people and have them judge you for it. That's the only prerequisite. It's about putting time in, not about shovelling dirt. Nobody wants you to only have to do it in the shit venues – but the reason shit venues are the best is because you're putting yourself out there for judgement but you're not really being seen yet.

Chris Rock said the most formative experience of his comedy life was Martin Lawrence opening for him at a big theatre in Chicago. Chris was famous before he was a good stand-up, he says. And he had been on SNL [*Saturday Night Live*], but he hadn't had a lot of success on the show and he wasn't that fantastic a stand-up. And Martin Lawrence got up there right before him and Chris says Martin Lawrence blew him off the stage. He said that his own opening act totally took him to task. Lawrence's performance was just so much better than his and – excuse my crass language – but Chris Rock said it was like watching someone fuck your wife with a bigger dick.

Chris Rock went back to Brooklyn and he had owned this carriage house and he put mirrors everywhere and he walked around the carriage house and worked on his performance alone in this room. And I think Chris Rock walking around an empty room looking into the mirror and seeing himself and just knowing that he wasn't a great comedian yet and that he had to be one – that's paying your dues as much as any person who's been doing it for a year and a half going to a crappy open mic night. That's what I think of when I think of a comedian working on his craft. I think of someone pacing in front of a full-length mirror and just being haunted by this really complex standard that they've set for themselves.

For many, being a comedian isn't something that you do – it's something that you *are*.

ADAM BLOOM

Make it a lifestyle, not a job, and then the comedy will flow naturally out of your brain. If you sit down to think about comedy, it means you don't think about comedy all day long. If you think comedy all day long, you will never have to sit down to think about comedy.

Zoe Lyons has a different point of view.

ZOE LYONS

Don't take yourself too seriously. Therein madness lies. Keep yourself grounded. I watch a lot of news and I look at trees. Genuinely, it makes me happy. I love a tree. I just came back from Australia and I spent four-and-a-half weeks in Australia. People asked me, 'What were the gigs like?' I said, 'The gigs were fine. The trees were amazing.'

I see a lot of comedians who could do with a bit more fresh air. It's not the healthiest of careers. 'Just go outside and look at a tree. Have a bit of sunshine.' My girlfriend's always saying to me, 'Don't forget to have fun'. There have been long periods where I forgot to have fun.

Don't forget to have fun. Don't take yourself too seriously and for god's sake, look at a tree.

Another option for a new comedian, as well as open mic nights, is stand-up comedy competitions. This worked well for Nathan Caton, who won the Chortle Student award.

NATHAN CATON

I did a bunch of competitions, not really thinking that anything would happen. The Chortle Student one, I didn't think I'd win. I remember getting to the semi-final and seeing all the other semi-finalists. I was thinking, 'Oh man, they're so much older'. I was 19 or 20. They were all like in their late 20s at the youngest. And I was thinking, 'Oh, I'm way out of depth here'. And I ended up getting through.

It might be quite annoying to others seeing this young, arrogant, cocky kid. I hope I wasn't cocky or arrogant. But I think it did help to start young. I'm now in my late 20s but I've got so much experience, so that has helped me out. I've seen so much in the comedy circuit and I've developed as well. A lot of guys don't start until maybe 28 or something. Whereas, even though I'm relatively young, I'm doing big clubs and got TV appearances and so on.

Neal Brennan stresses that it's only by setting yourself high standards that you can continue to improve.

NEAL BRENNAN

Listen to the laughter. Listen to what kind of laughs you're getting, meaning listen to the kind of laughter you're getting relative to the kind of laughs better comics are getting.

I remember doing TV shows before I was ready and if you're not ready, you're fucking not ready. You just know. They know it. You know it. You can't command them. I recently did a show and it was me and four guys who were really, really good. Then I put on a buddy of mine who was not quite as good. He just didn't do as well. The audience can feel it. There's something elemental about it.

There's just something – that non-verbal communication stuff where the audience feels like, 'I don't trust what he's doing with his hands' or something – you just figure it out. It just takes a while but you have to push yourself and do it all the time.

That's the other thing: do it. People now, they'll say, 'I'm going to do six spots by Tuesday'. It's 10,000 hours of practice makes perfect or whatever. You got to work your ass off. Set a standard for what you do and don't want to say. Is that a fresh observation? What am I communicating? Am I communicating that men are great or white people are great? What am I espousing?

For Robin Ince, it isn't just about repetition, it's also about self-belief.

ROBIN INCE

It's tenacity... you may not get it immediately, you may well die on your arse for a long period of time, you may find out other things, you might find out that the persona you've adopted is wrong. If you're going into it thinking you're going to be rich and famous and successful in three years, then you're going into the wrong thing. If you're going into it because you want to play the O2 Arena, then you're going into it for the wrong reason. The most important thing is that you do it because you must do it. And there isn't really any other choice, you can't think of anything else you really, really want to do and you are now going to risk your ego every single night.

I was once given a piece of advice early on: 'Once you've tried out a joke three times, if it doesn't work three times in a row, then ditch the joke, it hasn't worked.' That is a terrible piece of advice. If you've got something that you like, just keep going at it and you'll find it – it might be the tiniest thing, it might be an adjective, it might be the rhythm. There are so many ways you can get an idea wrong. To say that if you haven't got it to work in three times, ditch it, is ridiculous.

No matter how experienced the comedian may be, the process of working at and improving every aspect of the performance continues with every gig.

RICHARD HERRING

Now I really enjoy perfecting the show. I used to get bored of the shows and not do great performances of them, sometimes, when it was 100 days into a tour. Now I take every show and try to perfect it and enjoy the technical side of being a stand-up. So I see it more as an exercise. You want to make sure that people that come to see you have a great time. I depend on them to come back and see me again. So you want the best show possible. I'm always striving to perfect a show. Get every line right. Find new ways to perform it. I think you have to become slightly obsessed with the technical side of stand-up.

There are so many things to consider. You never hit an absolutely perfect performance because you will never get your perfect audience and be able to remember every joke and deliver it right. You've got to judge it a little bit by the room and by the audience, but also there's this sort of timing of everything. There are gestures. There's speeding up, slowing down. There's pauses and intonation. There are so many – whether you're pulling a face, whether you're letting a laugh ride. So it's just trying to find all those technical things. It's like juggling six or seven different aspects. When you're hitting it, you're not really thinking about it. Everything is kind of working and in some performances, you will be thinking, 'Wow, I'm really getting this'.

Andrew Maxwell has these words of wisdom for younger comics.

ANDREW MAXWELL

The number one key thing is, remember that you're the joke. You're the punchline. You're the weirdo in the room. Nobody else has gotten on a plane or train and travelled half a day to ask strangers for love. You're the weirdo. If you can maintain that, then it's a wellspring of humour. Where you see people go wrong is when they freeze up and anxiety or ego kicks in. You've lost your sense of humour at that moment. You've forgotten you're the fucking joke.

No matter how badly behaved that crowd is, you're the one who's living the ridiculous fucking life. They're normal. They just want a laugh and a drink. You're the fucking weirdo. You're the one who wants laughter from strangers. If you can maintain that, it gives you a moment to breathe on stage, a certain amount of grace, and then the well has no bottom. The jokes never end as you go through the travails of your life. Your life becomes more funny, not less.

And here's a vitally important tip from Tom Wrigglesworth about starting out.

TOM WRIGGLESWORTH

If I was to talk to the younger me, I would say: trust your instincts as much as possible. You've got to go with your gut feeling. Anyone that's got any good reaches a point where it's the essence of them that's being funny. And it's really hard to get there, because you've got to flush through a lot of defences and a lot of quite scary emotions within yourself to find this sort of essence. But once you've got that, you're away. Anyone who's been any good has found that. Everybody else is acting like a comedian.

We asked the same question of Andy Kindler – what advice would you give your young self just starting out?

ANDY KINDLER

I would have told myself: just don't wear the acid wash jackets. There's no reason. That isn't going to be in style long enough. So I would have done a lot of things with my clothing. I wish I could have told myself to not be so hard on myself. That's really the only advice I would give to people who ask me advice. Don't be hard on yourself. When you're first starting, you're like almost ready to cry every time you're on stage.

For one final tip, we turn to Moshe Kasher, who suggests that new comedians should…

MOSHE KASHER

Quit, quit, quit. Because it's a terrible life. There's nothing good about it. I'm serious. You should quit. If there are any aspiring stand-up comics listening, do not do it. However, if you can't not do it, then I would say get on stage as much as you possibly can and find out who you are.

There is only one piece of advice for comics starting – well, two. Quit and then if you don't, do it all the time until you figure it out, because you have to do more than get comfortable on stage. When I started, I thought I was the man. But I didn't realize even if you *are* the man, even if you're the most confident, brilliant guy in the world, it still takes years to figure out who you really are up there.

Deborah Frances-White talks to Robin Ince

DEBORAH FRANCES-WHITE: It feels like you're part of a humanist or scientific movement that has come about in the last few years. And it didn't used to be like that. It used to be all about 'the arts'! How did that come about?

ROBIN INCE: I think it probably still is dominated by arts – arts and alcoholism – but I think everything blends in together. I don't think there's any grand plan by anyone. The thing that really drove me on wasn't just about the science, but I didn't think that there was much out there in the mass media that was challenging in any way whatsoever. That old Reithian idea of giving people something better than they knew they wanted had gone. When Monty Python began and they got worried they were going too far, it was actually the head of BBC1 at the time who said, 'Oh, no, we should always be one step ahead of taste'. And I think a while back, it made a leap backwards in trying to second-guess what the public want.

When I put the first Christmas shows[2] together, I remember people thinking, 'I don't know if this is going to work', and then they sold incredibly. Then they became fourteen-night runs, a couple of nights at Hammersmith and so on. And what I do love about doing those is that you do see a tremendous level of excitement. People aren't just there for the celebrity element – whether that might be Dara Ó Briain or Brian Cox – they will happily watch a scientist or enthusiast doing some bizarre experiment or talking about the Hubble telescope. Because I think people are both more interested and more interesting than a lot of those who are in charge of what is fed to us, imagine or believe.

Do you think that's in some part a reaction to the homogenization of stand-up on the television?

---

[2]Since 2009, Robin has regularly curated a Christmas show featuring science communicators and comedians with a scientific or sceptical approach, under the banner *Lessons and Carols for Godless People*. Regular contributors include Barry Cryer, Josie Long, Ben Goldacre, Richard Herring and Helen Arney, among many others.

Well, things like The Book Club, for instance, I did that because the stand-up I was watching seemed to come across very sneery, and very cynical – not all of it, obviously – but a lot of the television stuff. *The 11 O'Clock Show*, and the stuff that came after it. I mean, I worked on *The 11 O'Clock Show*, you know, but it was kind of sneery, cynical and 'aren't they rubbish', in the same way as you sometimes go to a comedy club, and all you hear from the compere is about the fat bloke in the front row and then that couple there and something rude about them, and oh look, there are three men together and therefore they're *Brokeback Mountain* (which is generally said by comperes who aren't normally fans of the work of Ang Lee).

My favourite thing is to watch genuine passion, so I think a lot of it comes from that as well. I think that the homogenization amounts to fewer risks being taken. And one of the greatest risks is to reveal what you really believe, and do something that you can't merely walk off stage or walk out of the studio or whatever it might be and when someone goes, 'I didn't like that', go, 'Yeah well, it's just a thing isn't it? That's all. It doesn't mean anything to me. They're just some jokes that I do as an entertainer, that's it.' I like the fact that they should mean more than a bit of patter, a schtick or a job.

Figure 8 Robin Ince © Idil Sukan/Draw HQ

How do you make it accessible? How do you make science accessible? It is acceptable for a journalist to say to scientists, 'Well, you guys in the white coats... you boffins... I don't really understand this, but you explain it.' They wouldn't get away with saying to the Chancellor of the Exchequer on Newsnight: *'Well, I don't really know how it works! Something about money...' A journalist wouldn't do that. But they do say it about science.*

Yes, the attitude to science is very lazy in general. And indeed a lot of the things they may well say about finance and economics, as we've found out, are absolute rubbish as well, but they believe that they have the language for obfuscation, so they just do it anyway.

But it's totally socially acceptable to say I don't understand anything about that, but it's not about other areas. So how do you make that accessible? How do you bridge that gap for something seen as a bit inaccessible?

I am not an intellectual and I am not a scientist, so I am presenting it as, 'I have found out these things recently by watching something and chatting to someone and reading something and they sound fantastic and I am going to try and explain them to you, but you have to realize that I may well get this wrong'. So first of all, I'm on a level footing with the audience. I'm not approaching it as an expert. Two, I use lots of stupid voices and I jump around a lot. So I think the combination of those three things, not being an expert, jumping around and stupid voices, is very useful.

You're an evangelic enthusiast, basically?

It's what I'm genuinely like, and what I enjoy talking about. And then obviously everyone becomes something of an exaggeration of themselves on stage. Even when you're playing yourself, there is an exaggeration that is going to happen because you're being stared at by 500 people. That means that it's not going to be the same as having a conversation. Indeed, to have a conversation with an audience, you have to take some of the things you have when you chat with someone and they have to be exaggerated.

I don't think about these things when I'm on the stage. These things are only thought about when someone asks me.

So is your material just stuff that occurs to you during the day?

It's generally what I'm thinking about all the time. I'm reading things and I think, 'That's a good idea', or I look out the window and I see something in the distance and I wonder how that would work and think that would be interesting. So it's most of my life, just me looking at things and wondering how they work or what they do and then that quite often turns into some kind of stand-up idea.

So actually your inspiration is curiosity, really.

That's what I originally started with, but that's what then got lost as the 1990s kind of continued. It just kind of became that thing I did. My favourite gigs are always the ones I just improvised rather than wrote new material. And because I knew that I had the backbone of stuff that I could get away with generally, and then in my late 20s and early 30s, that's when I really started going, 'Hang on a minute, these are ideas that I really want to explore'.

I mean, I think it helped, the homogenization of the comedy circuit, because that was another reminder of what it felt like when I first saw people like Alexei Sayle or Claire Dowie or someone like that. All these people used to have an attitude, whereas now the attitude is – sometimes anyway – merely an attitude of commerce.

I love those American comics. I mean, Lenny Bruce, you might not be able to listen to him now and think that this guy is hilariously funny, but if you watch his way of performing and you watch his way of delivering ideas during his piece, you can certainly get the art of it, even if you don't laugh out loud. Or if you watch someone like George Carlin, or Bill Hicks – the way that they had of using their opinions to turn something into more than comedy. This was an agenda, this was a manifesto to an extent.

When do you think that power came in? I mean, it used to be vaude-ville. If you look at the origins of comedy, was it there, or do you think that it goes back to Swift and satire?

Well I suppose, the thing is it changes from being written down. You think of all the plays of Aristophanes, and what he was dealing with there in terms of the sophists and all those kinds of things. It used to be there in plays and novels and then you started seeing it in stand-up.

Now, I'm trying to think of how far back you can go. Apart from anything else, British stand-ups never really used to be able to have an opinion, because there were so many rules about what you weren't allowed to say. In fact, if you go back to 1948 and *The Little Green Book* of the BBC, impressionists had to have permission from whoever they were doing an impression of. That's what people don't realize, with someone like Mike Yarwood. The reaction was, 'My goodness, he's doing Denis Healey! But he's in the cabinet!'

The Americans had Mort Sahl and Lenny Bruce. I remember as a teenager seeing Bob Fosse's film *Lenny* with Dustin Hoffman. I was fascinated by Lenny Bruce. I'd just seen his book *How to Talk Dirty and Influence People*. And I thought, 'What is this book, and who is this man?' I didn't know much about him, I was a teenager and just excited by these counter-cultural figures, like Lenny Bruce and people like Hunter S. Thompson in another way. To my knowledge it was a kind of 1950s thing, in terms of stand-up performance, but it goes back over 2,000 years to Aristophanes.

In this country, the Lord Chamberlain's power to censor the theatre was overturned in the late 1960s.

Then you had things like *Oh! Calcutta*, which often gets overlooked. And I think you do see that post-war excitement of criticism and counter-culture and questioning the status quo. When you're given freedom, you can do incredible things with it. And then when you forget you didn't have freedom at one time, you don't really bother so much. We need to be careful to make sure that we don't become too lazy… and we say, 'Well, let's push this a little bit and see how far you can go'.

I get worried about the blandness in the mass media. I wrote something the other day about how Bill Hicks, Kurt Cobain, Lindsay Anderson and Dennis Potter and Derek Jarman, they all died twenty years ago. Sometimes you do need examples. I think what was great about all those people was that a lot of their work was about questioning things, and questioning the way the world is and the status quo. Even though they were all in some way mainstream figures – even Derek Jarman, who was very arthouse, he was known. Gary Bushell would write angry tirades against him in the *Sun*.

Oh god, yeah, the Dennis Potter Award people admitted not long ago that Dennis Potter would not win the Dennis Potter Award now.

I worry about us all getting dragged into the fact that we have to think about everything in money terms, and maybe you do need to do that advert and that corporate thing. You have to think about money. And I worry about that sometimes. I worry that's going to continue ironing out the kinks of culture. But that's equally why I'm trying to start up doing more weird clubs and stuff and not just the science stuff because that's all up and running now, but more stuff involving artists. I did a night the other day called 'Your Culture is Ailing, Your Art is Dead' where I had artists on stage talking about ideas and doing kind of weird stuff and then actual performance art and then comedians doing comedy and poets and that kind of thing.

With science, I think, when we started doing *Monkey Cage* on Radio 4,[3] a lot of critics were quite snotty about it. Partly because they were used to science being presented like: 'Hello, this is Science. We're going to be talking about Crick and Watson. We're going to be talking about it very seriously, because, you know, it's science and you have to treat it with veneration and blah blah.' And we were quite jokey with it and mucking about with it. And in the same way, with art you sometimes have this thing where people go, 'Well for art you really do have to talk a different language and it's not for everyone', but I wanted it to be quite… not frivolous, but you can be playful with these ideas.

There's a friend of mine, Charlotte Young, and she knows a lot of artists, and I want to put on a show where you go, 'This is art' and you don't have to go, 'Oh dear, did I say that name wrong?' or 'Do I not understand what that word means?' That's not what it's about. It's about engaging, and it's about curiosity. You can look at a painting and you know it doesn't mean very much to just know the name of the

---

[3] *The Infinite Monkey Cage* is the irreverent BBC Radio 4 science series which Robin hosts with physicist and science communicator Brian Cox. As of March 2015 it has run for 11 series.

painter. 'Well of course that's a Giotto, I'm very clever, I can tell a Giotto immediately.' But what's your reaction to it? What does it mean to you? Don't be scared of it.

People say, 'Football is the people's theatre'. And I think, well why can't the people have theatre as well? Can't people have football and theatre? There's this cop-out. I see that a lot: this is not for you. And people feel it with the science stuff. A lot of people who I meet, they say, 'I used to think that it wasn't really for me and that I couldn't really ask questions'. And that's one of the things that I always talk about in interviews and when I go into schools, is to say that there are no stupid questions. The only stupid question is one that you already know the answer to and you're only asking it to show someone up.

However stupid you think your question is, if you want an answer to it, the artist or the scientist, the philosopher, whoever it might be, may go, 'Well that's not quite how it is actually, you've kind of misunderstood the idea, but let me tell you what it is...'

When Josie Long and I and our friend Grace Petrie were on tour doing our *Shambles* tour, and there was a lot of mucking around and some politics and some being foolish and all of those kind of things, there was one night when we were looking at the audience and we were thinking, 'Ah, I don't think this is our audience...' We were doing a festival and they were very straight and the blokes looked like real gym blokes, and we thought that this might be awful. And then we went out and had one of the best nights we'd had, and we got talking to a lot of the people afterwards, as we often did anyway, and found out that all these people who on the outside looked tremendously mainstream, they had really vibrant ideas on the inside. Because of the town they lived in, they had to wear the disguise of the town. In some places you can't be overly flamboyant, but inside they were interested in so many different things, and there was nowhere we couldn't go.

I've noticed this in a lot of people, that we're all interested in seeing how far you can go. There are a lot of brilliant acts who can say 'you know when' and they have that fantastic broad thing of talking about parking or whatever, but sometimes it's nice, rather than saying 'you know when', saying 'do you know when?' And you can see the reactions. Do you do this? And the audience go, 'I'm not sure we do, hang on a minute...' and then a few people go, 'Yeah, we do'. And then other people quite like it because it will be an observation from a minority group, but which is perhaps such a weird behaviour that it's funny for everyone. And it's that thing of not seeing people as one big mass who've all had the same experience, and that everyone has had the same life and that you have no individuality.

PART THREE

Mastering more than the Basics

As you'll have noticed from the anecdotes and advice, working at comedy is something which continues throughout your entire career. No matter how popular or successful a comic may be, they are always still learning and working at their craft. This next section features advice about all sorts of different aspects of comedy. From handling hecklers to tweaking your persona to the intricacies of touring life, there is always some element of your comedy, on stage or off, that can be improved.

Chapter 7
Owning the Room

Owning the stage, microphone, noise, quiet, chairs and booze. It's all yours.

DEBORAH FRANCES-WHITE: Every room can be owned, but some rooms need extra thought. First, you have to decide on whether you will overtly own the room or whether you will look like the room is owning you, in order to own it. In other words, are you a high status school-teachery act like Al Murray the Pub Landlord, who tolerates no dissent and will eat a heckler alive? Or are you a low status clown figure whose comedy comes from their own ineptness and inability to understand the world, like Emo Philips?

If you are obviously high status, your job is easier to learn. Public speaking is the number one fear on polls about phobias. Number two is death. Jerry Seinfeld jokes that this means 'to the average person, if you have to go to a funeral, you're better off in the casket than doing the eulogy'. All commonly held phobias have their roots in life-or-death scenarios, because we were ten million years on the savannah and we've only been ten thousand years here at Jongleurs. It's easy to see why we're scared of snakes. Our ancestors who thought snakes were cute and cuddly had fewer children and those children died of venomous snake bites. We are the children of survivors. It's easy to see with heights. Even people who do bungee jumping do it for an adrenaline rush.

Public speaking is harder to understand. I don't imagine there were a lot of primitive toast-master groups. My theory is that if you were on the savannah even today and you wandered away from your safari party and came into a big open clearing and looked up and saw twenty eyes looking at you – you would probably be prey. The fear of public speaking is essentially the fear of being eaten. Think of a pride of lions on the savannah. They're not busy. They're not much up for pottering. They sit and stare, like audiences, and because audiences look like lions, comedians feel like gazelles. Twitchy and indecisive – keen to play with the microphone stand and shuffle about and look at the floor. Heart pumping, hands sweating – ready to run.

Come towards the audience. Lean on the front foot. It's hard to look scared of people you're coming towards. Open your body up. Take up space. The audience can't see how you're feeling – they can only see what you're doing. The other advantage is that you will quickly seduce your brain into thinking that you are not prey, but the lion in charge of the pride. No prey would dare to behave like this. Your heart rate will slow, your breathing will come more easily and you'll feel powerful in the space.

If you're a low status clown you are still a lion – but you are wearing a gazelle suit. You are in charge of the space. They must look at you. You can do this by employing 'certain uncertainty'. Your indecision is considered. You know exactly how you will prevaricate and for how long. Your comedic vulnerability is not indecisive. Watch Chaplin, Manuel in *Fawlty Towers* and Mr Bean for everything you need to know.

If you are in fact a gazelle pretending to be a lion, you will look edible. In a rough, impolite club they will look away and talk or even heckle. In a friendly room you will feel as if you are only half-lit. This has happened to everyone. When it happens to you, you will want to back away from the audience and move more. Do not. Come towards the audience, allow yourself to be still and then move with purpose. You can move with energy, but give your movements beginnings and ends. Vague wandering or pacing will make you look very good to eat or too small to be bothered catching.

Once, at a late-night club in Melbourne, I got intimidated by a drunk, chatty crowd and forgot this. They all looked away as if I were invisible. It was like an out-of-body experience and it took me ages to realize what I was doing wrong and get them part-way back, but it was a dreadful gig and I never really got it going again. Everyone else did a bit better than me, but the only thing they really went for that night was Henning Wehn in lederhosen being hilarious on the accordion and singing songs. He came off after a tight twenty and I said, 'Why didn't you do more? You were killing and you were headlining!' He said, 'Ask a German to do twenty minutes, he does twenty minutes. Exactly.' He even owned the room backstage.

However you own it, enjoy being in charge of it. Everyone is looking at you, so you can say what's on your mind. It's an amazing job. I remember compering the Melbourne Comedy Festival Roadshow, and David Quirk going out on stage and singing a few bars of 'Can't live, if living is without you', and then saying to the audience, 'Did anyone expect me to do that? No? Me neither.' Russell Kane and I were giggling backstage and he looked at me and said, 'This is an amazing job. We get paid to say whatever is in our heads. When you're out there, no one can stop you from doing anything.'

There's a power in that. If you remember that, you won't have to ask people to look in your direction.

ADAM BLOOM

Before I did my first show, I went to the Bearcat Comedy Club in St Margaret's every single Monday without fail and I watched and I learned from the mistakes of the new comedians. I learned about the ones who hold the mic too close or not far enough or too far away from their mouth. I was fascinated by how an experienced comedian could command the audience in a second and an inexperienced one couldn't.

It's all down to the borderline between confidence and self-belief. I learned from doing it, but you can't fake that. The body language comes with the confidence. But I at least learned a few basic things not to do. Things like, they would put their hand in front of their eyes because the light was blinding and that was showing their vulnerability of not being comfortable. They would mumble stuff into the microphone and look down at the floor and untangle the microphone – so their first impression would be looking at the floor mumbling and that's not good eye contact, getting a speech pattern across when you speak. The audience can hear every word clearly. So when you mumble the first thing you say, the first thing the audience gets is bad communication.

So, when I went on stage, I had five or six no-nos that at least I wasn't going to do. That really helped, because some comedians had messed up before they got to the mic. I saw a guy the other day who stood by the stage as he's being introduced, looking like a puppy dog, waiting for his owner's approval. It's like he had no status. You know what I mean? He stood by the stage looking up. He was quite sweet. He was sweet and innocent but he should have known better.

Neal Brennan explains the underlying physiology behind the process and even tries to game the system a little.

NEAL BRENNAN

I want to move. Eddie Murphy told Chris Rock, 'If you don't move when you're on stage, it gives the audience permission to look away from you – because they know where you're going to be'. So if you're moving, there's a primal thing of like, *this motherfucker could attack us at any moment*. I tell people all the time, 'This shit is not radio, man. You got to fucking move. You got to be commanding.'

I want to make eye contact with the audience. I want to shout, literally, because if you shout, it's another primal thing. People think, 'Well, this must be important'. And smile! A girl I was dating, I would give her $200, and for every time I smiled on stage, she had to give me $20 back. And the first time I lost $120. But slowly but surely, I got it all back. You just have to train yourself.

Human faces are programmed to mimic one another. So that's why I want to make eye contact with people because if I see somebody laughing, then I will remember, 'Oh, this is funny'. Then that makes me laugh and then it's a bit of a force multiplier in terms of you taking it into the joke. You take the energy of the joke. You're laughing. They're laughing. It's like yawning.

Harland Williams believes that the energy of your performance also plays a part in capturing the audience's attention.

HARLAND WILLIAMS

I think the keyword is 'energy'. I don't think it has to be high energy. I like to just use mental energy and stare a crowd down. Sometimes silence is louder than yelling. Sometimes a really long silent pause is more impactful because people are waiting. They're waiting. They don't need to be overwhelmed. They need to be underwhelmed sometimes.

While you need to bring your own energy to the performance, part of a good comedian's job is to test out the energy in the audience as well, and to find the best way to make a connection between the two.

ADAM BLOOM

Probably, my talking fast was a defence mechanism to start the audience getting to buy in. But also my energy is big naturally. I'm an excitable person. The other night I went on, low energy audience. I said, 'Hello'. I got back nothing and I said, 'Hello' again. They said, 'Hello'. That's such a powerful technique. It's so simple. It's saying to them, 'I just said hello and you didn't say hello back again. This is a two-way thing. So please respond because this is not just about me. It's about us.' They have then been told what to do. It's actually quite passive-aggressive because I'm saying hello twice. So I'm actually saying, 'Hey, don't be rude. I said hello to you. Say hello back to me.'

Sometimes you need to get the crowd back in the middle of a gig. It's often worse to call attention to the fact that you are losing the room, so Hannibal Buress has a more subtle way of reasserting his authority.

HANNIBAL BURESS

If I was in bar shows or club shows where people were talking – and I still do this now, because I don't want to break out of my joke to address people talking in the second row – so I say a word in my joke louder. All of a sudden, I will just say a certain word in the joke louder to get their attention, just to kind of keep people in.

While you have the microphone, you are the person in charge – but Orny Adams suggests it's important to ensure that the audience knows that, too.

ORNY ADAMS

I don't allow for any distractions. If there's talking, texting, I stop the show and I just stare at them. To me, it's unacceptable. It says something to the performer. If it's in the front row and somebody's phone lights up, then it trickles all the way to the back: 'The front doesn't respect, so we're not going to respect.' It's horrible. You have to say something. And some people just don't get it. Some people just think it's a part of society now.

But we have such ADD. People can't be away from their phones. You can't even take a shower any more. You come out of the shower, you've got forty-two text messages. 'Where are you? What happened? Is everything OK? Are you mad at me?' 'I was in the shower. Sorry I didn't tweet about it before I got in.'

Different nights of the week also tend to attract different sorts of audiences. Daniel Kitson often refuses to schedule his shows on Friday and Saturday nights, due to the crowds often being drunk and inattentive and ill suited to his particular brand of delicately thought-through and intellectual comedy.

NAT LUURTSEMA

It's drunk audiences versus non-drunk audiences, isn't it? That's the dividing line. I know what I'm like when I'm drunk. I'm like, 'Next! More! Make me laugh.' I don't really want to think, I want to relax. I sympathize with that. My mum's a teaching assistant and a waitress, my dad's an accountant and a barman. They're knackered, they work two jobs and they have done for years. If they go out in the evening, if they wanted to go see a stand-up, I know who I'd send them to go and see. It's not who I'd go and see but it's who would make them laugh and relax them and make them have a good time.

I do see that if what you've got is a bit more delicate or is a bit more thoughtful, then the circuit is not the place for you – although there's a lot of great comics who can make it work. I feel like my personality changed a lot on the circuit. I feel like I got much more hard. I got much more aggressive. I don't cry in front of people ever any more and I used to be quite normal about that, but I've had enough nightmare gigs where I wanted to cry and I couldn't because my friends were backstage.

I was so frightened in my first year. I used to sort of wobble on stage and clearly be frightened. I couldn't take the mic out the mic stand because my hands were shaking too much and I get a bit dyspraxic when I'm scared and I lamped myself in the face a few times. I think I was so clearly frightened that my status was really low. Then when I started enjoying the stage and my real obnoxious confident side came out, that's when audiences were a bit like, 'Yuck, what's this? Hit it with a brick. We don't like this.' It didn't fit my jokes any more.

Mark Watson explains how the different audiences on Friday nights in his early career had a huge impact on the style and choices about his performance.

MARK WATSON

When I started, that was an issue for me. For whatever reason, Friday nights are normally the most infamous ones. I think people just live, work and drink in that slightly manic desperate way that British people have and yeah, it used to frighten me a bit because it's not really my environment. I used to wish that I was really much older or like certain types of comics that are old. If you're going to be an old, grizzled, fat guy or American or having some point of difference, you can deal with it. If you're just a skinny guy barely out of university going up in front of those graduates, you do feel quite scared and it's not easy to be personable.

Partly that's why I adopted a Welsh persona when I began. Partly, it was just a gimmick to stand out, for about the first three or four years in my career when I was always in clubs. So I used to talk in a quite broad Welsh accent. My family is Welsh and stuff so it wasn't really like doing a character. It was the exact same material but I just used this bogus accent and that was a response to the fact that those environments that you're playing in are quite threatening. Because if you go out there with a point of difference like that and say, 'Look, I'm not one of you guys at all, I'm Welsh', somehow that's better than saying, 'I would like to be one of you guys'. If you're going to be low status, you want to go really low status.

A lot of comedians have done that. If you're nerdy or fat or whatever sort of quirk you have as a person, you will probably play it up as a comic. The other thing I used to do is be much louder. I'm still pretty frantic and chaotic on stage, but in those days I learned to just shout my way through gigs if necessary. Especially hosting. And when I started, people could still smoke. So you would have like these plumes of smoke in the air. People are chatting and chatting. Over a few years of that, you learn that sometimes you just got to get your head down, yell at them and then you're away.

Stephen K Amos tells a similar story. He too came to appreciate that too much manic energy can contribute to losing a room rather than holding it.

STEPHEN K AMOS

When I started, I was very animated. I used to run around the stage all the time. Then I did a show with a comic that I hugely respect and he said, 'What are you doing? Look at it from your outside. You are a man of your mid-30s and you're jumping around the stage. Why don't you just hold your stance, stand in the middle of that stage, let them come to you?' It was great advice.

So for some bits of the show, when I'm being quite poignant and serious, I'm not moving around. I'm standing there. I'm not leaning into them. They're coming into me. I used to also do this thing when I did rowdy clubs where I'd shout loud into the audience. Another comic friend of mine said, 'Why are you shouting? If your jokes are good, lower your voice. Bring them into you.' Little tricks like that work. It's just about showing that you are there for a reason. You're the man with the mic. You've been doing it for quite a while and, essentially, you're funny.

What Stephen is describing is the difference between purposeful energy, which can be very still, and chaotic, unmotivated energy, which can look like nervousness. A naturally high-energy person offstage may need to control and purposefully direct that energy on stage, while a naturally laconic person may need to generate more fizz and verve once they step up to the mic.

TOM WRIGGLESWORTH

I'm very relaxed on stage, but I flap about quite a lot. I'm trying to rely on my stage persona to be just me. But that's always a lie. It is an act, isn't it? So you've always got to crank a few dials up, otherwise you can suffer from being too underpowered and too low-key. You have got to make yourself shine. Me on stage is as close to me offstage as is currently possible.

There's an interesting thing that's happened. I used to get really aggressive. All new comedians do it. They react so aggressively to any sort of heckle. Even if a joke dies, you'll see a new act turn on an audience with far too much ferocity than is actually called for. And it's fear on the part of the comedian; it's absolute fear. If they feel they're being rocked or having the rug pulled from under them a bit, they lash out. I'm so much more mature now in every way that, if someone doesn't like something, it's absolutely alright as long as they're not causing a fuss.

Heckles are, in context, welcome. I'll just chat to them. I'll just try to find out what the motivation behind that particular heckle was, rather than slam them down and threaten to slay every female member of their family. I'm much more interested in working with it in a nicer way, I guess.

We will return to the subject of heckling very shortly.

The size of the room also dictates the size of the performance. What works in a big theatre may not work in a more intimate club and vice versa. Stadium gigs are hugely profitable for the acts that can book them, but very few see it as an ideal setting for stand-up comedy.

PHILL JUPITUS

It's not about the act being greedy. If there's a demand to see them, fine. I just find it so strange that people go. Imagine you're in Row Z of the O2 watching something, and it's the people who go to the gigs who buy the DVDs, who have gone to the room, paid a lot of money to sit in the room and watch on the screen, but they want to be there. It's about wanting to be a part of something. I think that's very post-Live Aid, U2 at Red Rocks, Glastonbury. The fact that Glastonbury is on telly every year, and you're watching something and you wish you were there.

I look at comedy in a large room and I can't think of anywhere I want to be less than in a room of 18,000 people watching one person talking. That to me is like Billy Graham or evangelists. It's like there's a Messianic thing, you know, going on.

I don't wish to do anyone else down who does arena comedy, Russell or Michael or any of 'em. And even Eddie does the arenas as well, and I did one once, I did Wembley for Eddie. And it's an amazing feeling but I can't understand doing an hour in those sorts of conditions. Me and Jack Dee had a chat about it and we think the optimal size for stand-up is 500 people but you can push it up to 1,500. That's workable. But 500 is the optimum. Leeds City Varieties, that's the perfect-sized room for comedy. Five hundred people there's an intimacy. You open your eyes a bit wider, the person in the back row sees you doing it.

I'm more nervous in tiny rooms than I am in arenas. A hundred and up I'm fine, but, you know, the twenties, no. I mean, it's just you and twenty people in a room. That's a large dinner party.

Even very successful comedians can feel awed when the room isn't familiar. Panel show *Mock The Week* is famously a tough test for younger comedians. We asked Nathan Caton about his experience.

NATHAN CATON

I was petrified leading up to it because I got the news at the start of August, when I was in Edinburgh, from my agent saying, 'You're going to do *Mock The Week*. It's the first one back next month.' So I had a whole month of it just playing on my mind and thinking, 'I got to write to some topical jokes'. I just spent so much time reading every single paper trying to go over everything.

Around the weekend before, the nervousness started kicking in. I felt, 'I've got to do this nice. It's a proper TV show. I'm around the big boys. Don't flop. Just don't flop.'

And then I got there on the day and they started recording, Micky Flanagan on my left, Andy Parsons, Dara Ó Briain obviously in the middle, and then Stewart Francis, Hugh Dennis and Chris Addison. Luckily, I knew Micky and Andy from the circuit. They took care of me. Micky was amazing. 'Yeah, it's all right, mate. Just say anything and try to make it funny, all right? Just try and get your word in, OK?' And then I had my first joke. It got a decent laugh but not massive laugh.

It was – do you know the thing where they ask, 'What do these initials stand for?' It was CATL. I said, 'Cameron Attempts Tight Lyrics'. I mean, people laughed a bit, but nothing major. I thought, 'OK. Oh gosh, all right. Cool. Try another one.' There's now a window of opportunity. I could talk. 'Cameron is a Tosser. LOL.' And that got a massive laugh. They gave me a round of applause. I felt like a whole weight had come off my shoulders. 'Oh gosh, thank you. I can do this.' And Micky was like, 'Yeah, that's good, Nathan. Nice one.'

Then once you get that first big laugh, it's kind of like doing stand-up for the first time all over again. You wait for that first big laugh and it just eases you in. And after that you feel all right. I mean I was still nervous, but because I had that memory of that first big laugh and round of applause, it got me through. That was a chance for me to show that I *am* funny, that I *can* do this. I *do* belong here. But man, it was petrifying.

The bigger gigs generally have an extra frisson to them, but some comedians do get to the point where really nothing fazes them any more.

PHILL JUPITUS

Sometimes I like to play. Did you see the *Live at the Apollo* that I did? Before I went on, I thought, 'let's have a laugh'. I was a little nervous. I thought, 'Maybe, this will be the thing that will get me off television'. And with that state of mind, that this could be the biggest disaster of my fucking career, 'let's have a laugh' was the thought literally, as the thing started to go and there was smoke all around me, and it started to rise, and I saw the light coming up my feet and my legs. I am looking down and I saw the light come up my legs, and I was walking on stage at the Odeon where I saw my first-ever live gig. It felt like one of the most stupid things I ever did in my life to be on telly doing stand-up. And I was so relaxed – I am a father of two from the Home Counties. I'm walking on stage at the Odeon. That's what Jon Bon Jovi does. I was doing what Jon Bon Jovi does.

You know that way I talk about the clown? The clown is me on stage. I did a gig where I read poetry and I went on stage. Robin Ince, Hammersmith Odeon again. I was reading poems, and a very hysterical lady went, 'We love you, Phill', and I looked up, very lonely, and said, 'The clown's not here'.

I see that Comedy Phill is a very separate entity and I keep him separate. And he belongs on stage and he feels very sexy and he feels irresponsible and he feels powerful and he feels silly and he feels all these things. You let all these things out of you on stage. You can't predict if he's gonna come or not. Sometimes he doesn't turn up. But *Live at the Apollo*, he was there and then when I filmed, I'll stand by fucking *Quadrophobia* until the day I die – I think it's one of the best bits of work I've ever done – and that *Live at the Apollo* was on a par with that. That was a good bit of work, *Live at the Apollo*. Bearing in mind I wasn't allowed to swear, I think I did some fucking great work because I need swearing.

The term 'status' was co-opted by improvisation guru Keith Johnstone to describe the physical ways in which people compete, often unconsciously, for power in social situations. It became a very useful way to express relationships of all kinds. In *Fawlty Towers*, would-be high status Basil Fawlty dominates the cringingly low status Manuel, but is in turn put in his place by the rather more effortlessly high status Sybil.

When it comes to stand-up comedy, it's important to consider how your choice of status will play out in your relationship with the audience. The relationship between an audience and a stand-up comedian is an interesting one. Although the comedian has the advantage of the larger space of the stage, the added height and the spotlight – not to mention the power of wielding the microphone – the comedian's persona need not be high status over the audience.

In a typical double act, a high status 'parent' character tries to curb the chaotic impulses of a low status 'clown' character. It's tempting to look at solo stand-up comedians as one half of a double act, with the audience being the other half. So, while some play high status, chiding the audience about their lack of insight or absurd habits, many others play low status, revealing to the audience that they find the world a bewildering place.

Lewis Black's stage persona is the epitome of high status.

LEWIS BLACK

My act took a long time for me to find. It took me a long time for me to find my voice on stage. I kept trying things and doing stuff. I was changing outfits. I was wearing this kind of outfit or I'm wearing a lumberjack shirt. I'm wearing this. I'm wearing that. I'm just trying anything and meanwhile my voice is all over the place and then I'm working this room that I ran with some friends in New York City and I get up on stage one night and I come off and a friend of mine, a comic, Dan Ballard, he says to me, 'You know, you're really angry and you're not up there yelling'. He said, 'When you go on stage, I just want you to yell your entire act'.

I remember the first time I tried it – just like, '*You idiot!*' I started to yell more and more. When I would yell, I would literally turn my back to the audience and walk up stage and yell at the wall. Then once I got comfortable, I just yelled directly at them.

For other comedians, the need for vulnerability is more important – at least, on stage.

ANDY KINDLER

I went to Australia. I got up on stage. I said something bad about myself and they roared. I killed with self-deprecating material. It felt almost like coming home. That was what was amazing. I had so much fun there because they enjoy when people are saying negative things about themselves. That's how I grew up, with Woody Allen and Albert Brooks and Carson and Letterman. They would do a joke and they would comment on it. Richard Lewis, he would do a joke and he would comment. I'm much more attracted to that kind of bravado.

I love Chris Rock but I love Chris Rock in a club more than I love him in a big hall yelling, because I feel like that kind of bravado to me is not funny. I mean, not that he's *not* funny doing that, but it's just he sells it so hard. So I think vulnerability is much more engaging and something I really relate to.

Of course, we all have egotistical sides to ourselves. We need to watch it. Some people don't, they just get taken with themselves. I'm taken with myself but I keep it private. I have a mirror in my room on the ceiling and occasionally, I will get up and I go, 'Looking good, looking good. You're a funny man. You're a funny, funny man.'

The best comedians are probably the ones who can flex their status along with the rest of their persona. They appreciate that the audience has paid to see someone comfortable on the stage, happy to be placed in this dominant position. But they also appreciate that the most truly confident people are precisely the ones who can admit how lost, helpless and frightened they sometimes feel.

Stephen K Amos often plays with these expectations. He's been known to come on speaking in a Nigerian accent, acting in a very high status and very aggressive manner. Then, later in the set he changes back to his normal accent.

STEPHEN K AMOS

I'm absolutely very much aware of status and perceptions and genders, how we see each other, how other people see us, how others see you rather, because to me, it's all about commanding that room – be it from what you're saying or be it what you believe. An audience will just immediately take the lead from you. The first two minutes is very important with a stand-up. The audience are going to get you and get what you're all about. If you can flip with that and change people's expectations, then, wow, that's a great thing.

John-Luke Roberts on the Alternative Comedy Memorial Society

A snapshot of an alternative comedy club[1] in the 2010s

The Alternative Comedy Memorial Society was conceived or discovered at the Edinburgh Fringe in August 2010 when Thom Tuck and I met to discuss putting together a night like the Alternative Comedy Memorial Society (although Thom wanted to call it the Captain Planet Repertory Theatre, which was briefly its subtitle before it quietly vanished). The aim was to create a night where experimentation was encouraged and failure celebrated, and where the audience would be raucous *but respectful*. We wanted a place where audiences could see things that were genuine one-offs, and comedians would feel safe to try out their stupidest ideas.

We both had folk memories of Simon Munnery's Cluub Zarathustra, and actual memories of Robin Ince's Book Club, Captain Dude and the Dude Patrol, Laffs-and-Broccoli and Josie Long's Sunday Night Adventure Club, and had found a little gap of time where there seemed to be a space for a new something-like-that.

We came up with various sly tricks to get the atmosphere right.

1   We would have a call and response catchphrase: after each act on the bill had performed, Thom and I would shout 'A Failure' and the audience would shout 'A Noble Failure'. This was a clever psychological trick to make them feel they condoned what was happening, and would be legally considered accessories.

2   A different foreign act would open each show with a set in their own language. This would bewilder the audience into a defenceless state. We would then translate the set into English and, whatever the act had in fact said, the English translation

---

[1]Whatever that means.

would be Ed Byrne's routine about the Alanis Morissette song *Ironic*. We would then accuse the act of plagiarism.

3   Heckles would be permitted, but only from a pre-approved list. These included: 'We appreciate what you're trying to do', and 'That's a Tim Vine joke, surely'.

4   We would book far too many acts for each show. Having done this, Thom would then book five more acts.

5   As well as changing guest acts each week, there would be a board – a bunch of acts who would perform most weeks and nominally have some sort of democratic power over the club. We never got round to sorting this democratic power out, which is likely for the best. The board included, at various times, Isy Suttie, Bridget Christie, Josie Long, Sara Pascoe, Tom Bell, Nadia Kamil, William Andrews, Alexis Dubus, Ben Target, Tom Golding, trumpeter Steve Pretty and Jonny and the Baptists.

6   At the end of each show, all the performers would get together to do a live performance of an episode of the mid-nineties cartoon *Captain Planet*. This lasted, in retrospect, for a surprising number of shows.

We started in early 2011, running fortnightly on a Tuesday at the New Red Lion pub theatre in Islington (which is now a Co-operative super-market). It worked; people liked watching and acts liked performing. Things worked at ACMS that wouldn't work anywhere else (and indeed didn't, as several acts found out to their fury). The room was great – acts would chaotically stand around the audience through the show, able to join in or disrupt as need be.

After the New Red Lion closed, we performed on a barge, a big top and a recently renovated Australian bar, before settling into the Soho Theatre. In Edinburgh, we played the Pleasance's lovely Ace Dome, before moving into Stand One, which felt like our spiritual home. We were then thrown out of our spiritual home and into the Stand's Yurt, because Daniel Kitson wanted his time slot back and, fair's fair, he is very good.

At Edinburgh in 2013, Ed Byrne stormed the stage to shout at a German man for nicking his act, and Tim Vine performed a set so peculiar that no one was able to heckle him with 'That's a Tim Vine joke, surely'. In autumn of that year, Simon Munnery performed his club act, *The League Against Tedium*, at Soho ACMS. Channel 4 made a TV pilot with us, called *ACMS Presents a Board Meeting*. We'd created the night we'd wanted to and had loads of brilliant oddballs do ludicrous things for us. Similarly minded nights that had started around the same time as us – Lost Treasures of the Black Heart, Lolitics, Weirdos – were flourishing. We lost out on a Chortle Award for Innovation to American millionaire Louis CK. It felt like the sensible time to stop.

So we carried on for a bit.

The ACMS is currently in a pleasantly dusky state. Most of our board (especially the bloody women) are successful enough to be busy all the time. Our shows now pop up unexpectedly, and then lope off, tail triumphantly between the legs. We have loose plans for a hubristically large final show. And then we'll start the ACMSMS.

Chapter 8
The Best-laid Plans

DEBORAH FRANCES-WHITE: One of the things I love most about stand-up is working out how to play different gigs. Small rooms. Big rooms. Outdoor gigs. Rooms with pillars. My first-ever Edinburgh solo show, I regularly had around eight or ten attendees. So I treated it like a dinner party – got all the names, made a seating plan, introduced people. I could usually have a great time if I kept referring back to what I knew about the punters and involved them. My rule is that if you can't touch a stranger, it's not an audience, so I like to find ways to get people to sit closer to each other to create what we in the industry call 'an audience'. Although we all know we've had the best nights of our lives at heaving concerts, buzzing parties or crowded restaurants, most people would rather have a mediocre time than willingly sit next to a stranger. We've had mediocre times before. We're comfortable with that.

The first time I played a music festival, I watched comedians I loved and respected die or play to largely uninterested audiences for two days. The crowds were a little drunk or high and were sitting on the grass, not really meeting them half-way. I watched the rock bands soar and the jokes fall flat. I decided (almost certain I'd crash) to take a rock star approach and go to the edge of the stage like a lead singer and play to the people outside the marquee, over the heads of the front row. I didn't ride the laughs, just like the bands didn't wait for the audience to sing along – they just kept going. It worked brilliantly and I was amazed and relieved. They got onside because I wasn't asking them to do some of the work.

At the Edinburgh Festival they want to do some work. They'd be annoyed if you didn't make sure they were on board and leave some ambiguity. The same people will be at both venues but audience science means they'll respond in different ways. Audiences are odd. No one knows why different audiences respond differently on different nights. My friend's play opened with a video which included a clip of Jeremy Paxman on *Newsnight* saying, 'So how do you feel about a coalition of losers?' in a scathing voice. Some nights that would get a big laugh, some nights a medium-sized titter and some nights nothing at all. Jeremy Paxman wasn't bringing a different performance. It was a clip off the telly. No actors had sullied the space bringing a negative energy. That sizable audience just decided it was funny or not. Collectively. Where they'd been that day. How difficult their journey had been. How hot the room was. Their average age. Who knows?

There's no question that an individual seeing the same show in two different audiences might have different reactions and laugh at different things. I can only advise that you don't take a low-energy audience to heart, and I have no idea how to follow that advice myself. If you work it out, let me know. I do know you can sometimes win around an audience who don't really want you there and there's no more satisfying feeling.

I was once booked for a music festival where the audience were so high on ketamine, they were really just in the comedy tent for somewhere to sit out of the all-encompassing mud. They were looking at the acts like they were lava lamps. The host of the sweet indie show I was meant to be opening was trying his best, but some of the audience got aggressive and started shouting 'cunt' at him. A young woman dressed as a fairy crashed the stage and dry-humped him. A glassy-eyed man dressed as Santa Claus was shouting, 'I've got AIDS!' repeatedly. The compere – a wonderful comedian – got so sick of it, he shouted, 'Sit down and shut up you Trustafarian cunts!' and then brought me on.

I was aware the event was meant to be for alternative comics who'd prepared special material on an offbeat theme they'd been given. I'm very experienced as an audience wrangler because thirty minutes or more of my tour show was working with the audience, so I knew I could take them in hand in a very high status way, but I felt that would leave the rest of the comics dangling and would make it impossible for them to do their prepared stuff. I just went with my instinct, came to the mic and sang, 'All you need is love...' And the audience replied, 'Da da da da daaa' and we sang the whole song together till there was some love back in the room again. I did it because it was all I had. And it worked. It might not have. Another day, someone could have thrown a bottle at my head. That's what makes this job so exciting.

Learning to 'trust your obvious' is worth doing. Your brain will hand you a comeback for a heckler or a sassy remark about a dropped glass and if you learn to trust it, it will start to offer you more stuff. It's all about speed. The first thing you think of, delivered with huge confidence, will get a much bigger laugh than something far wittier said with hesitation.

The most exciting discovery is that you can make something out of anything. I would work with people in the front row of my show *How to Get Almost Anyone to Want to Sleep With You* and one night I got a guy who would only give me one-syllable answers, which was quite limiting – but I thought: what if that's the feature? So I made him into a Bond villain and would repeat everything he said while miming stroking a cat, which the audience really went for and he found really funny. (I never, ever want to make someone I'm playing with feel uncomfortable.)

After the show a TV producer said, 'You were really lucky with that guy in the front row tonight. That was so funny.' In reality he was giving me nothing – but nothing can be something, if you see it that way. No matter who I talked to – talkative, mute, sassy, shy, single, married, gay, straight – people always said, 'You were so lucky with the people in your audience tonight'. I had that in reviews. Like Oscar Wilde and George Bernard Shaw always came and sat right in the front row and did the work for me.

At first it annoyed me, but after a while I started to realize it was a compliment because it meant it looked easy. To be honest, when I first started stand-up all I'd ever done was improvisation, so ad-libbing was the only thing I could do. I was terrified of material. Writing something worth saying in my bedroom and dragging people out of their houses to hear it because it was so important seemed way more difficult than making something up on the spot – but it was only because I'd trained my brain that way.

Here's an easy exercise you can do to learn to trust your obvious. It's one I learned from Keith Johnstone, the legendary improvisation teacher.

First, point at things and say what they are. Clock! Window! Pencil!

Next, point at things and say the last thing you pointed at. I'll start you off. Point at the floor. Now point at the ceiling and call it the floor. Now point at something else and call it the ceiling. Keep going. If you lose it, start over.

Finally, point at things and say what they're not. Point at the chair and call it a banana. Point at the sink and call it your grandma. Point at the dog and call it a dressing table.

The first exercise is easy. It's what you've been doing all your life. It's just to get you into the rhythm. The second exercise is hard at first but once you get into the pattern of remembering the last item you pointed at, it probably becomes easy. Most people find a rhythm or strategy.

The third exercise, for most people, is by far the hardest. Even though in the third exercise there is no wrong answer. Or more accurately, the third exercise is the hardest *because* there is no wrong answer. If there is no wrong answer, how do you know the right answer? It is easy to be paralysed by choice. Also your brain will probably have tried to create right answers by making its own constraints, like 'you can't repeat words' or 'the words have to be original' or 'long words are better than short words' or 'if you've just said apple, it's boring to say orange', even though the only instruction was to call things anything but what they are.

The best way to train your brain to give you its first idea is to start with a letter of the alphabet. If you put nothing into Google it won't offer you all the websites there are, it will ask you to narrow it down. Your brain is a search engine. Offer it something. Decide you will call things what they're not, but everything will start with the letter M. Point at something; don't think up good words starting with M, just make the sound – 'Mmmmm' and let your brain offer you the rest of the word. It will. 'Mmmmuppet', 'Mmmmouse', 'Mmmother', 'Mmmary'. Be curious as to what your brain gives you. If it offers you 'meringue' twice in a row, that's a call-back. If it offers you a nonsense word, that's whimsy. Enjoy whatever it gives you. Open your mouth, make a sound and it will offer you something. Wait it for to offer something brilliant while you censor out the obvious and it won't.

Point at things every day and say what they're not for two minutes, but use a different letter each day. Notice how much easier it is if you do it with confidence than if you do it half-heartedly. If you act like you're good at it, you get better quickly. After you've done this for a week, try going through the alphabet. Aardvark! Ballet! Cattle! It's important to point at things, not just list things, because it lets the brain free-associate. By week three you should be able to take the letter constraints away altogether and just open your mouth and have something come out. Your brain will be used to making a sound first and then allowing your mouth to finish up. This is like going to the gym and developing the ad-lib muscle for when you want to riff or play with the audience.

Go to improv classes. It's good for the soul and it will train your imagination to play off the cuff. But also you'll realize that the audience are so much more willing to laugh at something you've just come up with – because they were there at the moment of invention, so they're complicit. They love watching it. It feels like magic to them.

Bad improv is worse than almost any other sort of theatre, but great improv is incredible and anything you ad-lib on stage while doing stand-up the audience will give you extra points for and it will make them truly love being in your company. They love watching someone who trusts themselves so much, who is so fearless that they'll open their mouth and say the first thing that occurs to them about the guy in the third row or the air conditioner exploding. Then they're not just watching comedy. They're watching a funny high wire act. And who doesn't love a funny high wire act? More than that, as Thom Tuck recently told me, you remind them they're watching something live. You make them remember this isn't TV. They're here. They're in the room.

TOM WRIGGLESWORTH

I think it was my fourth gig when I actually finished without any wheels on the wagon whatsoever. I felt awful. Awful, but it was nowhere near enough to put me off. I've been booed off quite a few times. I've been booed off twice in one night. It just makes you feel sort of angry with the world. But you've got to get to a point where you realize it doesn't matter that they hated you. I've seen audiences hate really good performers. I've seen audiences love really rubbish performances. I've seen that whole gamut. But you have got to protect the ego a little bit and it's not easy getting booed off.

I think it's inevitable that you'll die. It's like having to take the rubbish out; you've just got to do it now and again. It's part of being a grown-up, really. The bar gets higher, that's all. But the feeling is fairly similar. But I've never died, touch wood, in a spectacularly important situation. (I've just signed my own death warrant, haven't I?)

One or two comedians even plan to die at early gigs.

HARLAND WILLIAMS

Eventually I stopped worrying about bombing and not getting laughs and just thought, 'You know what? I'm going to present myself. I'm going to present the show and you're either coming in the door and having fun with me or you're not.'

Believe it or not, I used to go up on stage and bomb on purpose. I learned from it. I would go up and bomb and I would eat it but I would realize I wanted to know what it felt like to go as low as you could go. That way I could learn what's it like to be at the bottom and never fear if things went bad because I had already taken myself to the bottom. So I knew and it became familiar and safe terrain for me. Once I had found it on my own terms on purpose, then whenever I fell down there by accident, I wasn't scared of it and I could wander around in it and slowly crawl myself back out.

It taught me how to swim when you're sinking. It taught me how to claw my way to the top and get air. It's like when you're drowning and you frantically claw your way to the top. So I would kind of do that on purpose and the more I did it, the longer I could hold my breath underwater it seems. So yeah, that's what was great about bombing on purpose because you had just learned that stuff. You have to learn it on the fly, so it's instinctual.

It taught me not to be scared of the dark. It's like being in a cave with a flashlight that starts to flicker and go out. When it goes out, you're terrified, but I just realized when the light goes out way down there, I don't have to be scared because I will find my way into the light.

Sometimes even a very experienced comedian may just be in the wrong place at the wrong time. If you've worked hard to carve out a niche for yourself, you can have devoted fans turning up to see you, but if one night a crowd is in that hasn't seen you before, it can be disorienting for everybody. Having served your time in the clubs can help you out, or it might just be a hindrance.

ROBIN INCE

I haven't been on the circuit for a while. I think the circuit was incredibly important. Even when I was doing some of my science shows, I always have in the back of my mind when the next laugh is. I'm overly paranoid about it if I haven't had a laugh in twenty seconds. I can get a big laugh and then in about thirty seconds I think, 'Come on, you've got to find another one now, I don't care if you've told them about particle physics or not'.

So in that way, you can't just be self-indulgent. You need to involve them and you need to entertain them. One of the things that can be overrated is sometimes laughter itself. Some of my favourite acts to watch are ones where you get a while since the last laugh, but look how enthralled people are.

I remember walking out to a gig in Birmingham as the compere and the front row, and they just looked and everything about me was, 'Oh god'. And I just went on and on and on and pushed it as much as I could and by the end of it they were, 'Aw, that was great mate, we weren't really sure about you at the beginning…' And you get some times when, rather than being browbeaten, you think, 'I'll get them… and if I don't get them, then I shouldn't worry too much but I'm going to try everything'.

The first time I played the Belfast Empire twenty years ago, I was booed on. It was Christmas week, 600 people, getting booed on, with stuff being thrown at the stage. I was booked for thirty minutes and I did about forty. With them just hating me and throwing stuff at me. Typical Belfast temper: if you stood your ground, they hated you, but they'd buy you a pint because you stood your ground! You just go, 'Right, I'm never going to win them round, but I'm going to bloody stand here for the whole of my contract and maybe more'. When I hit thirty minutes of just dodging bottles and I turned to where the dressing room was, and I said, 'Oh what's that? Patrick Kielty's just given me the nod. Says it doesn't normally go that well for an act from London, so he says do another ten.'

Adam Bloom has a surefire way of dealing with a bad gig.

ADAM BLOOM

When you're having a bad gig, you try anything. I get my cock out. That works. I will keep my cock out. Comedians are very artistic about what they do, but the bottom line is we do what works.

Eventually, the bad gigs get fewer and further between (or you give up). But the process of facing the fear of being on stage while people stare at you expectantly can have profound and long-lasting effects.

SARA PASCOE

My body's actually changed because I got an overactive thyroid and that's been caused, apparently, by too much stress. So my adrenal glands now don't work and my thyroid works for it instead which means that my body doesn't really feel nerves any more. It's just gone. Sometimes I wish that thing would kick in where you would get this kind of hit of different neuro-transmitters that made you slightly sharper or more energetic and I don't get that any more. I sometimes have to remind myself – speak a bit faster, look like you've got some energy. And I have to consciously do it.

When you go on stage you have to kind of not care. No matter how many people, no matter who's there, you have to not care. Even that thing of, 'I hope I don't have a shit one because that comic I like is here', that's enough to make stress come out in your system. That's enough to make your body go, 'Uh-oh, danger!' And your body doesn't know the difference between 'Richard Herring is in the audience' or 'There's a predator nearby', so it reacts the same. That trembling thing which some people get is fight-or-flight and you're having to restrain it.

What's so interesting about the brain is that we have all of the ancient pathways of three million years ago when we were just apes. The amygdala, which deals with fear, that's a very ancient part of your brain. So a tiny stimulus message to that part and it reacts like, 'Okay, go limp, there's a predator!', or 'Get the fuck out of here – evacuate!' So that's what you have to struggle with because the rest of your brain knows it's not a lion, it's just Richard Herring.

Desmond Morris wrote about why, for all actors, stage fright doesn't go away. If someone is looking directly at you, that means they want to fuck you or they want to fight you. Those are the only two explanations in nature. And so walking out in front of lots of people staring at you is the most unnatural thing. He says actors and performers are wired wrongly. Because the thing that you should fear the most in your life is the thing we want. And someone else said, 'Never doubt that you are the maddest person in the room because you are the only one facing the wrong way, and the only one not laughing'.[1]

Sometimes a bad gig forces a comedian to abandon their prepared material and start improvising. Lee Mack observes that all comedians recite prepared material on stage, ad-lib on stage, and recite prepared material as if it is an ad-lib – but the proportions vary wildly from performer to performer.

---

[1] We think this was Jimmy Carr. It appears in the book he wrote with Lucy Greeves, *The Naked Jape*.

NAT LUURTSEMA

Some of my best moments in my life have been just reaching for the right word or the right punchline, just landing it, and everyone laughing and you're thinking, 'You think I wrote that down, you think that's rehearsed', but as if… as if I could do something so… make it look so spontaneous. That's probably the thing I don't like most about stand-up, is making it look spontaneous like you've just rollicked on stage and you're just like, 'Here's just some spontaneous shit I've just come up with'. That makes me feel dirty but it's the job and you have to.

It doesn't have to be something unexpected happening that forces a comedian off-piste, nor does it have to be the writing-on-stage process which we examined earlier. Some comedians just like improvising.

ADAM BLOOM

A lot of comedians are just good writers. I saw Harry Hill, who's one of my heroes, the other day socially and he said, 'Panel shows, I can't do them. I can't think on the spot in those situations.' But his joke-writing is world class, absolutely timeless, legendary comedy.

I can just about cover not improvising over seven minutes. If I'm on stage for twenty minutes, I *have* to improvise. Usually at about ten minutes in, I feel like I'm lying. Then an imaginary glass wall starts to go up between me and the audience. I feel like we're not connected any more. So I have to improvise to keep the gig alive for me – otherwise something happens to me and I glaze over. The audience senses when we get detached and the laughs stop happening because, although I'm saying the words, there's not any truth in my voice. When that barrier goes up, I hate myself because I know I've left it too long.

When I do a seven-minute set at a festival like Montreal, I'm happy not to improvise because I've worked on my material, I'm thinking about memorizing the order, to change each day a little bit, each time until

I get it right. So when I'm doing that much stuff on stage and it's only seven minutes, not enough time to get bored. Twenty minutes without improvising, I will. Even if I'm storming the pants off a gig, I will start to feel bored.

For some comedians, spontaneity is less about the audience and more about their temperament.

PHILL JUPITUS

It's a zero preparation thing. It's totally a zero. And I think it's better. The first idea out of your mouth is usually the best. And when I did the tour doing the improvised characters,[2] sometimes I'd do something brilliant one night and I'd try and do it again the next night. Never as funny as the first time it came out of your mouth.

And as a cartoonist as well. The pencil line... I used to do pencils and then ink over them. And then I thought, what if I ink straight, commit to paper. It's about commitment. Ink, straight to paper. Which is terrifying. You can't rub it out, you have to start again. So now when I cartoon, it's ink straight to paper, because your first line is your best line. And it's like that in performing as well. The first time out of your mouth is when it's freshest, and when it's the most organic. And that's again why I envy people who can craft and hone and perfect because I've fucking not got the patience as a performer.

When you plan to include improvised material (which isn't quite as contradictory as it sounds) you create a different relationship between you and the audience.

---

[2] In 2012 and 2013, Phill toured a show called *You're Probably Wondering Why I've Asked You Here* in which he appeared in front of an audience in costume as a series of characters and spontaneously answered questions from the audience.

RICH HALL

I try to improvise songs on stage because you can take what someone does, which is generally mundane, and make it exciting. Most people have comparably mundane jobs compared to comedy – or at least they think so. They're not, but they're watching the guy on stage and they think, 'Well, I'm just … I'm a dry cleaner'. But you can take what they do, say dry cleaning, and elevate it. Then they're nervous because they think you're going to belittle them. But in fact, you do the opposite and really build it up because it's ridiculous high epic proportion and that generally is pretty funny.

I remember watching a musician in London, American musician, who I really like, and they came out and did about five songs at the Shepherd's Bush Empire and then someone yelled out, 'Talk to us!' It was a really amazing thing to hear from the crowd. The show was great but they just wanted that person to say something about being at the Shepherd's Bush Empire or being in London, and they did.

I kind of think that was one of the best pieces of advice I ever got was just watching a show where someone was yelling, 'Just talk to us!'

Ad-libbing has an added element of danger which, when done successfully, bonds the performer and the audience more tightly than some pre-prepared sets. Harland Williams thinks this is the spirit of what comedy is all about.

HARLAND WILLIAMS

I feel like to just have everything pre-planned in your head, that's not the spirit of comedy. Comedy happens in the moment. Comedy is a flow. It's energy. An old lady walking down the street who trips over something and falls. She didn't wake up and plan that. It just happened to her and everyone around got the joy of laughing. If someone walks into a plate glass door, they didn't plan it. It just happened in that moment. So when

I'm on stage, I try to have moments that aren't planned and just happen and there's a real pure comedic energy to that.

I sometimes will do a whole show where I just make it up and sometimes I will just do 20 per cent or 40 per cent, whatever I'm feeling.

While you're still learning to handle your nerves and remember your jokes, it can often be too stressful to add another degree of difficulty in the form of trying to ad-lib. But once your confidence has grown and you feel more at ease behind a mic, it's an excellent skill to have in your back pocket.

MARK WATSON

I used to virtually never improvise when I started. For the first couple of years, partly because you only do five or ten minutes on stage, so there's really no time to mess about. You can barely get your three jokes out and then say goodbye. These days I do it quite a lot. It's not so much confidence – it just becomes second nature to mess about a bit more because you're comfortable on the stage.

When you start out, even twenty minutes on stage feels like a marathon and all you've done is five minutes. You think, 'How will I ever get twenty minutes together?' Then when you've got twenty, you think, 'I can't imagine how I'm ever going to do an hour'. But after a while, you realize it's not really about writing millions of jokes. Obviously I've proved that point by doing thirty-six hours on stage so I think I'm qualified to say that you don't need that many jokes. You just need to be good on the stage.

The crossover for me, in terms of when I became comfortable ad-libbing on stage, was starting to compere. I didn't do that at all for a long time. I was intimidated by the whole idea of it because you're also in charge of the evening and in some ways it feels like a big ask. But once, someone was ill or something and I got asked. So I got promoted from doing five minutes to suddenly hosting the evening. I think I was the only one that got there through the traffic or something. I definitely wasn't a good enough comedian to do it, so it must have been a logistical decision.

That was being thrown in the deep end of it. Having got away with that, I started to do that more and more. As a compere, you've really got no choice but to chat with the audience and before you know it, you can do it.

Moshe Kasher talked to us in more detail about how the need to ad-lib, to make the show feel alive and spontaneous, is opposed to the force that needs the show to be solid and have structure.

MOSHE KASHER

There's nothing good about watching a comedian who's an amazing writer but doesn't know how to perform and vice versa. When I started, it wasn't that I didn't know how to write, I just didn't know enough about stand-up to know some basic things like how to keep your writing tight. Eventually, I started tightening my act. Then at about five years in, I thought to myself, 'Now let me loosen this'. Then I went on this journey where I started trying to just have fun on stage no matter what happened.

In San Francisco, the club that everybody would go to was The Punch Line. You would wait a year to get on stage – it was a big thing. Everybody was freaked out by being there and so everybody would do the same seven minutes every single week. My friend Brent Weinbach is an amazing, brilliant performer. He started going up on that stage and experimenting. He would go up there and just do the craziest, weirdest things – and he would fail sometimes, but he was the only person that was trying to do something outside the box. I would see him and I would think, 'I'm going to go on stage and not do any material. I'm going to see what happens.' No jokes. Just ad-libbing and finding out what happens on stage there. It might not sound like the most revolutionary idea in the world, but for me at the time, especially culturally, nobody was doing that because everybody was so terrified of bombing on that show.

I think that was when I really fused as a comedian. I had the loose. I tightened it. Then I unloosed it to find that I'd created some kind of little carbonite, lightsaber-y kind of thing. So that's what my act is like now. I have very, very tightly scripted stories that I will drop in a moment's notice, or if something cool happens in the room I will just go with it. The more fun I'm having, the less jokes I'm telling, basically.

One common source of ad-libbed material is interaction with the audience, or crowd work. Todd Barry's act includes a lot of crowd work and he barely makes a distinction between ad-libbed crowd work and prepared material.

TODD BARRY

In a way, jokes are just ad-libs that you've memorized and written. It's about whether you're quick on your feet. It's not about whether you're screaming or yelling or your jokes are long. It's just whether you can talk to someone and come up with something. It also depends on the night. Part of the reason I thought of doing this [fully ad-libbed] tour was because I just did a special and then thought, 'How can I tour without worrying about repeating material? How about I don't do any material?'

And of course, what was ad-libbed tonight can become reliable material a few gigs later.

MOSHE KASHER

I call them Riffingtons. Riffingtons and Rantingtons. So Riffingtons are riffs. That's the crowd interacting stuff. The Rantingtons, that's a whole other thing. That's when you're not even interacting with the crowd.

You know the Grateful Dead? They play their set and then they do what's called 'going into space'. So in the middle of their song, they would go in a space where they would let go of the structure of the song and just sort of float away and just do improvisational playing for an hour. So I like to go into space but it only happens once every third show or fourth show. Rantingtons are rare. Riffingtons are everywhere.

One thing I think I'm very, very good at and always have been good at is finding fake segues. It will almost always seem like I meant to do what I'm doing. I don't know how or why I do it but if I'm going off on a thing, I always find some click back into my material that makes it seem like I've been planning on doing that the whole time. It seems very fluid, so sometimes people don't know what I wrote and what I didn't. To me, it's very obvious because, with the stuff I write, I talk very fast and just it seems scripted to me. When I'm out in space, I'm slower.

Stephen K Amos will also write gags which are specific to the venue.

STEPHEN K AMOS

When I did my last tour in the UK, I sent out a tweet for each town. What should I know about so and so, so – say Lowestoft? People would send me facts that I could then turn into jokes or find ways of incorporating them. In fact, when I did Lowestoft, there was – in the local paper, they were asking people from the community to come around to a local newsagent where they were staging a mock terrorist attack. I was in bits because it was just so bizarre. Of all the places in England to conduct a mock terrorist attack, Lowestoft I'm pretty sure is not high on the agenda.

Finally of course, a comedian may have to extemporize when dealing with hecklers. Many comedians strive to create an intimate atmosphere, a conversational tone. They want the audience to feel part of the gig. However, that can lead to audience members talking back. But skilled comedians know that simply making a lot of cruel jokes at the expense of one audience member may turn the rest of the crowd against you.

MOSHE KASHER

I like making fun of people but I want it to be fun for them, too. I've always disliked it when a comedian ruins someone's night in order for everybody else to have a good time. I think that stinks. Sometimes, you find yourself doing it by accident. You think, 'Oh, this guy will swing with this', and then they don't.

I think the secret is that I make fun of myself a lot. So hopefully that opens up for everybody to be able to get made fun of a little bit.

Most comedians who deliberately include the audience in their act do so benevolently. If audience members intrude into the act uninvited, then usually all bets are off.

DANIEL SLOSS

My rule that I've made up is that my set is much like my house. If I invite you into it, you're more than welcome to join in. Put your feet up. You're welcome. But if you break into it, I will fucking kill you.

If I'm ever talking to audience members, it's always very friendly. But if you heckle, I go very dark, very quickly, because nobody expects it because I'm so innocent-looking. Then when they heckle, I'm like, 'Now, I'm going to destroy your character'. I quite like it. It gives me licence to say the worst possible things your mind can come up with. I say dreadful things when I get heckled and I love it. I love how shocked the audience gets. I love the guilty laugh.

I did a gig in a music festival in the UK and some guy heckled me. I turned and went, 'Right – my next five minutes are going to be destroying every fibre of your human being'. So I just really ripped into him. The audience loved it. At the end of it, I told him, 'Honestly though, it would be great if you could go home and kill yourself. I would feel nothing.' There was a six-year-old in the front row, who was like, 'Yeah!' When you can get a six-year-old to cheer someone killing themselves, it's wonderful.

Sometimes comedians try and ignore heckers. Others have a suite of put-downs at the ready. We asked Jenny Eclair what we would hear if we tried to heckle her.

JENNY ECLAIR

In actual fact, all you would hear is me saying, 'Pardon?', 'What?' Because I can barely hear, I'm almost deaf now. So it's pretty pointless heckling. I say, 'If you have anything to say, write it down on a slip of paper, pop it at the front of the stage, I'll have a think about it and I'll email you back when I've thought of something funny to say. It might be two weeks though.'

So I kind of lay down rules. I like an audience to know what's in store. Because there is many a time you go to a theatre and you think, 'How long is this going to be? When are they going to stop talking?' – so I tell people exactly what's going on.

Andrew Maxwell marvels that anyone would attempt to heckle an experienced comedian.

ANDREW MAXWELL

Well, I'm curious about them. A heckler, by their nature, is an optimist. They're absolutely certain this is going to work. They're pissed, you're sober, you've got the mic and the lights, everybody's paying to see you. They're fucking eight rows back. You've done it for, in my case, twenty-odd years. They've never done it before. But they give it a go. They fascinate me. I'm like – what the fuck?

To be honest, if they get a good one in and they get a big round of applause, fair play. If there was a good one, you'll be laughing too. They don't have two. They never have two. Sometimes you got to kick them out. It's my house. You're in my fuckin' house. If you're an absolute cunt, I'm kicking you out the room. And a lot of times those sort of people, they can't believe that a little man is telling them what to do. Usually rotten egotists. But they're fucking leaving my party. I always have them out the door.

The comedian's stage persona makes a difference about whether people will heckle and the kind of heckling they are likely to get. Jim Jefferies cuts a very imposing figure on the stage.

JIM JEFFERIES

There's a group of people who would be too fearful to heckle me because of my reputation. There's the people who want to see me do it, so they heckle me just to see me do it. They're happy to be put down for ten minutes and they think it's great and they're laughing through the whole thing, even though it's bugging the shit out of me. They're so happy to be called a cunt by me. Then there's the last group that have been brought in by their friend and really don't like what I do. The angry hecklers. Ones that want to be ribbed will normally yell out something they consider to be funny and interrupt. The ones that hate me will normally yell out something hurtful and then it will just get nasty.

My policy with hecklers is that I try as much as possible to do it off the top of my head. That comes with all the emotions, whether you're angry or having a shitty day or whatever. If my brain turns up blank, then I go to my pool of comebacks that I've used before.

I have a list of three or four ones that I go back to. If I rip into someone for five minutes, there will probably be two lines I've used before and the rest will be off the cuff. Sometimes I'll be a bit tired and just do those two lines and get back into the jokes and ignore them.

As we saw earlier, Orny Adams has no tolerance for his own mistakes and even less for hecklers.

ORNY ADAMS

If I get heckled, I shut it down really quickly.

There's not a lot of room for heckling in my act and I'm not the type of person you want to heckle because I don't turn it into an antagonistic thing. I turn it around so the audience gets behind me and that person is the villain. But you want to do it really quickly and then get out or hope that the club throws him out of that venue.

At Just For Laughs [festival in Montreal], I was on the ethnic show and everyone was like, 'What ethnicity are you?' 'I'm the Jew.' And I'm not a very Jewish-type personality. That's not my essence. It happens to be who I am but not what I put out there on stage. So I would walk out on stage and say that. 'I'm the Jew.' And then people would cheer and I'd say, 'I didn't even know until I got the show'.

Now, Saturday night on the second show, I walk out and I say, 'I'm the Jew'. And somebody yells, 'Fuck you!' from the balcony. I can't even see the person. So now I'm dealing with anti-Semitism off the bat. I've got twelve minutes. I'm not doing an hour. I'm not in front of my audience. I couldn't even see the person. It was like a sniper shot from the back. It sounded like they were serious. It certainly felt anti-Semitic to me.

Now, I've got to shut him down and I've got to win back the audience and I've got to do twelve minutes. It's just not a fair situation. And I said, 'I don't know if that's the right thing to say when somebody walks out on stage'. I said to the host, 'Let's do it again'. Everyone claps and he goes, 'Orny, come on to the stage now. This comedian is very funny. He's the Muslim on the show, Orny Adams!' And I walk out and I go, 'How's everyone doing?' And they cheer and then I look in the balcony and say, 'Fuck you!' And then they stood up. They loved it.

Having a pre-existing relationship with the audience makes a huge difference, but even very experienced comedians can face the kind of challenge which Orny Adams describes.

RICHARD HERRING

You still occasionally don't do the right thing with heckles. Some of them are used in the wrong mood or you're sensing that you're losing the audience. It's just something you learn by doing it. The answer is not to get angry. It's to realize that, if you pretty much just say anything, people will be impressed. People are overly impressed by ad-libbing and they imagine everything is a script.

I remember very early in my career there was a guy who was heckling. He was sitting at the front, and the stage I was on was raised. His head was right by my foot and I kind of tapped him in the head with my foot. It just created a very bad atmosphere because it looked like I've kicked him. I think I probably kicked him harder than I meant to but I didn't hurt him. That's a bad way to respond, with a physical attack.

So, as you become more well-known as a comedian, your proficiency with handling hecklers increases, but so too does the percentage of people in the audience who know you, who like what you do, and who are perfectly happy to sit and watch and laugh. So the anti-heckling skills so arduously acquired may not end up getting used that often.

MARK WATSON

The funny thing about heckling is that, when you get to the stage where you're so proficient at comedy that you could really deal with it, it's not really an issue any more. Once you're touring with your own show, it's very seldom that you get heckled in a theatre environment. If you invite the audience to comment on something, you will get something. I will chat. The audience will ask questions but there's not much genuine disruption. I've probably had about two or three what you call hecklers in the past two or three years touring.

But in the early days, I never really had standard heckle putdowns. A lot of people quite rightly, or at least understandably, will just go for these lines like, 'I remember my first drink'. There are about ten or twelve approved heckle putdowns.

When I was a young comedian, I was more idealistic and thought, 'Oh, I would never do that'. I would force myself to try and find a more reasonable way of doing it. Looking back, I think with those audience members, there's not really any point in dignifying them with that effort. So I totally see why veteran stand-ups without even thinking just do one of those lines, as if to say, 'I'm not really talking to you at all. Let's just move on.'

Those rough clubs in a way are about the process rather than serving any artistic dreams you might have. It's more about getting up there. You do the putdowns that you ought to do. You do the punchlines where you ought to. It's much more orderly and like a job basically and there are still comics that just do that circuit and do it, like a job, very efficiently.

Lewis Black has another strategy to deal with hecklers.

LEWIS BLACK

Be quiet and let them hang themselves. And they will. They will do it on their own. That was my first major lesson. You can't figure them. You have the stage. They don't have anything unless you're biting it bad. If you're biting it, there's nothing you can do – once they smell blood, they're going to come at you. But if you're doing well – you're rolling along with a heckler, I mean – for me now it's easy because I literally just look in the direction of where they might be sitting and that pretty much does the job – the audience already goes, 'Ha-ha!'

Then you just wait. You let them say what they want, let them talk themselves out of. If you can't think of something immediately, they say something else. Eventually, by giving yourself the time to think, you can nail them.

Jenny Eclair knows exactly when she developed a sweary style on stage.

JENNY ECLAIR

There was a time in my career where I was trying to make people like me that I wouldn't get into a lift with! So you would be doing these pubs and clubs and there would be like football crowds, really rough. And also university gigs were quite tough because they are always, just mental – everyone drinking too much – and they were hard. It was a less civilized time in some respects. You know, Northern men were Northern men.

They would shout, 'Get your tits out', or you would come on to a barrage of, 'Fuck off, fuck off, fuck off!' It was footballery… I dealt with it by coming on shouting and swearing. That's why I became a shouty, sweary, stand-up comic because if you came on sort of mincing on and stopped to breathe for a couple of seconds, people would go, 'boring'. I am not making that up.

If I had to do one of those gigs now, twenty minutes at the Comedy Store or whatever, I would be ill with nerves. I'd do it, but it would spoil my entire weekend. I'd want to do the earlier show. If they said it's the Saturday night, midnight show, I'd be poorly all weekend with the anxiety of it. There's a bit of me that doesn't really approve of people like me doing the circuit anyway. I think that the kind of performance that I want to do now doesn't suit the circuit particularly, and it's not my job to bore people. I have this terrible people-pleasing thing, so I would immediately try to find the lowest common denominator and then come off stage hating myself.

Finally, when a gig is over…

GARY DELANEY

At some clubs they have a show manager who will write their reports on how you did. My instinct whenever anybody asks me how a gig has gone is to be honest and tell them what my inner monologue was on that gig. That is always negative and neurotic, for that is my nature.

So, if I'm giving you an honest assessment of how my gig went – even if the gig went really well – I will say, 'In the middle, I tried something new. I probably shouldn't have done that. We're talking and then I lost them and then those girls didn't like me and I'm pretty sure…' Which is fine if you're talking to somebody who watched it, paid attention, knows everything about comedy and then knows enough to make an independent, genuine assessment of how you did and that you did a good gig. But you cannot assume the person you're talking to or the person writing the report has that knowledge of comedy.

So a couple of the other guys said to me, 'Whenever anyone official, anyone industry asks you how it went, it always went great'. And they told me to forget my insecurities. They are for yourself, maybe your close friends. Don't parade those in public because you will only harm yourself. Because you don't know if the person asking you has any genuine, accurate opinion of what happened on that stage. They might not have even been in the room. All they might have to go on is what you said. If what you said is just a list of your insecurities about it, that's what will be their impression in that show report or whatever it is. It's not just the show manager. It applies to whoever. So they told me to lie.

PART FOUR

Lifestyle

How living on the road changes your life, and why painters and novelists don't sleep in a different town each night.

DEBORAH FRANCES-WHITE: I was in a cult when I was a teenager; a cult that said I would never die because Armageddon would come and I would live forever in a paradise earth. I left it because I came to the realization that I was going to die and that I had better do something with the one life I had to live. Since then I've always juggled quite a lot in my career. I say yes to almost everything to make up for lost time and because I'm acutely aware of my own mortality. I can always tell when someone else knows they're going to die, usually because they've been in an accident or very ill. I heard a story once that Mark Watson, who does incredible marathon stand-up shows and writes novels and all sorts of crazy things, was complaining that he was tired. So Tim Minchin asked him why he didn't cut back and he replied it was because he'd had a feeling for a long time that he'd die young, so he wanted to get as much as possible done. Tim asked Mark if he'd considered the reason he might die young is that he was working himself into an early grave.

No matter how you approach stand-up it will probably affect your health. You're a shift worker. You have to travel a lot. You're away from your home, your family and your pets – all the things that happiness metrics tell us matter. You don't see as much daylight as other people. You probably drink too much because you mostly work in bars and after your set is done, you want a drink to come down. I rarely smoke except at the Edinburgh Festival, where I poison myself with cigarettes. My doctor asked me if I smoke and I replied, 'Only after gigs,' and she said, 'Oh my god – if you do stand-up comedy, of course you need to smoke! That must be so stressful.' I'm not sure that's the official NHS line, but it is what she said.

There are people who let it kill them and there are people who just look a bit pale and ill and there are people who counteract it with water and running. There are people who are perpetually single. There are people who constantly cheat on their partners and there are people who insist the whole family come on tour. I don't think there are really any answers, except your own. You know how much your own home means to you. You know how hard it is to leave your dog. You know whether your boyfriend will quit his job and look after a baby in a tour van if you hit the big time.

Gigging is fun if it's local and infrequent, but if you want to make a real go of it, at some point you'll have to go on the road and I think that's probably a lot of fun if you're a guy under 25. Some day it'll get easier because you'll get a TV show or you'll start writing sitcoms or you'll do more corporates which are better paid or you'll get a voice-over agent. Or it won't, so you'll stop and get a proper job. Or you'll die cold, empty and alone in a Premier Inn on the M6. But if that happens, you'll die unaccountably happy because it was the only choice you could have made. And you might even get a two-line mention on Chortle, even if they do spell your name with an 'i' instead of an 'e'.

STEPHEN K AMOS

I've never been one of these comics who have just been driven for success. Maybe because I didn't come into this wanting to be A Comedian. I did it by chance, really. I didn't plan to be a comedian. When I started, they didn't have all these comedy shows you can get on, panel shows that will make you a star. I was quite happy doing a room above a pub for fifty people and having a laugh and seeing what happened.

But now there are people who come into this who are being groomed for stardom, people who are on a mission, people who are quite ruthless in their approach, and maybe that's where I should be because I could be bigger than I am if I was more ruthless.

That's fine, because there's a lot of us in this playing field and you pick who you want. You pick who you're drawn to and as long as there are racist issues in the world, I will still talk about racism. As long as there still is injustice in terms of sexuality and homophobia and intolerance, I will still talk about that.

For many working comedians, gigging is a huge part of their life. Many, like Neal Brennan, aim to perform almost every single night.

NEAL BRENNAN

My friend Dov Davidoff, a comedian, said stand-up is the only thing in the world that if you don't do it for twenty-four hours, you get rusty. One of the analogies that I always think of is that stand-up is like being a lion tamer and you just got to be around lions, man. If you're not around, the audience can sense that – 'We can attack! We can take this motherfucker!' So you have to be more used to it than they are. You have to be, 'I'm here. All I do is stand-up.' My brother made the observation that the thing with stand-up is, if you do it enough, you will be comfortable on stage and uncomfortable at the grocery store.

It makes me laugh how comfortable I am on stage. It makes me laugh how I can wake up from a dead sleep and someone will say, 'You're on in a minute'. I would be like, 'OK'. I'm just used to it.

Orny Adams believes that he has to be physically fit to survive the rigours of performing his show frequently.

ORNY ADAMS

When I do my hour, I spend so much energy that after a weekend of doing it, I could be in bed for a few days. To me, comedy is very physical. I think performing is physical. I think even if you're standing in front of microphone and not moving, it is physical. I've studied these chess masters. They talk about how chess is physical and how they work out to stay in shape so they are in chess-shape. And to me, that's what you have to do. Sometimes, before my show, I do yoga in the green room. I have to go upside down just to get to that place.

So, I work out really hard. I think I got that originally from Mick Jagger who would run twenty miles the day of a show. You've got to be in that sort of cardio shape. You've got to have that body and breath control. And I find it more taxing as I get older, which is something new. If I'm doing an hour, at about thirty minutes I slow it down a little, catch my breath and then continue on.

For some comedians, being on stage is almost like a drug.

NAT LUURTSEMA

The problem with me in stand-up is that I love stand-up, I love being on stage, but I can't take the loneliness, the isolation. I've done it for seven years now. From pretty early on in my career I went pro. Not that I was existing particularly well off it, but it was my full-time job from six months in. That's six-and-a-half years of driving all over the country all by myself. It breaks me and makes me depressed. It makes me so lonely. It's not really a life.

But I still think there's nothing more exciting or sexy to me than the whole room under my control. I love when I make them laugh. When a gig is going well and I'm in charge, that's the best I ever feel. It's the calmest I ever feel. It's weird when people ask, 'Aren't you terrified being on stage?' No, no, no. That makes sense to me. It's all the difficult worries and stresses of life that are backstage with you. I can't handle them. As soon as I've got on stage I've only got one thing to concentrate on. As soon as the gun goes, it's just about winning that race. You can worry about everything else later. You have one goal now and that's what you have to do. That's what I like. That calms me down.

Roseanne Barr feels the same thing even more strongly.

ROSEANNE BARR

> Roseanne Barr was already a hugely popular stand-up comedian in the USA before her self-titled sitcom starting in 1988 gave her worldwide fame. When the show ended in 1997, Roseanne wrote books, hosted a talk show and returned to stand-up in 2005, playing her first-ever UK gig in Leicester, England.

Here's another thing I love about comedy: as a woman, I don't have any place to force my will on people, so I do it on stage. I've had nine to fifteen thousand people or more, and to be one lone being controlling that room with nothing but your own body, your mind and a mic is high, spiritual shit.

Comedy is a spiritual act, really. You give the audience something, they take it, and they leave something behind for you. It's a perfect exchange.[1]

While gigging in the evenings can impact on your social life, it's usually going out on tour which changes a comedian's lifestyle the most. For some, it's a grind; for others, it can be the most rewarding part of the job. But for almost all, it takes quite a lot of adjusting to.

MARK WATSON

I quite enjoy the actual process of touring in some ways. I quite like going to new parts of the country, although there now aren't many human habitations in this country where I've not done a show. What I don't enjoy about the adventure of touring is that your real life goes to hell a bit. If you're away from home for most of the week, you obviously don't see

---

[1] Taken from *Satiristas*, op. cit.

your family as much, so then you get in trouble. Your bills mount up, your paperwork. Basically, it's not a very functional way to live as a human.

So you can only do it so much. I've been touring almost perpetually for about five years now. It has been good from a career point of view but it's not an easy thing to combine with actually living a normal life.

It's not easy to keep material fresh if you're repeating it forty or fifty times, pretty much on consecutive nights. But every audience is seeing it for the first time. So you have a real responsibility to make sure that each show feels as fresh as the first one was. It's easier for me than it is for some people because my style is quite sort of shambolic anyway. So, to some extent, it looks like I never really know what I'm doing anyway, which is has its drawbacks but it's quite handy in terms of keeping material spontaneous, because I always seem as if I'm just going off on one. I very often look as if I don't have a plan. And of course, sometimes I actually don't have a plan. I build in quite a bit of improvising and try to play with the audience. As much as anything else, to keep it interesting for me.

Alex Edelman sees very little of his family since his move to London from America in May 2014, but his parents have been very supportive.

ALEX EDELMAN

I think my parents are thrilled, actually. On the most superficial level because, you know, they're professionals. My mom is a lawyer with, like, four advanced degrees, and my father is one of the smartest professors – he has joint tenure at both Harvard and MIT, I'm crazy proud of them. And they're really intelligent people but they want their kids to do something a little unique and I think their goals as parents have actually changed a little bit to make sure that their kids are happy and able to do what they want to do.

We had this big discussion before I left for London – I just dropped everything in May and moved to get ready for Edinburgh. I had to have this big sit-down with my parents where I'm like, 'Look, I'm gonna drop all my copywriting work and script-writing work and freelance work and just go and try to write this show in London and I'm gonna be away for a long time and I don't know what my financial or health situation's gonna be…' I'd never had to have a conversation with my parents where I'd said, 'Look, in four or five months I might be calling to ask you for money'. They were so cool about it. I was almost ashamed, honestly. They have been so supportive that it's almost a joke.

Having family that's supportive of stand-up is the new having a father that doesn't support your stand-up. Everyone I know who's a young comedian, their parents are cool with it. And the people who have parents who aren't cool with it are now the rarity. This is the twenty-first century. If your kid wants to do stand-up that's not an issue any more. There are people who sit all day and search for fucking YouTube videos.

I do try not to work on Friday nights. I think my parents would rather I didn't. I know that sounds so weird. And I'm not more observant than when I started doing stand-up, I'm just observant of different things. I try to put on these things called tefillin every day, which is like these Jewish prayer boxes. My parents aren't psyched at me working on Friday nights and other comedians I know who are Jewish aren't psyched with me working on Friday nights, but they understand what it is and they understand who I am.

The practical issues of getting to and from the gig also create tricky situations for some people.

SARA PASCOE

I really like touring. I don't like the car journey, so I get the train. In a car, it just tends towards negativity. And it doesn't matter who you put together. People bond over who they don't like or who they don't think deserves what they've got and that's really negative, especially before a gig. And if you've driven there, it means you have to drive back which means that one of you will not have done well, or as well as the others, and then that's an awkward drive.

If you've had a bad gig and someone else had a brilliant gig, you can't blame the audience. You can't say, 'I thought they were stupid, horrible people', because for someone else they were the perfect audience. Also, I'm very lucky, and I'm in a position that some – people who have been going a lot longer than me – would say wasn't fair, or that I'd got it very easily or very quickly. So there are certain gigs that I think, 'I really hope this is okay, just so that that person who I know doesn't rate me doesn't have another reason not to'. People love it if they think your career's going better than theirs, but then they do better than you at gigs.

The tour schedule can mess with a comedian's head – on stage and off stage.

ROBIN INCE

I've got really used to spending time on my own. And there are little moments of madness, and there are times you want home comfort, and there are times that you think, 'I don't want to leave the house now, I don't want to be on tour the whole time'. But once you compare it to a lot of people's existence, to have a job that you have chosen to do and that you like to do and that you have control over is a rarity. You only have to go to a party filled with people who have very normal jobs and listen to what they say and listen to their priorities and what they have to do for their boss, and you go, 'No, this is good. This is better.'

But some people would prefer that anyway. There are those who would know that they have to do something and they have to do it a fixed time. Some people like pattern. I don't. I like to go, 'What the hell am I doing now?' Someone the other day in my gig said, 'We'll come and see you in Bedford'. I said, 'When am I in Bedford?' They said, 'You don't know?' I said, 'Of course I don't know. I know where I am tomorrow. I know I'm getting on a train to Newton Abbott tomorrow. I've no idea after that. Because each day I wake up and look and go, "Oh right, I'm going there next".'

You then have that thing where there *is* a certain routine in that once you go on stage, you may go off on tangents, but there is the routine that you have to constantly find laughter here and here and here and here, and the amount your brain works. Brains use an enormous amount of glucose and energy and all of these things, when you're standing on stage and having to go through all those ideas. You know, sometimes you have about five different things going on at once in your head? And then every now and then you have a moment when you almost freeze because you realize, you go beyond instinct. You think, 'What am I doing? I'm standing in front of these people, I'm saying these things. But I've just realized where my head is. I've realized what I'm looking like. This is preposterous.'

Some comedians limit their touring, but others, like Moshe Kasher…

MOSHE KASHER

I tour pretty constantly. It's lonely and it could be boring. It could be frustrating.

If I go to a place, a cool city, I come to somewhere like London, then it's great! I have friends here. It's a swinging place. I go to somewhere like middle-of-nowhere America – and I'm sure the same is true for middle-of-nowhere England – it's just like you're in a mall parking lot and a hotel. You trudge across the mall parking lot from the hotel to get into the mall to go to the Panera Bread and have a cup of soup. That's your big moment.

Robin Ince feels he is just making up for lost time.

ROBIN INCE

I think it's partly down to boredom threshold. It's never in terms of financial ambition or ambition of celebrity, I just like doing lots of different things.

Like a lot of comedians, I also I spent a lot of time in my twenties not doing very much. You sit around and then you go and do your gig and you count that as a day's work – standing on a stage for twenty minutes. So, really, probably since my late twenties in particular, I've felt that I should be making up for lost time of laziness.

Life is finite, as far as I'm concerned. Get on with it. So that's one of the things. I like nearly all the things I do. There are some that make no money whatsoever, but that's never my first priority. The reason I sometimes do four shows a day in Edinburgh is because I have the opportunity to be somewhere where you can put on four different shows. And probably then go off and do shows with your mates as well in the evening or whatever.

And you know, if you can, and you have lots of things in your head, then you might as well turn them into things. So whether it's me reading the letters of Richard Feynman one moment or shouting topless with Michael Legge in an angry show the next, or doing stand-up about Charles Darwin after that – you know, while you've got the opportunity, go for it.

I was in a big car accident when I was three years old. Maybe it's that. For my autobiography I'll work back and find the most exciting narrative for sales purposes. I think I've always been – since the age of seven or eight – aware of mortality. But most of the people I know who do a lot of work know that they're inherently lazy. So the only way of not being lazy is by doing far too much. So therefore they become workaholics precisely because of their utter laziness.

For many, while the travelling and the hotel rooms are a grind, the opportunity to bring their material to new audiences is a joy.

NATHAN CATON

All the travelling stuff is annoying but when you go on stage, you kind of forget about all that. It makes it worthwhile.

Sometimes, I change my set around. So if I start with something, I might end with it the next night just so I don't get bored of saying it, because there have been points when I've done that certain joke so many times that while I'm saying it I feel like, 'OK. This shitless piece of crap again. Yeah, here we go, blah, blah, blah, the same punchline. Boom!'

Also, I read a lot of papers when I'm travelling so I'm trying to have some topical stuff. Or if I'm in a certain town and I'm there for a while, I might walk around, trying to get some material about that place just so it feels fresh. Not just to the audience but to me as well when I'm performing it because you have to like what you perform, otherwise it will sound dead. So I'll just do some jokes about the town or something like a topic on the news.

When I did my own tour, before every gig I would get there early, walk around, and then buy a local newspaper and look for some bizarre news – because every town has got something bizarre that goes on. There was one town where someone was stealing dairy products from the local supermarket. Who does that? Who thinks, 'I'm going to steal some cheese today. I'm a gangster. I want mozzarella and parmesan.' You also sometimes meet people who know weird facts about the place you're in. And that can give you some comedy gold.

And, of course, touring provides an income for comedians who have got past the tens and twenties in comedy clubs but who haven't yet developed lucrative TV and movie careers.

RICHARD HERRING

At the moment it's how I earn most of my money because most of the other things I do are for free. The tours and the DVD and previewing is how I basically make most of my money. I might write some scripts and do few TV bits and pieces but it's mainly the touring. I mean, I've done solo tours now, pretty much every year for the last twelve years and they've gotten bigger and bigger.

I usually tour completely on my own. I don't have the support acts and I don't have a tour manager. So it's very solitary. If you're in a darkish place, it's kind of depressing. I'm glad the way it has happened because I've had – as a solo act especially – to build up from very small audiences. I'm now getting 300, 400, sometimes 700 or 800 people come to see me in places, which is fantastic.

When you're touring around, driving hundreds of miles and thirty people come to see you, that's quite hard. But also when you're driving around and 500 people come to see you and then they will go home and you have to go back to your little Premier Travel Inn on your own, it's a massive bumpy comedown. Now, I find it quite amusing but seven years ago, I was finding it very solitary and quite hard.

If you are combining TV work with touring, you face another interesting challenge – how much material can you repeat?

TODD BARRY

The reality is, if you do a TV special and then you go do a show somewhere, the chance is probably 2 per cent of the people have seen the special and half of those people don't care if you repeat the joke. It's just the occasional guy and a blog or Twitter, someone that has expectations. Also people get things just wrong. You could do thirty minutes of new material and three old jokes and someone will say, 'I've heard everything you've done before'. It's like, well, there's no way you had heard everything I had done before unless you saw me in New York within the past two months or something.

It's nice when people want to hear something, but even if someone said, 'I want to hear this joke, and this joke, and this joke', and I just said, 'Well, I just did an hour of new material. Did you enjoy it?' 'Yes.' Well then, you can't lose. But you can also only write as fast as you can write.

Apart from the local comedy circuit and going out on tour, the other opportunity which comedians have to perform is at festivals. But not all festivals are equal.

SAM WILLS

We've got one comedy festival in New Zealand. It's a wonderful festival, but at our festival, when you do a show, your season is four days. That's normally the thing. So that's the longest run you do, four or five days. Then, at the end of that four or five days, you go into development for your next year's show!

I developed my show in New Zealand and I got it up and running to an hour long, then made it work for there. Then I took it to Australia and I toured it for three festivals over there, running it out, making sure it worked. And I got promoters to see it over there who I knew were from Edinburgh, so when it came to me going to the venue of what I wanted to go to Edinburgh, there were all in Adelaide picking over who wanted to see the show, who wanted to be at the show. Then it was up to us to decide who we wanted to go with.

I saw a lot of others people's mistakes from Edinburgh, people who were coming back going, 'I lost a lot of money and I got a three-star review and nobody knew who I was'. I think for me that was the thing, nobody knew who you were. So many people come here doing shows and it's like nobody knows of you.

So by the time it got to me coming to Edinburgh to do a show, I was already known on the circuit enough that people were going, 'Finally, you're bringing your show. I can now tell people about it.' I already had a word-of-mouth behind me, which is the key.

The Edinburgh Fringe is the largest arts festival in the world and is a hugely important showcase, especially for UK comedians, where a successful Edinburgh run can create a career.

ANDREW MAXWELL

The gag that I always say is that it's exam time for clowns. You've got to get an MOT every year for your car. It's all too easy to let your sharpness as a performer slide. And here you're not allowed to slide. Simple as that. You can't win the league by only playing home gigs.

It gets bigger every year. That's a good thing. It's got so big that there's different divisions. If it hadn't have gotten as big at the top end, there wouldn't be room for a Free Fringe level to exist. It's great that one year somebody can make a name for themselves on the Free Fringe, then get into the more established venues.

The thing I like about Edinburgh is you can be found here. That's why the bigwigs do show up because people really are discovered here, as opposed to Montreal. It's a great place to be, Montreal, but I wouldn't go there thinking you're going to get a deal out of it.

Overseas comedians may not know quite what to expect, coming to the Edinburgh Fringe for the first time.

TODD BARRY

I've done it twice. It's one of those mixed bag things. It is pretty rough. First time I did it, I did a full month. Then the second time I did it, two weeks. Second experience was a little better.

Waking up every day and wondering what a 23-year-old has written about you who doesn't even understand what kind of show you're doing. People who are just pointing out there are empty chairs. That's like, well, yeah. I didn't say I was going to sell out every twenty-five shows. So shitheads like that.

So there's that and you wonder who's going to be there and whether they're going to get you. But as I got a little more well-known, I would actually get real fans showing up.

Last time I was there, I did a 3.00 p.m. show, put on by the guys at The Stand who are great people and everyone likes dealing with them. But still, it wasn't like packed houses. It's just kind of a grind really.

I think it's a great thing to do. I think it reinvigorates your act – because there's people over here who have just been doing the same thing over and over again or just start to get a little fed up with the States and then you go, 'Why don't you go to Edinburgh where you have a clean slate?' and they don't even know you or they might not know you, and start over basically, but with the skills you've had for doing comedy for as long as you have.

Alex Edelman moved to the UK in order to bring a show to the Edinburgh Fringe, but not because he wanted to crack the lucrative UK market in particular.

ALEX EDELMAN

For me, what prompted the move was the fact that you guys let comedians do an hour, and there wasn't really an outlet for me to get on stage all of the time for an hour. I must have previewed my Edinburgh show thirty times. That's thirty hours of stand-up comedy and I was doing sometimes three hours a week leading up to the festival. And then when I got to Edinburgh I must have done more than a hundred shows, because I have a hundred recordings I need to listen to still. That's stage time that is not available in the US. And my perspective on it as a US comedian is that it puzzles British comics a little bit. Because for me, I don't think the obligation of a stand-up is different in a five-minute spot or an hour-long spot. Sure, you've stretched your legs with longer bits in a hour-long spot but your laughs-per-minute should still be the same. Your dedication to writing strong punchlines should be the same. So for me it was just an artistic opportunity that I could not pass up.

Daniel Sloss told me that he thinks that one month of the Edinburgh Festival is equivalent to two years on the circuit because for most comedians it is. Thirty hours of stand-up comedy. That is so much more than you get in your first two years. You're a different comedian by the end of it.

Some comics choose Edinburgh as a way to avoid the club circuit.

SEAN HUGHES

In 1990, Sean Hughes became the youngest person to win the Perrier Award. Two series of *Sean's Show* on Channel 4 established his status as one of the most important figures in the booming alternative comedy scene of the 1990s. He went on to spend six years as a team captain on *Never Mind the Buzzcocks*, write three books, and land acting parts that included roles in *Agatha Christie's Marple* and *Coronation Street.*

I still don't like club comedy. I've never liked it. It's kind of speed dating, really, isn't it? Four (usually white) guys talking about sex and drinking escapades and the like. I just felt that wasn't really what I wanted to do and I just started developing ideas and I wanted to say things.

I found when I came to Edinburgh, I thought, 'Oh my god, this is where people actually develop ideas'. It's not about getting a TV show. It's properly developing stuff.

My third year, when I won the Perrier, was with *One Night Stand,* where I was one of the first to do a kind of theme show. I wanted to have the arc where there's a beginning and an end. Before that, people were just doing two club sets and stringing it together. I just thought, 'No, this is so much better'. That was the first time I felt, 'This is me, this is exactly what I want to do'. And because I wasn't confident, I just thought that if this didn't work out I would probably stop doing comedy because I didn't like the clubs that much. That was a wise decision and everything just went big after that.

Edinburgh also means you get reviewed. Usually, a lot. And the reviews you get in local and national papers may not bear much resemblance to the reaction you get from the crowd. Andrew Maxwell has a class theory about the difference between a reviewer and a typical audience member for one of his shows.

ANDREW MAXWELL

Working-class people and middle-class people come around to a comedy show. They'll both laugh. But it's all about afterwards, the drinking in the bar afterwards.

Working-class people will get the round of drink in. Two couples, the two lads who've known each other from school and their wives get on great. This is all they have to say: 'Ah that was fuckin' great.' 'What he fuckin' said to that fuckin' fireman.' 'Who wants a drink?' Conversation closed. Everybody's happy. The evening goes on. They're delighted. Maybe, 'Round of of applause for Bridgette. It was your idea to get the fuckin' tickets in the first place.' Anyway, great evening.

As part of middle-class culture, people have to talk. Working-class people talk but they don't *have* to talk. The middle-class people will leave the gig and if you haven't set thoughts and pieces and ideas, within the show, constructs and ideas for them to take away, they have nothing to talk about. In television it's called, 'What's the takeaway from this show?' 'Interesting. It's a very good point he made about that, actually. I never really thought about that about Scottish independence. He's clever. I wonder if he'll get any flak off duh, duh, duh for that?'

But if you leave middle-class people just going, 'Yeah he's funny. He's funny', and they have nothing to say, they'll instantly feel stupid. And if you make the middle classes feel stupid, they will despise you. They don't mean to. It's just – who else is to blame? Somebody's got to be blamed and that's what I'm getting from reviewers.

The extraordinary disconnect is if you're an improviser. You go, 'I made everybody laugh their bollocks off for an hour, spun gold out of fuckin' air. How is this three fucking stars four days before the festival ends?' Because you haven't given them anything to talk about, it's a giant cultural chasm.

Sara Pascoe marvels at the difference between an Edinburgh Fringe audience and an audience almost anywhere else in the world.

SARA PASCOE

Edinburgh is completely different in terms of audiences. You would never, ever anywhere else have to have an audience who's already seen three shows that day – or five shows that day, depending on what time you're on. It changes people. When people brag to me like, 'We're seeing ninety shows in four days!', I think, 'Well, then you've done everyone a disservice, because you're not even giving yourself a coffee break afterwards to take in what's happened'.

It's the same for reviewers. A reviewer in your show will have seen 200 shows in the entire festival. How can anyone's judgement be what it would be if they'd seen one thing and allowed it to actually percolate and affect them? My theory is that people who have audience interaction always do well at the awards – people who get people up on stage. People like Adam Riches or Dr Brown or The Boy With Tape On His Face. Because it doesn't matter how many shows you've seen, an old lady being got up on stage and made to do a dance is always going to be hysterical. If you have become desensitized, something like that will break you out of it and you'll think, 'That's the only show I laughed in'. Everything else just becomes words thrown at you.

Edinburgh is a trade show, so your show is the product. And Edinburgh is asking, 'How can we market it? Who are we selling it to? Who wants to buy it?' And that's what the whole star-rating thing is as well. We don't write for reviewers. We write to entertain people because we think we've got something that might be universal, or if not universal then at least really mean something to some people. And a reviewer does not fit in that category. But the judgement thing is just a tax you pay so that more people can hear what you have to say.

Why, then, do people become comedians? Sometimes, even they don't seem to know.

PHILL JUPITUS

I wish that I had gone to uni still but I think if I had I wouldn't be doing what I'm doing now. What I've done is… I think I've got a very odd personality and I found a way of monetizing it.

Phill Jupitus talks to Eddie Izzard

Eddie Izzard is one of the most popular stand-up comedians in the world, known for his rambling, improvisational style and surreal flights of fancy. He notably shunned British television, building his reputation in clubs and theatres, but now can be seen on *QI* and other shows. He has also worked as a dramatic actor in many film and television projects, including a starring role in *The Riches* and appearances in *Ocean's Twelve* and *Thirteen,* and has plans to run for public office in the future.

PHILL JUPITUS: How you been anyway, what you been doing?

EDDIE IZZARD: I just came back from Spanish class.

Oh yeah! So, the gigs in Spanish…

Yeah, so I did twelve minutes by the end of it. I worked out a way with my brother, he's the language expert. He translates all the shows but, also, he chooses German, French or Spanish that I can do. There's sort of a very advanced way of speaking, the equivalent of saying, 'So I calculated the interference that might be caused by my consternation'. You know, to have that in a sentence in your stand-up, rather than, 'I worked out that this would cause trouble'. You know the difference between those two sentences? So he'll go into the ones that are much more grab-able. It was weird the first time I got a script, because my stuff is all so fluid, like yours is. Do you ever write your stuff down?

Well no, funnily enough, I've been archiving, I found some written-down bits and I found an old recorder today. Remember, you used to walk in the park? And I remember you telling me the first way you used to write was going for long walks and recording it. I found an old recorder with really nascent ideas of stuff from five years ago.

It was because I only found out on the move. When I was in a flow I could hit stuff. Whereas if I went to writing it, it wasn't going as fast as my brain and I wasn't in the zone. 'So what's up… with… pigeons…

why… full stop.' And that wasn't hitting anything. In sketches I could write that way, but stand-up I couldn't, so that's why I was walking round doing it.

I saw Second City in Toronto doing their thing, and they do this set show which is an hour twenty or something. But then at the end of it, they do half an hour of spitballing, of improv, but there's a woman at the back recording and writing shit down, and that forms the basis of the next show, all the bits that come out. I didn't realize this was the way that they worked. Imagine if someone had been annotating the Comedy Store players for the last thirty years, the stuff that they would have – the keepers!

In stand-up, we have no end. We have no denouement in a stand-up show. All we can do is take the pace up and go on a rant and then say, 'That's all from me tonight!' or you say, 'I'm gonna finish up with…' You know, it's quite difficult to get closure after lots of little bits. A bit like rock and roll, they have these three-minute, four-minute, five-minute numbers, and you end up with all these little bits. Then you come back on for the encore, you do three, then you come back on and you do one, and there's some sort of set thing.

I find that in my stand-up, if you have the characters that have turned up, and if I got them all to come back in the final scene, then it actually feels like an end. So I try and always get people who have turned up during it that are interesting to turn up at the end and say things. I think it started with *Definite Article*. It was the big bang, god lights a firework, and all the characters were there, reacting to the fireworks or something like that. Then there was a salmon at the end.

So I constantly get them back in. I was doing that in *One Word Improv*, I was saying at the break, 'What characters did we like in the first half? Shall we try and get them back in the second half?'

Improv is just people writing down stuff, but without writing it. Talking down stuff. It's all the same thing. You can do that in drama, you know; you could get up and just get some people dramatically improvising and then saying, 'Johnny just killed his own brother… go!' and then see what they get out of that. 'Do we like it? When she came in, what was she about? What the fuck was the reason for that?' You could use it either way. But it is interesting that all creativity comes from that, and music is that way, people jamming and then you like this bit of a sound or we like that bit of a sound…

I got addicted to the improv thing with the show I did with Deborah Frances-White, Voices In Your Head, where there's an offstage director. You should do it, you'd love it! Four people on the stage and you're called out one at a time and it's like, 'So you're Mexico's leading budgie expert' – 'Yees, oh yees this ees true.' And you're asked a question by her and then she sort of directs but you build the character as well. And I did this with her and we really, really got on well.

As a show or a developing show?

Yeah, we did it as a show. The characters are on stage and she's offstage in the dark. We can't see her, she's just literally the voice, through speakers. Then she did that with me on my own, so no supporting cast at all, an hour of me on stage and she made me be different people. We had a rack at the side of the stage just with different jackets and hats, and we did that in Edinburgh for a month and it was just, the chaos of it, the up and the down, some of the best moments I've ever had on stage, in that show. She knows that there's a painting I really like by John Singer Sargent called Lady Agnew of Locknaw. She got an actress to play Lady Agnew!

  So what happens is, I don't know what's coming up, I'm told to walk into the room. She tells the audience that they're gonna fuck with me, so the audience shout shit at me and it's stuff where I don't know what's happening. It's a really immersive sort of way of getting stuff out of people. There's something about the solitude of stand-up.

There's something about the solitude of stand-up that's not so great for you?

Well no. What I find is… I can't understand how Lee Evans works, for example. I really respect that he's this machine. It's that: do the huge show; take six months off; then do the next show; take six months working it up; tour it; DVD; repeat. Literally, that engine room of just doing that, you know.

Figure 9 Eddie Izzard © Idil Sukan/Draw HQ

No I couldn't do it like that.

And he writes as well.

I mean I should write. Last time I was working with Sarah Townsend. She was reacting to stuff and saying, 'Why don't you change this? That's a good thing. No, you've repeated that before so dump that. Head in that direction. Keep that. Stronger characterization.' She was very tough on me and I would do the characters but they all had the same voices and she would say, 'Make them distinctive'. As soon as I did, in fact, they would come alive, it was very interesting.

But this is what I'm wondering, about the language thing. Is that to make you almost start again?

Well, in a way, I know it keeps me on my toes. It means that I must be battling hard if I'm going into Germany, France, Spain. The way I've created it, and I've put subtitles on the DVDs for about ten years now, which doesn't perfectly work. And now my brother's started examining the subtitles. Some haven't been written exactly correctly or they've got the wrong end of the stick or they won't put the bad swear words in that I want.

Really?

They ignore the bad swear words, they do light ones. So, that doesn't really matter, the English ones is what they all really wanted in the end. The French people wanted the French subtitles, but they wanted to check on certain words. But it does make you start at ground level to an extent. It makes you work really hard.

You know, I've been trying to do this universal comedy so I talk about dinosaurs, gods, food. You can talk about everything, it's just your references can't be British. That's the only thing that I've actually blocked. And sayings and puns, they go out the window. Actually when I'm creating, when I'm on stage, I'll go, 'That's a good idea!' For instance, I thought to show how Hitler was to the Germans, with an Austrian accent, that was a bit like someone coming in with, say, a Yorkshire accent who was an extremist to everyone in Yorkshire. 'Hey, y'know, why don't we murder everyone? Just bloody murder all these people. We don't like 'em so let's just kill 'em', with that kind of Tetley's voice. But that wouldn't work outside Britain. So that came into my head and I put it to one side.

When I interviewed you before for Time Out *[in 1997], you'd just done Sean Connery in France and you were really bemused as to why the Sean Connery bit wasn't working out.*[2]

It was a French guy saying it didn't make any sense. Whereas for the bilingual people it was fine. Initially my audiences were at least 80 per cent bilingual. In the end in Germany it was 95 per cent German as the mother language and down to 5 per cent English speakers. The further afield you go, the more it doesn't really matter. In Romania it was all Romanians probably and a smattering of English people. So it definitely keeps you on your toes.

But it is political beneath it, like people saying Europe is terrible and horrible and I hate Europe. But I'm saying, 'Look, you know if it's there, you can actually earn money out of it, you can actually develop things, you can develop bonds, bridges between countries'. That's my positive way of looking at it, but it's actually business. I can now play for the whole of Germany, Austria, German part of Switzerland. I can play for the whole of France and into the French part of Switzerland. Spanish, I get Spain and the whole of South America. It's actually good business sense, so there's a number of things going on, but creativity is at the bottom of it and this positivity thing. Spain loves it, the French love it and the Germans love it. So, it just means that I'm not on the machine thing. I'm on this experimental, out there thing. And it also makes gigs in English fucking easy.

So, if you've spent a month or whatever away in Paris, then suddenly you come over here…?

Hollywood Bowl came after Paris. It was three months in Paris in French, then four gigs on the roof of the De La Warr Pavilion in Bexhill, to do the outdoor gig…

---

[2]Eddie's act included an impression of Sean Connery, the humour of which was entirely lost on an audience who had only ever heard him dubbed into French.

On the roof?

Yeah, on the roof. Because if the Beatles had lived in Bexhill that's what they would've done, that's what I say. And then I did the Hollywood Bowl. So that was my training. And that was like altitude training really, because you're doing gigs in French, that altitude of brain work. Then the gigs in English in the Hollywood Bowl are just walk out there and talk.

I'm interested in the kinks that might happen. Do you start talking too much, too many ideas suddenly, if you're back in English, after doing two months in French?

No you're just as calm as a cucumber. The gig at Hollywood Bowl was just… the Greeks got it right, the amphitheatre does work.

I did one on my last tour, and it was roasting hot and we were losing people, because I was doing three-part shows and in the intervals, people started shipping out. In the middle I was like, 'Look, you're either not getting it or you're really hot'. And they went, 'We're really fucking hot'. And I said, 'I tell you what, why don't we do the last bit outside?' and they went, 'Yay!' and none of them left and I just had to shout a lot outside!

There was another thing I definitely wanted to talk to you about, which was the scale of comedy now. I was talking to Jack Dee about this, about optimum size of audience, and the figure we hit was 500. Enough people for it to have the mob feeling, but small enough crowd for every single person in the room to be able to see your eyes. To see the most imperceptible flicker and by using that logic, we reckon the best venue to do comedy in is City Varieties in Leeds.

Well, you see, Hollywood Bowl was just a fantastic gig and, at the time of doing it, I just thought it could've been a crapper gig. But it felt like a great gig and afterwards people seemed to react to it like it was a great gig.

I've seen people at the gigs there, it's warm and it's beautiful, the weather's amazing. It's like, if Glastonbury had guaranteed sun. So any amphitheatre will work well. I believe the one in Greece, I wanna play there, it's 3,000 and I think that will kill too.

I'll tell you, when you hit Italy you gotta do the Coliseum in Verona. If you're ever holidaying over there, go see some opera there, because it's a proper Roman coliseum.

I saw Aïda *there and there was the most amazing thing that happened. There was a storm, so we sat there in fucking rain macs. It was curtain-up time and just pissing it with rain, lightning, everything. Just people sat there, and they said, 'We'll give it an hour and a half for the rain to stop. We've spoken to the met in Italy and they say it's gonna roll out', and it did. But the storm went behind the stage. So the storm went away, we were watching the show and the storm's moving away from us. So when* Aïda *started, there's a fucking full storm going on behind it, full lightning and everything.*

Well, yeah the Greeks got it right. Isn't that interesting? The Greeks got it right way back when, and we've just been trying to undo the wheel, and if you go back to it, everything should really be an amphitheatre.

Yeah, yeah, yeah. But every space politicians have to speak is based on an amphitheatre. If you think about Congress… er, Parliament isn't, Parliament is confrontation, it's people facing each other. The physicality of our Parliament, I think, may have done us down.

Well, it doesn't seem to affect anyone, because they're gridlocked in Congress and they've got an amphitheatre, so it doesn't really help.

I suppose not.

I mean, in the end, it's political systems, I think. It's not that that system is wrong, it's just human beings. I'm just now looking into financial training. Michael Lewis has this book out about what the trade is doing, where they're going. You say, 'I want that stuff, buy that stuff'. When you press 'Buy', through the computer systems that they have, they come and say, 'What about that stock?' 'OK, I'll buy it first.' But they nip in and buy the thing before you've bought it [so they can sell it to you at a higher price]. What the fuck? And they think this is OK, because they're all rocket scientists, all the cleverest people in the world.

I need to know stuff before I go to politics because I came from accounting and financial management. I mean I can do that, passed my accounting exams without even working on them. But I had As in O Levels and A Levels, and then I just got a zero at university.

Whatever systems we come up with, in say politics or maybe finance, laws against being bad finance, humans will sit and work at it, until they twist it round to their advantage. That is what's going on. The decent people are trying to make things go positively and the more twisted people are twisting it to a negative with a black heart. Saying, 'More money for me, less freedom for these kind of things', or stealing it when you're trying to buy it and then selling it back to you at an inflated price.

That's the game. The whole thing has changed. It was about eighteen years ago I spoke to you [for Time Out *magazine], you were working to five-year plans. Did that stick? Did you keep doing that?*

The truth is I'm working on a fifty-year plan that I can change in half an hour. That is the best way to plan. Fifty-year plans are totally adjustable. So you know where you're heading but you can change. Someone can walk in and say, 'This thing has happened', and you go, 'OK, let's cancel this, do that, and do that'. I've had to cancel a tour because a film came up. I had to pay a hundred grand.

So I do plan ahead, but it's certainly adjustable. It's a military thing. If you have a plan and you say, as soon as the battle starts the plan will go all out the window, so you got a direction of a plan, then people can improvise around it. It's what they teach.

Is it easier to keep to the plans with the operations being totally you, with everything coming from you? It's weird because you're the resource, but you're also the captain. You're the ship and the captain of the ship.

That's the thing, and that's why running the marathon last year required…

Marathon singular? I thought there were thirty-six?

Forty-three!

Forty-three!?

But someone's got to do it and someone's got to plan it. Other people did the fine-planning it, but my thing was just run round the country, run to every capital and that's it, quite a simple plan.

I remember at the time thinking that I don't know anyone who's quite as reactive as you. If you have an idea it will be acted on incredibly quickly.

Or incredibly slowly. I had the run idea in 2002 and I ran in 2009. I was trying to find the right time to go because I'm also trying to move things forward in Hollywood and films and then how do I do that when I'm doing this? My idea, my plan for the languages, it was eleven years to get in and do the German one. I told them in 2003 I was coming, and I did it this year, 2014. The French one, I thought of it in about 1996, '97, and I did my first one 2011.

I always thought when my career craps up then I'll back off. I have this whole Clint Eastwood plan. You know Clint Eastwood in *A Fistful Of Dollars,* when the guy who does the coffins puts him in a coffin then gets him out of town, and then he learns to shoot left-handed? I thought that's what I do if my career craps up at some point. I would go off to lick my wounds and I'd go to France and I'd just do [gigs in] French and then I'd go to Germany and that was gonna be my Clint Eastwood learning-to-shoot-left-handed plan.

So, it's almost like a story. Everything's got to be a fun and interesting adventure.

Another thing that's a subtext to the whole chat with you is that we had a chat like this nearly twenty years ago. Have you noticed the change, over the intervening couple of decades? Or have you been driving the ship in the business?

Part of the reason why I did the first arena tour was – why should rock and roll have all the fun and all the venues they want up to stadiums? I mean a shit stadium is a shit gig. But over the intervening period they've worked out how to do stadiums. And you can only get good at something by doing it so that's why I pushed. I wanted to push 'us' all up into that gear. And then suddenly the whole thing of the roadshow going on tour, *Live at the Apollo* going on tour, BBC1, is that all the broadcasters have blocked stand-up on mainstream channels. Not allowed, not allowed, not allowed, oh that's cheap, put it on, put it on.

This is the weird difference of those two things that have happened almost around the same time. I do like having that top end, even though the small gigs can be fun. I like playing both, because the Stones were doing that, so I thought, 'Well I'll do big ones and small ones'. And they actually play the same, if you get good screens. I have a tall one that just does what the small one does, with me on the stage and the big me is the same thing and the audience will be editing. They can zoom in or zoom out with their own eyeballs. And therefore it's still a live gig. In the Hollywood Bowl, we believe the best gig is at the back. We believe in the O2, the best gig is at the back in fact, because you get the whole event and you can see quite clearly what's going on.

I still haven't been to watch comedy in an arena yet.

Well, yeah, I wanted us all to have that, and now we do the most in the world because Americans don't really do arenas, but we should have that top level that we wanted. And we can only get good at it by doing a lot of it.

At that time when we started there were a couple of hundred comics. There are a couple of thousand now easily, I reckon. Especially if you go up to Edinburgh and look at it.

There's always between sixty and eighty venues. The biggest club scene in the world. What Hamburg was for the Beatles, London is for us.

What I found, going away from it then coming back to it again now, is that the way your brain works on stage when you're performing does not change, but I find that I'm less bothered now. I used to be more bothered when I was younger.

On stage?

Yeah, there was more anxiety, there was an anxiety about doing well. And now I'm like, 'If you don't dig it, fuck you, I simply don't care'.

I love it as much as I ever did. I think when it's at its best, stand-up is unbelievable to watch because if someone really opens up, either themselves or an idea that no one has ever thought of, there's nothing like it. I went to see Kitson's show,[3] and he thought, 'Right I want to do a show at the National Theatre that's two hours and seven minutes long where I don't speak'. And the way he did that was by using forty-two tape recorders that he bought online on eBay and secondhand shops and he put chunks of the show and one at a time he plugged them in and turned them on and they did the show, then he'd go out the back get the next one, plug it in, turn it on. And he did that for two hours and ten minutes. It was one of the most unbelievable fucking things I've seen.

And the audience really liked it?

Fuck yeah! Three different narrative strands going on, fucking incredible, and at the end of the gig there were six projectors he'd turn on, with screens showing images, and forty-two tape recorders running chunks of the show that he'd turn on and off from a central plug board. Fucking unbelievable.

I was with Dylan Moran and he brought up the Death Star Canteen and said he'd been listening to it. I said I'd forgotten about the Death Star Canteen and he said, 'Really!?' So I had it on my phone and I listened to it and I thought, it is actually quite funny isn't it? So I went on stage in New York, and I played it to them and they laughed at the same parts that they laughed on the recording. You could just stand there and hold the tape recorder and just do your set that way, and Kitson has just taken that to its logical extreme.

So there's the acting, there's the politics bit, how far is that down the road?

That's 2020. Which means at 2019 I've got to really plan. Well, I've got to start. I'm campaigning, I was campaigning today. So, there's a lot of training to do. You *can* just sort of jump into politics and train on the job.

---

[3] Daniel Kitson's show *Analog.Ue.*

You can, depends how you get elected. But, I've been campaigning since 2008, so this is the first complete cycle of campaigning that I've done.

Is this as an independent?

No, Labour Party. So I've been a member of the Labour Party since 1995 and I'll be going for a Member of Parliament or mayor of London in 2020. There'll be a general and a mayor's election at the same time. The dates are all tied together.

So is there a sense of urgency…

Yeah, the film thing and getting the languages down. Spanish is developing now because I can Skype with my brother. I've got a French gig tonight, I'm putting in the new show, because I'm going to Cologne for the seventieth anniversary of D-Day. And I'm going to do a gig, at seven o'clock I'm going to do an hour in German, and at eight o'clock do an hour in French, then at nine do an hour in English. I've already tried this in Yale University about two weeks ago and it does work. You get a bit scrambled and you tend to swear in the last language you did.

Are they all the same three sets or is it three different sets?

Yeah, it would be *Force Majeure*. *Strip* was the previous show, it was the first one I did. So at the moment, tonight, I am frontloading in the end of *Force Majeure* into the *Strip* show and then finishing off with *Strip* which I've got down to a tee. It's interesting because my French is good enough that I'm looking at the translation… In German I had to get it down to, I can't translate all these words, because I had to learn the whole thing like a play and my German was not good enough. It was survival German. So we wrote the whole thing down, got a transcript from an English show I did, then got that transcripted out. It was like, 'Yeah that's a bit too waffly, what are the exact words you want to say?' So I got it to a script. I had someone at the side of the stage giving me *Zeilen*, which are lines, so, 'Zeile bitte'. So I did that, and it means that the same line will come out in German. So I will say the same thing in the same show, but as I get better and better I can ad-lib around it… In French I can completely ad-lib, but in German, it's very slow.

In Spanish all I can say is what my order is... sugar, I don't know what sugar is. See, my vocabulary is not good, I've only had seven lessons. But I can learn the show. It's an interesting thing. I can learn in German – here's the best example: I learnt the show like a memory trick. Exercise, not trick, exercise. There is comprehension in it, I know what I'm saying, but I can't use them separately in a different sentence.

And meanwhile I'm doing German conversation lessons and then I'm doing German comprehension with memory because you have to remember the words you are doing. And I'm cooking my show like a soufflé; I cook my German language like a soufflé to reach the level of the show. So it's like a building level – my German is on the fourth floor now, my French is about seventh floor and my Spanish is... horrible!

Is there gonna be any more?

Russian!

Russian?

And then Arabic, and then Mandarin Chinese would be after politics or before if I get the system, because I did German in January and doing Spanish now and I got twelve minutes in one week. But also the learning curve is cumulative, so you actually get faster and faster. So I think in a month I could learn the show in Spanish, then I could be performing in Spanish. I could get that in a month and I could work on shows with my brother on Skype and then Russian and then Arabic – we were born in Aden [in Yemen]. So we could go to Cairo, Cairo or Beirut, because Cairo is a bit all over the place at the moment. But Cairo's the place, so it's got to be 'Cairo Egyptian' that I'm learning, so that, even if I go to Beirut, I'd have to learn whatever they're saying on the streets of Cairo. And the swear words are important.

I have this great bit in the Spanish thing. You know lions are so fit. You never see a lion running along saying, 'Oh I've hurt my knee!' And then in English I'm going, 'Go, get him, get him, get him!' and 'get him' in Spanish is '*Conseguir le*!' But they said be careful because '*conseguir le*' in Mexican Spanish means 'fuck him'!

There must be an astonishing amount of goodwill for the effort that you're making at these gigs. And it's also like the tension with the 'Come on, Eddie come on!'

It's hugely positive. This Edinburgh, there was a French guy who did an hour in English, first time ever a French guy has done an hour in English. And then that guy from Russia did an hour in English, first guy to do an hour in English, Francesco De Carlo, Italian, hour in English – and of course Henning Wehn, who kicked the door open with this entire language thing and proved to everyone that Germans do have a sense of humour and even the British will pay money to go see a German do it, which we never thought we'd do.

I think a mainstream comedian could go to France and do it. They'd have to learn French well and then have to check all their local references. It's the references that are the problem, they'd have to check all their references and learn all the new French ones so it would take forever to do it. Whereas if you talk about gods, dinosaurs, pigs with guns, fish taking over the world, you go to Moscow and they go, 'Guns? Guns, yeah OK we know about these things.'

But is the language shift forcing a creative shift as well? Is it making you think of the act in a different way, doing it in a different language?

It's tightening up the act, because there is a certain waffle to my stuff. But there's a danger, so it's nice to have a tight form and a loose form. Some plants, you prune them hard and then they come back strong, and that's what I think everyone should do. Improvise now, build your set, and then hack it back, edit it back and then grow it again and then that will grow stronger, just like the trees. Growing of comedy and growing of trees and pruning is the same thing. Which is an interestingly holistic approach to material.

You phoned me when you'd heard that I'd stopped doing stand-up and you seemed quite irate about that.

I don't know about irate… I was, I was… what's the best way to say it? It's not concerned, it's more… I wanted to point out something – and I did this with Alan Davies as well – that you're both great at what you were doing and if you get off this gladiatorial combat thing that is stand-up… We train like ninjas, we train like mercenaries, you know. You can't just pop back into it, you can have it for the rest of your life. So I just wanted to say that it's a loss to the world if you guys don't do it, if any of the great stand-ups don't do it, it's just a loss to the world.

I am a student of comedy, a student of creativity, a student of energy, and I feel I've got a good heart. I want everyone else to come on because if they're doing really well, it keeps me on my toes. 'Christ what do I have to do?' I met a guy in Hamburg, one gig in Hamburg sold out in two, three days, which means I can tour the whole of Germany. I get to Hamburg and there's this guy there – thin, lean guy just standing at the door, checking in and he sits down, seems to know the people working there. I say, 'Hello' and I realize he's a stand-up and he's come to see me because he does surreal stuff and there's not much surreal stuff in France and there's not much surreal stuff in Germany. Supposedly these countries love Python but they don't do it and I think it's that they have no home-grown Pythons or Goons there. We have the Goons here, which influenced the Pythons, which influenced everything surreal ever after – and they never had that particularly in France and they never had that in Germany. So, they feel that if you do that there's going to be no audience for it, but there *is* an audience in the student population and that's where they need to break through to. So I've persuaded this guy to go to Edinburgh, so then I can tour with him so that we can build up the surreal audience in France and then it will exist.

France doesn't have to think this way. Dada was all across Europe wasn't it?

Yeah completely.

I was gonna say, the interesting one was Yacine.[4] His parents are from Algeria. His parents came to the Olympia.[5] Now the Olympia is a 2,000-seater and it's a cross between Albert Hall classiness and Brixton Academy street-ness. Edith Piaf played there, so did David Bowie, Jimi Hendrix…

---

[4] Yacine Belhousse, a Parisian comic, who supported Eddie at the Olympia show.
[5] A music hall in Paris.

The Clash.

The Clash. You know, a lot of great people. I was playing a 140-seater, this is a 2,000-seater. Antoine de Caunes,[6] who people of Britain know, he came to see me after I'd done three months in 2011. I came back 2012 and I did a couple of gigs just to see where we were and he said, 'You've got to step this up!' And I went, 'OK, well, there's a 350-seater I know, I can come back and play that', and he said, 'No! We go to the Olympia! I know the guy, 2,000-seater, I can get you in there, then we just got to sell the tickets.'

I'd already played one before which was 860 and we'd had to paper[7] half of it because I'd played three months earlier and I'd used up all the goodwill. I thought I had trouble with 860 – how do I get to 2,000?

But what happened was that the French performers and some actors and people who know the grass roots and the cable media and the online media and this kind of thing – not the mainstream media – they sold this for me. They went around saying you got to go see it. It became the thing to go to. We still had thirty tickets to sell on the last day. And I was sitting with French people and British people, 200 years since the Battle of Waterloo, French and Brits working together to sell this show, it's a beautiful thing. And I got up there and I watched Yacine doing his show and his parents are up there watching, they're laughing and they laughed at my stuff as well, which means that an Arabic family is laughing at my stuff, which means Cairo is going to work, and I was sitting down with my brother leaning on this gorgeous place, top floor and I'm looking up, looking across doing like I did back at Edinburgh Festival where I was getting six people a night. And I'm looking at them going, 'I cannot see a single seat not filled, we have sold even the last thirty tickets.'

You know, we'd come a long way and we'd got all this negativity from UKIP and let's pull out and separate and who are these other people? And I'm saying, 'No! We've got to make this work!' If we don't make this one work, we don't learn how to work together, then how the hell is the world supposed to work? If we're all gonna separate off to different places, even Scotland, even though they want to separate

---

[6] French-born presenter of *Eurotrash* on Britain's Channel 4.
[7] In other words, give away free tickets.

they want to stay in Europe – they want to just be part of Europe from a different perspective.

But that's not what UKIP was saying – 'Pull out, head for the hills!' Little Englanders. We are big Englanders, we should be big England, big Wales, big United Kingdomers! You wanna change Europe? Be inside it. It's called this bureaucracy because no one's allowed to lead it. Because no one allows anyone to lead it, because they say, 'Well, that would be the super state', and they get paranoid about that. So, if we do not make it work in Europe then the world will not happen. We are the most advanced continent of making things work together.

If we could get this right and we're heading forward, then Asia can do it, South America, North America, Africa eventually, then all the continents have an agreement with each other and then there's a level playing field for everyone and everyone has a fair chance. Everyone has a chance, everyone has security, no one's fighting over borders because it doesn't fucking matter any more.

It's the only world. Someone's got to have a world vision. And you can have a world vision, but you're not plugged into politics. And it's not something you can actually utilize in British politics but I'm trying to hold that in my head, and I'm trying to build bridges, and doing the gigs in different languages is definitely a bridge-builder.

And Yacine said, because he's from an Arabic family, that the fact that I want to do it in Arabic means something, and I know it's going to resonate. It resonates for the Germans, the fact I said I was going to do a gig at Cologne on D-Day. Adding the hour of German is important – it's the future. And Germany is invited to those commemorations. So I'm passionate about that project and I will keep doing that, you know, forever, and trying to build those bridges. And Russian is the most important to do.

So when the politics happens, if/when it takes off, what happens to the stand-up?

The stand-up has to go into hibernation. Everything goes into hibernation and it depends what momentum you have going into hibernation, when and if you come out of.

But you're gonna be on an up.

Well, that's the plan.

You've got six years, mate. The only thing against you is fucking time. I mean you've only got one life to live.

I want to get the drama to a good place as well. *Last Christmas*, *Treasure Island*, *Hannibal*, the Dustin Hoffman film. I'm doing much better work there, so I bring that up so if I have enough momentum going in it should have a little bit of a roll when I come out.

Are you aiming for producing or directing at all?

Producing yes, I need to make films in these next six years. That's why the clock is ticking and I've only not done it earlier because I didn't want to do crap. I've got about four scripts, four stories in my head in different levels of development and I've got to get them out.

I went from doing surreal comedy in Germany to doing a film with Dustin Hoffman and Kathy Bates. That's pretty good, it's a pretty good place to be.

But you're a real one for that, in a very positive, having a go…

And you will go and you will fail, or semi-fail, and then you do a second one and you fail less badly, then gradually… the first one was shit, then the second one…

But the thing now is that, I would say there appears to be certainly more shape to the plan. There's the political side, there's the stand-up, there's the actor, there's these three prongs now that are definite. We see these as the things. Is there anything that I'm missing?

Running?

You see the thing is, you've been out doing your stuff and doing your thing, whereas I've just been a dad, so…

I was planning to have kids in my fifties. So I'm still trying to work out how I'd do that. I see the energy that's required. It is tricky, but I thought I'd get stuff over, and then I could get to it in my fifties. You see, I'm not going to be moving around in 2020.

There's that! They're gonna know where to find you.

Yeah and I think there's quite a good crèche in Parliament.

Which would you rather, MP or mayor?

It doesn't matter. They would be different things. They're both representing people. If people are good enough to vote for me then I will do the best job I can. I would be happy to stand anywhere and I would be happy to be Mayor of London. If I had a choice, I'd like to be Mayor of London. But if there's a sitting Labour mayor that wishes to go on and they're doing a good job… then that's a little tricky. But whichever way it is it doesn't matter.

I've thought about it because, one is obviously a higher profile and whatever, but I still have to learn how to make that work and not lose myself. If Labour happened to get into power all the way through 2020 that's different. So we shall see. If one of our guys is doing something decent, that's great, that's what I want for us. I'd like this career, though. I would have it.

I just want to be trained up to know how to do it, because extremists are always coming back up in financial crisis. And there will always be crisis and the crisis will always come from people fucking with the system, that's where financial crisis comes from. Something fucked with the system, people working out how to be cyber-greedy.

Am I right in saying there's not been a book yet?

No. I wrote a tour book which was slightly twisted. It was with Dave Quantick. And I thought it was going to be an interview thing but in the end he took himself out of it and it was just me saying stuff. So that's not what I thought it was gonna be, it was like a ghost-written thing. I mean it was my words but… Then they brought it out as if it was my biography, which was wrong, because it was just supposed to be a tour book of America.

What I would like is a European chat show, in the sense of someone going out to another place. I have been thinking of a political one, like a Jon Stewart one. Have this political edge before I go in and I don't really want to become the chat show guy.

I might have to just make sure I see you every five years, because I just have to. It just wakes you up to the possibilities of it.

Well that's it. I trawl my mind for things to do that work for me and work for someone else. So I'm coming back from my fourth language and I'm doing my second language tonight. It's the one I did on Wednesday as well.

So where's the gig tonight?

Soho Theatre.

Oh right, so it's tonight in French, so the audience will be curious bilingualism fans.

Yes – I checked. It's usually a smattering of pure French people – only a smattering because I have to be very big in Paris before the 400,000 French people over here will come.

Do you get, 'He won't really do it all in French' from English fans coming in?

No, not from that point of view – just that they didn't read it. They just go, 'It's in French? I didn't know!' Well it's written all over it! It's there!

I'd imagine now that the fan base are more than OK with checking what language you're doing tonight.

No, because there's new fans. There's people that just come to you and say, 'I didn't even know you did this!' With the German show, we did

Q&As because I could only get thirty-five minutes after the first night. And someone asked, 'Why the fuck are you doing this in German?' and I had this whole 'Mein Führer' thing at the beginning where I said, 'I just wish I could tell you now, this is what I said in German and I now say in English and am gonna put at the beginning of the French shows, Spanish shows'. I did this because a number of years ago we stayed at a place in Santorini, a Greek island. There was an ancient volcano and it blew out the whole side of the island and now it's very beautiful. Three thousand years later and you watch the sunsets go down, quite fast, like half an hour. It's near the equator and you can go to this beautiful place, but you can also swim in the water in the volcano. You go out to the steaming rump of the volcano and they say, 'Would you like to swim in this warm water?' Everyone was shouting in French, in German, in Spanish, Russian, whatever it was. And I just thought, 'This is young Europeans here. All Europeans and they're not just about to go to war.' I thought, 'This is good, this is people having fun and what can I do to help this?' And I thought 'Right, I can do the gigs! I can do the gigs in French!'

Because they started happening in Paris. My promoter wasn't wild about the idea because there were 200,000 English speakers in Paris. And I was going 'There's sixty million French speakers in France – let's go!' And that's where it started. I thought it was putting my money where my mouth is. It's coming out on a limb, it's positive you know. I'm a British European transvestite. This is my political statement with my fingernails.

And I campaigned actually, on Tuesday and Wednesday, campaigned in lipstick for the first time ever. Zero reaction. My lipstick was the same colour as Labour Party colours. Great, it's boring. If we can get to boring then we've made it. I've campaigned in lipstick for two days and everybody else isn't bothered. Brilliant. So we're up and running. It's cool. I had to work out these two different looks, so the blended look of kind of boy/girl.

Yeah. But you've been sort of easing towards that. It's really nice, the mix, the mix is getting good.

Yeah, it has to be sharp. I have to be lean, I have to be an athlete. Because I've been so tired the last two weeks. I've just worked intensively on Spanish and campaigned intensively, then I have to go home. Funeral yesterday then back to campaigning this morning. Now I'm gonna go sleep then I'm gonna go do the gig… and in my sleep learn Spanish… and French.

You are really good on the advice. You said that thing about speed of thought. One of the things you said, that what the punters want is speed of thought, because there's thousands of new comedians. What's the one piece of advice you'd give a new comic?

Stage time. Yeah. Build a stage, get on it, do stuff. It's hours on stage. How many films you've made if it's films. How many paintings you've done if it's paintings. It's how many songs you have sung. Stage time if you're a performer. Studio time if you're recording. It is just the time, because you will be shit and then you will be less shit, then you will be medium then OK then better. Some people just do genius straight off but they are not analysts, they won't know why they've done it. Most people develop instinctive on one hand, analytic on the other hand. If you can develop both of those as equal you can do amazing things.

Nelson Mandela learnt Afrikaans and he said, 'If you talk to someone in a second language you can talk to their head if they understand the second language, but if you talk to them in their first language you talk to their heart.'

There you go, and you say you can't do endings. I seriously still can't, especially with stand-up. I don't know why.

Well with stand-up, just put all the characters in at the end.

Thanks and Acknowledgements

Deborah Frances-White:
First of all, massive thanks to all of the comedians who agreed to be interviewed for this book. Thank you for your time, your honesty and your good humour. And extra thanks to Paul Provenza for permission to use extracts from his wonderful book *Satiristas* and to Phill Jupitus for assuming the role of interviewer and chatting to Eddie Izzard for us.

Huge thanks to Tom Salinsky for his unfailing help and support in shaping, structuring, arranging and proof reading this book. We were of course late delivering it, but without Tom we would have been so much later.

Thanks to publishing gods David Barker and John O'Donovan at Bloomsbury for letting us do this at all and Eve White for helping to make it all happen.

And big thanks to our dedicated typists who tirelessly turned hours of audio into pages of text: Emma Beale, Devon Harland, Peta Griffiths, Nadia Kamil and John McLeod.

Marsha Shandur:
I'd like to say an ENORMOUS thank you to Deborah Frances-White for inviting me to make this very exciting book with her. Thanks to Tom Salinsky for going above and beyond in his work on it. Thanks to Eve White, and to David Barker, Emily Hockley, the unfailingly patient John O'Donovan and all at Bloomsbury. Thanks to tireless transcribers Brendan Donald and Prexie, aka 'Transexpert', from Fiverr who constantly stunned me with her professionalism, hard work

and efficiency. Thanks to Lucy and Andy Picken, to Kat Georgiou, to Nathalie, Devon and Dillon, and to Zoe McGrory.

Thanks of course to all of the wonderful comedians who allowed themselves to be interviewed for this project, and to everyone who helped those interviews become possible – in particular: Mel Brown and Sacha Taylor-Cox from Impressive; Danny Payne, Andrea Wong, Emily Carlstrom and Matt Corluka from Just For Laughs; Megan Pugh from Chambers Management; Victoria Lepper, Nathalie Laurent-Marke, Emily Saunders, Lauren Marks, Emily Gay and Lisa Thomas from Lisa Thomas Management (for, among others, Mark Watson from markwatsonthecomedian.com); Aimee Reilly and Alison from Alison Peters PR; Helena Hewett and Beth Kahn from Avalon; Gaby Jerrard; Debi Allen and Sally Homer.

Thank you to Xfm for letting me do *Marsha Meets…* and to all my exceptional producers for that podcast – in particular Ed Barfoot, Graham Albans, Chris Fitch and Ben Jamieson, who as well as all being master researchers were experts at talking me down from the ledge when I was standing in the studio, whining, 'SEND THEM HOME, I'M TOO NERVOUS, I DON'T WANT TO DO IT'.

Thank you to Pam Lostracco for designing us such an *astonishingly* beautiful cover. A massive thank you to Val Takeda, and to Jill Farmer of Jill Farmer Coaching, without whom my half of this book would be just a pile of un-transcribed, un edited interviews on memory cards lying, avoided, on my desk.

Finally, thank you to the extraordinary Natasha Ward, to Paul Dixon for his patience and support, and to Ilija Tomic, Rosie Brandon, Briar Brandon, Robin Brandon and Akira Shandur. May you all laugh a *lot*.

Index

Note: a comedian's name preceded by an asterisk (*) refers to an interview with that comedian. A comedian's name with no preceding asterisk is simply a mention of that person.

The first interview with each comedian is accompanied by a brief biography.

Page reference in italics denote an image.